Women in
American
Journalism

Women in American Journalism

A New History

JAN WHITT

UNIVERSITY OF ILLINOIS PRESS

Urbana and Chicago

Manufactured in the United States of America

1 2 3 4 5 C P 5 4 3 2 1

∞ This book is printed on acid-free paper.

Library of Congress Cataloging-in-Publication Data
Whitt, Jan.
Women in American journalism : a new history /
Jan Whitt.
p.   cm.
Includes bibliographical references and index.
ISBN-13 978-0-252-03354-4 (cloth : alk. paper)
ISBN-10 0-252-03354-X (cloth : alk. paper)
ISBN-13 978-0-252-07556-8 (pbk. : alk. paper)
ISBN-10 0-252-07556-0 (pbk. : alk. paper)
1. Women journalists—United States—Biography.
2. Women in journalism—United States—
History—20th century.
I. Title.
PN4872.W47   2008
071'.3'082—dc22   2008009042

For
Willard D. (Wick) Rowland Jr.

Contents

Acknowledgments

No research is original in the truest sense of that word. Most ruminations rely upon the ideas and efforts of others. To express gratitude to everyone who contributed to my scholarly interests and worldview would be impossible, of course, so I thank the following people and acknowledge that they are important in their own right but are also to some extent representative of all those who deserve recognition.

This book is dedicated to Willard D. (Wick) Rowland Jr., Ph.D., dean emeritus of the School of Journalism and Mass Communication, University of Colorado at Boulder (1987–99) and now president and CEO of Colorado Public Television (KBDI-TV/12) in Denver. His belief in interdisciplinary inquiry, celebration of diversity, commitment to scholarship, and generous mentoring have shaped my vision of the purposes and contributions of the academy.

Among the scholars who shared their wisdom and their example, I especially am grateful to Eric Gould, who was chair of the Department of English at the University of Denver and taught courses in modern literature when I was in graduate school; Rachel and Andy Moore, who were caring mentors and gifted teachers when I was an undergraduate in the Department of English at Baylor University; Robert D. (Bob) Richardson Jr., who taught American literature and directed my dissertation at the University of Denver; and Robert Trager, associate dean of graduate studies in the School of Journalism and Mass Communication at the University of Colorado, who has made mentoring an art form. Those named in this paragraph represent individuals who encourage and promote women colleagues. We notice.

Among the women whose commitment to historical research paved the way for so many others and whose formidable presence brightened the journey, I especially thank Maurine H. Beasley, Shirley Biagi, Diane L. Borden, Elizabeth Burt, Barbara Cloud, Caryl Cooper, Janet M. Cramer, Judith Cramer, Pamela Creedon, Hazel Dicken-Garcia, Kathleen Endres, Sandra Haarsager, Nancy L. Roberts, and Ramona R. Rush. Thank you for your friendship, scholarship, and sisterhood.

Among the colleagues and friends who have encouraged me and many others over the years I thank from the bottom of my heart David Abrahamson, Brenda J. Allen, Del Brinkman, Richard Byyny, Carole Capsalis, Robert Collmer, Thomas Connery, Sara Davidson, Tom Duncan, Katherine Eggert, Barbara Elmore, B. Glenn George, Todd Gleeson, Michael Grant, Elissa Guralnick, Sarah R. Hankins, John Hartsock, Mary Klages, Paul Levitt, J. R. LeMaster, Patricia Limerick, Heidi Loshbaugh, Carol Margolin, Nancy Matchett, David McHam, Polly McLean, Susan Moran, Sandra Moriarty, Graham Oddie, and Garrett O'Keefe.

I also thank Lana F. Rakow, Patricia Raybon, Wendy Redal, Karen Risch, Elizabeth Robertson, Michael Robertson, Jeffrey Robinson, Norman Sims, Elizabeth Skewes, David Sloan, Joanna Starek, John Stevenson, Rodger Streitmatter, Patricia Sullivan, Quinn Sullivan, Leonard Teel, Larry Weisberg, Marianne (Mimi) Wesson, Michael Danny Whitt, and Terry Tempest Williams. Thank you for walking the walk.

I also want to thank journals and publishers for giving me permission to reprint my previously published material from the following publications: "Burning Crosses and Activist Journalism: The Unlikely Heroism of Two Mississippi Editors," *Southern Studies* 9 (Summer/Fall 1998): 87–108; "Portrait of an Artist as a Young Woman: Eudora Welty's Early Years in Media," *Southwestern Mass Communication Journal* 15 (1999): 26–38; "'The Truth About What Happens': Katherine Anne Porter and Journalism," *Journal of the American Studies Association of Texas* 26 (October 1995): 16–35; "A 'Labor from the Heart': Lesbian Magazines from 1947–1994," *Journal of Lesbian Studies* 5 (Summer 2001): 229–51; and "Focus: A Journal for Lesbians," "The Ladder," and "Sinister Wisdom" from *Women's Periodicals in the United States: Social and Political Issues*, ed. Kathleen L. Endres and Therese L. Lueck (Westport, Conn.: Greenwood, 1996), 94–98, 156–63, 351–56.

I am especially grateful to the Commission on the Status of Women (Association for Education in Journalism and Mass Communication) for selecting the proposal for this work for the 2005 Mary Ann Yodelis Smith Feminist Scholarship Award.

INTRODUCTION

The Secret Sharers

Women Outside Mainstream Journalism

The introduction to many academic treatises is an explanation of how the scholar's work is different from research that came before. The conclusion often summarizes the researcher's discoveries and suggests future study. In deference to the tradition of storytelling that lies at the heart of *Women in American Journalism: A New History,* however, this book's beginning and ending will be untraditional. I will share part of my personal story as it informs this study and suggest reasons for more work in the history of women in journalism being necessary, rewarding, and inevitable. Ideas for future research appear throughout the manuscript and in the conclusion as well.

After completing my dissertation defense in 1985, I walked out of the English department at the University of Denver and decided to reward myself by buying a book and going to lunch. I purchased the first edition of *The Norton Anthology of Literature by Women,* edited by Sandra M. Gilbert and Susan Gubar, walked to a restaurant, and settled in for a blissful hour of reading— reading not required by any professor toward any particular end.

I scanned the contents page in the anthology, expecting to see familiar names and titles of familiar poems, short stories, essays, and excerpts from novels. Along with the names of well-known women writers—Louisa May Alcott, Jane Austen, Anne Bradstreet, Emily Bronte, Elizabeth Barrett Browning, Emily Dickinson, George Eliot, Margaret Fuller, Christina Rossetti, Mary Shelley, Harriet Beecher Stowe, Elizabeth Cady Stanton, and Mary Wollstonecraft—there were also a startling number of names I didn't recognize.

Having completed a bachelor's degree in English and journalism, a master's degree in English, and a Ph.D. in English, I was flooded with the all-too-familiar panic that most academics experience when they realize they have a diploma but much more to learn. At that point, however, I couldn't register for another class or earn another degree. I was at the supposed pinnacle of American higher education in a field I was expected to have mastered.

I fought back the feeling that I had failed myself and other women scholars by reading too much by Herman Melville and William Faulkner and too little by Toni Morrison and Alice Walker. What if I were asked to teach a course in women's literature? What if my students discerned how much I didn't know? What could I do to fill in the gaps before I was found out?

Now, more than twenty years later, my reactions and fears on that day seem, mercifully, to have belonged to someone less confident and more naive, certainly not someone who has gained tenure and taught for almost three decades. Publishing and discussing ideas with colleagues, I have learned the boundaries of my knowledge and have discovered the joy of defining what I don't know.

I have taught literary journalism, media history, women and popular culture, and writing in the School of Journalism and Mass Communication, the Undergraduate Academy, and the Division of Continuing Education at the University of Colorado since 1988. Also at CU, I have taught courses in lesbian-gay-bisexual-transgender literature and culture for the women's studies department and for a residential academic program, American and British literature for the English department, and the literature and journalism of the West for the Center of the American West. I am now more confident in what I know and more sure of how to appropriate what I do not know.

Into this seemingly safe world came the idea to write a book about women in journalism, referring only briefly to the names of those more familiar to undergraduate and graduate students—Ida Tarbell, "Nellie Bly," "Annie Laurie," Katharine Graham, and others—and including women who have been overlooked. I would, I decided, challenge the intellectual identity I had carved out by writing about *other* women, specifically those of the society news and women's pages, often vilified even by those who worked side by side with them; women of contemporary literary journalism, often overshadowed by Norman Mailer, Hunter S. Thompson, Tom Wolfe, and others; women journalists who have turned their backs on print media and made names for themselves by writing fiction; women of the alternative press, who have advocated for the downtrodden; and women of the lesbian press who often have faced financial ruin and have been forced to use pseudonyms and suppress the names of those on their circulation lists.

What was I thinking? Why would I leave a comfort zone—an area of accepted research into the lives and work of somewhat familiar women journalists—and risk exposure again? As I began to write a series of articles for publication in journals and collections of essays, I experienced the throat-clutching fear I remembered when I scanned the anthology of women's literature. Even names considered mainstream in American journalism history—Jane Cunningham Croly, Elizabeth Timothy, and Anna Catherine Maul Zenger among them—were largely unfamiliar to me. I have taught courses in media history organized around the development of ideas (e.g., literacy, religion, and progressivism), around global events (e.g., wars, stock market crashes, and political corruption), around eras of newspaper history (e.g., the penny press and yellow journalism), and around famous men of the press (e.g., Benjamin Day, Horace Greeley, William Randolph Hearst, Adolph Ochs, Joseph Pulitzer, and others). Too often, I realized, I have considered the perspectives of women in journalism as ancillary to the great ideas originated by men, the great events driven by men, and the great newspapers and magazines owned and run by men. Even for me, the women of print media often were faceless, obscured by the shadows cast by better-known, more powerful giants of industry and media—all of them decidedly male. If that was true for me, how much more was it true for my students? Moreover, given the fact that a majority of students in communication programs are women, how did they define themselves in their media world?

In my pilgrimage I turned to women in the American Journalism Historians Association (AJHA) who had written about women and their contributions to newspapers, magazines, and public relations; to women in the Association for Education in Journalism and Mass Communication (AEJMC) who had presented papers on women's press clubs; to women who added the names of unfamiliar women writers, editors, and publishers to the next edition of their media textbooks; to male scholars such as Rodger Streitmatter who had retold the stories of African American women journalists and lesbian magazine editors; and to many others lighting the way for academics such as I and the students who filled our classes. Gradually, I met women on the printed page; they were often without faces but no longer without voices.

As I began to read their sparse narratives, I realized the value of the oral histories of women of my own generation. I began to conduct interviews with those whose names appeared only briefly in biographical indexes. I also began to seek out family members of women journalists who had died before becoming widely known and to unearth the narratives of women journalists who had gained some degree of public recognition before passing out of vogue. In the process, I understood how little I knew and how rich would be my journey.

Telling the Untold Stories

Women in American Journalism: A New History has only a brief conclusion. The research questions necessarily are part of each chapter; furthermore, it is impossible to summarize potential scholarship about women in journalism when so many stories remain to be told. Although much of the research may be conducted in libraries and special archives, interviews of contemporary women are essential. It is time to look behind men such as James Gordon Bennett and Lincoln Steffens and examine the literature and journalism of their female contemporaries. As Virginia Woolf suggested in *A Room of One's Own* (1929), William Shakespeare may have had a sister who wrote a sonnet or play. Who was she? Where are the letters and diaries and first-person accounts that will bring her to life once again?

The reservoir of writing by women grows daily with the efforts of readers who discover Ellen Goodman and want to know more about her intellectual predecessors; of academics who seek out the stories of lesser-known reporters and editors for papers to be submitted to refereed journals; and of professors who want students to read about more than colonial newspapers, the assassination of William McKinley, and the identity of Deep Throat.

When an anthology of women journalists is published one day, some of us will experience deep satisfaction in recognizing not only the names of celebrated women columnists such as Maureen Dowd and Anna Quindlen but also the names of white civil rights journalist Hazel Brannon Smith and African American journalist Betty Wilkins of *The* (Kansas City) *Call. Women in American Journalism: A New History* is a modest contribution to what I hope will be a new era of attention to, and recognition of, the women of American journalism and literary history. Even now, books such as *Women and the Press: The Struggle for Equality* by Patricia Bradley are contributing to the discourse about gender and race and ethnicity in media.

In graduate school, a male classmate pointed out how often I and the other women in our class began statements about research findings with disclaimers. Embarrassed by his accurate observation, we collectively vowed never again to frame our comments negatively or to present research by focusing on its limitations. Certainly, women historians owe no apology for a tradition of research that now informs the field of media criticism. In attempting a manuscript designed to encompass the stories of women celebrated in traditional journalism as well as accounts of those not as well known, however, an introduction that does not include a hearty disclaimer is misleading at best and unprincipled at worst.

To maintain that particular women truly have become "mainstream" in American journalism history—and thereby imply that others remain on the periphery—is unsupportable, and I make no such claim in this book. In fact, in spite of the work of prominent women historians such as Maurine H. Beasley, Elizabeth Burt, Janet M. Cramer, Kathleen Endres, Sheila J. Gibbons, Therese L. Lueck, Nancy L. Roberts, Ramona R. Rush, H. Leslie Steeves, and others, women in journalism history often remain largely invisible. Editors of history textbooks and professors of media history continue to emphasize familiar names such as Horace Greeley, William Randolph Hearst, Adolph Ochs, Joseph Pulitzer, and other men central to the development of the early press, the penny press, the yellow journalism era, objective journalism, the "New Journalism," and contemporary journalism.

Women in American Journalism: A New History is not a definitive or exhaustive chronicle of the history of women in American journalism. The articles in *American Journalism* and *Journalism History* and books published by media scholars remain the primary resources for those interested in the contributions of women to newspaper history. *Women in American Journalism* is, however, a study of often overlooked women in journalism and of others who—like the literary journalists included in chapter 3—are representatives of more controversial genres of news reporting and writing. Rather than being simply a descriptive phrase, "the secret sharers" in the title of the introduction is, in fact, the thematic heart of this study. Although I pay tribute to scholars who work in mainstream women's journalism history and rely on their efforts, this volume is an attempt to broaden the conversation about the women in overlooked areas of journalism history.

In Search of the Secret Sharers

The title of the introduction is an allusion to *The Secret Sharer,* a tale by Joseph Conrad, a novelist and writer of short stories, who was mesmerized by what lies beneath the sea and what lies buried in the human mind. Best known as the author of *The Heart of Darkness* from which the revolutionary film *Apocalypse Now* is drawn, Conrad was fascinated by what people might learn about themselves in isolation from others. Unflinchingly, he probed what lies within the secret heart of every individual.

Captivated by the unpredictability of the human psyche and by the complexity of human thought and behavior, Conrad created protagonists whose natures are defined by dualities. His central characters exist not as heroic, integrated selves but as fragmented people who often achieve heroism in spite of an internal struggle that threatens to immobilize them. In *The Secret Sharer,* Conrad traces his central character's stream of consciousness and describes his internal torment: "And all the time the dual working of my mind distracted me almost to the point of insanity. I was constantly watching myself, my secret self, as dependent on my actions as my own personality. . . . It was very much like being mad, only it is worse because one was aware of it" (383).

Like Conrad's often-tormented characters, women in American history have been themselves and yet not themselves. By internalizing the descriptions of who they are in the minds of others and by accepting much about the visible social structure, women have been challenged to discover and, perhaps more important, remember and protect their essential selves. Throughout history, they have been aware that they are watching themselves. That sense of otherness—of a self that exists as it observes itself and struggles to integrate what it sees—constitutes the peculiar duality of a woman's consciousness. As Conrad observed in quite another context, this fragmentation must have been very much like being mad, but it is worse because women are aware of it.

The women who sought careers in journalism were, of course, no different from their sisters in other societal roles. Born into a world that minimized their contributions to the profession, few women journalists were able to gain recognition in American newsrooms; even fewer were able to alter prevailing definitions of news and industry practice. Once they became part of the news machine, women sometimes became female versions of their male mentors or were relegated to types of news coverage believed to be more appropriate for women, such as feature articles, gossip columns, or society news. Female audiences were similarly mischaracterized and marginalized by American newspaper editors and publishers. In this study, I will cite scholars who argue that this is still the case.

In spite of the difficulties they encountered and continue to encounter, women journalists and readers have throughout history reminded American society by their very existence that communities of women are richly varied and are capable of having measurable impact on the industry. Like the protagonist in Charlotte Perkins Gilman's "The Yellow Wallpaper," though, a woman's desire to make her mark in American journalism often left her feeling fragmented and, like a character in her own story, watching and analyzing herself. Was she who she was presumed to be? If not, who was she, and how would she translate her essential self into something acceptable to her family, employer, readers? Was news what she had been told it was? If so, would she be able to recreate it as well as her male counterparts? If not, would she be able to redefine it?

It is no accident that madness surfaced as a central theme in literature and drama during the nineteenth century. Male and female writers alike treated the topic as a symbolic escape. In Conrad's story, the protagonist says his fragmentation "is like being haunted" (395). "It was, in the night," writes Conrad, "as though I had been faced by my own reflection in the depths of a somber and immense mirror" (374). It is this "somber and immense mirror" that concerns us as we deal with women in American journalism history. What did these women see as they looked at themselves in their private mirrors and through the lenses of others? Few considered themselves part of the mainstream. Some were even more peripheral than others. Yet certainly all are worthy of being afforded the opportunity to surface, to speak, to become more recognized for their contributions to American journalism history.

Chapter 1 summarizes the stories of the women reporters, columnists, and photographers who are most likely to be known to media scholars and evaluates their collective contribution. Although the list risks being encyclopedic, recognizing the role of women currently in the literature is important in defining what has become familiar in media history and what remains on the periphery.

The women who worked as society and women's page reporters and editors are the focus of chapter 2. Alternately celebrated and vilified, they transformed American journalism. Writing the news of interest to women and news perceived as being of interest to them, editors of society and women's pages were touchstones for readers and symbols for male newspaper editors and publishers. The impact of their contribution was still felt in the twentieth century as newspapers such as the *Chicago Tribune* and the *Lexington* (Kentucky) *Herald-Leader* experimented with women's sections and as former women's news reporters and editors made major contributions to mainstream journalism.

Chapter 3 discusses three women best known as "literary journalists," reporters who transformed news coverage by using literary techniques such as narration, description, and dialog once considered the particular province of fiction and then became recognized for writing extended nonfiction. The work of Joan Didion is the best known in this genre, but other women, such as Sara Davidson, Jane Kramer, Adrian Nicole LeBlanc, and Susan Orlean, have won literary and reporting awards and are transforming society through their observations on contemporary culture.

Chapter 4 deals with representative women who turned away from careers in journalism and made their mark by writing fiction. In some cases they spent only a short time in American newsrooms. In other cases they belittled journalism. In all cases the time they spent writing about the "real world" factored heavily into their fiction. Although some, such as Willa Cather and Margaret Mitchell, have begun to receive their fair share of recognition as former reporters, others, such as Edna Ferber, Katherine Anne Porter, and Eudora Welty, are rarely identified as writers who spent time in the newspaper industry.

Chapter 5 focuses on women who chose to champion their causes in the alternative press, and the stories are organized not by chronology but by theme. The story of civil rights journalist Hazel Brannon Smith, the first woman editorial writer to win a Pulitzer Prize, introduces the chapter. The environmental press is represented by Phyllis Austin, a long-time journalist and activist with the *Maine Times* and now the *Maine Environmental News*. The early feminist press is represented by Caroline Churchill, editor of and reporter for Denver's *Queen Bee*. Betty Wilkins, rejected for membership in a prominent Denver press club because she was black, gained her reputation as a writer for *The* (Kansas City) *Call*.

Finally, chapter 6 deals with the founders of the lesbian press, especially those who edited the newsletter *Vice Versa* and journals and magazines such as *Focus: A Journal for Lesbians, The Ladder, Lesbian Connection,* and *Sinister Wisdom*. In spite of financial hardships and infighting, lesbian newsletters, newspapers, magazines, and journals continue to reach a segmented audience and to remind heterosexual society that *Maxim* and *Vogue* are only part of the landscape.

Throughout this study I have made every attempt to recognize the fact that women have not long resided in mainstream journalism history—if they can be said to reside there at all. Textbooks and professors of history continue to relegate women to particular chapters or to particular sections of the syllabus. However, this study argues that as women become more accepted as a part of the complex and ongoing text of media history, there is a parallel narrative that scholars also need to address. That narrative—which includes the contributions of lesser-known women to society news and women's pages, to literary journalism, to fiction, to the alternative press, and to the lesbian press—is rich with promise.

Women in
American
Journalism

1

Familiar Women of
American Journalism History

Telling the stories of women on the outskirts of traditional journalism history requires knowing which women have been accepted into the mainstream and understanding why their inclusion is considered of primary importance. Since the 1990s, the names of women have become more familiar in media textbooks, although it is important to acknowledge that inclusion did not come naturally or easily. Assembling the stories of the not-so-secret sharers required the individual and collective efforts of numerous women historians, including Sheila J. Gibbons, Agnes Hooper Gottlieb, Susan Henry, Therese L. Lueck, Kay Mills, Sharon M. Murphy, Ishbel Ross, Madelon G. Schilpp, H. Leslie Steeves, Linda Steiner, Gaye Tuchman, and others.

Although a survey of the work already completed in women's journalism history cannot be comprehensive, this chapter will suggest why particular women have become more familiar figures in that history, what areas are central to further research, and how this volume stretches the boundaries of contemporary historical and biographical criticism. At the heart of this chapter lies the philosophy of journalism history pioneer Maurine H. Beasley, a philosophy that she articulates persuasively in a landmark article entitled "Recent Directions for the Study of Women's History in American Journalism."

Although Beasley deals primarily with whether Eleanor Roosevelt should be considered a journalist—and concludes that she should—she also suggests that as women in traditional newspaper history receive their just due, historians must include others on the periphery as well. Her argument is especially compelling when she writes that "a wider definition of journalism itself is needed than the traditional one that involves reporting and commenting on conflicts and controversies mainly of interest to a male-run world." She suggests that a "broader definition, more appropriate to women's experience, has to include the presentation of informative material that has wide popular appeal" ("Recent Directions" 208).

Beasley's perspective makes possible—indeed, makes necessary—the inclusion of work by women in literary journalism, women who left traditional journalism and made their reputations in the literary world, and women of the lesbian press. Other women in journalism, such as those who wrote and edited society news and women's pages, may already be a significant part of historical study; however, their role is minimized even by women historians, and they often are slighted as having had little impact because they are perceived to have reified the status quo by celebrating the woman as wife, mother, and homemaker. Women of the alternative press also are gaining recognition, but their roles remain secondary to those of women who wrote for mainstream metropolitan dailies. They, too, are appropriate for this study. As Beasley observes, "Widening our concept of journalism allows us to take into account more fully the way women have participated in all areas of the field, whether oriented to the presentation of 'hard' (front-page) or 'soft' (feature) news. It lets us go beyond news *per se* to the involvement of women in allied activities like public relations which include an understanding of and participation in the journalistic process" (Ibid. 209).

Beasley borrows from Gerda Lerner's four stages in the conceptualization of women's history—compensatory, contribution, transition, and synthesis. She summarizes Lerner's categories by writing, "The compensatory stage represented the identification of women previously omitted from standard historical accounts. Moving beyond it, Lerner described the contribution stage as the evaluation of women's achievements in a male-dominated world, the transition stage as the reworking of various historical categorizations from women's perspectives, and the synthesis stage as the integration of the history of men and women's experience" (Ibid. 210).

In this volume, the categories of most interest are the contribution and transition stages. The compensatory stage is problematic when dealing with a well-known figure such as Joan Didion, who, although not omitted from "standard historical accounts," is sometimes disregarded because she does not fit the traditional definition of a "hard" news reporter. Although she writes about war in San Salvador, for example, she does so from inside a nearly deserted mall where taped music plays eerily in the background. Didion deals with the essence of hard news—breaking coverage of significant world events—in her political and war coverage, but she employs literary techniques such as description, narration, and dialog and experiments with voice, chronology, and vantage point. The compensatory stage also does not emphasize study of other well-known figures such as columnists (whether entertainment or politics is their subject matter) or those who opted out of the male-dominated newspaper world and began writing fiction. The contributions of these women must be acknowledged, though, and the transition stage makes it possible to rethink dominant "historical categorizations" in light of news and information by, about, and of particular interest to women.

Beasley is correct when she argues that "women, like minorities, have been studied mainly from the standpoint of chronicling the difficulties they have overcome in order to succeed in a male-oriented field" (Ibid. 211). However, many of the women in this study—most obviously those involved in the lesbian press—did not try to succeed in a male-oriented field. They opted out of that field and created their own genre of news-gathering and news dissemination. They did so by audaciously redefining what constitutes news and by reaching a target market invisible to establishment media. By broadening the definition of journalism history, we may, as Beasley states, ally it "more closely with social history, an area of study crucial for understanding women's experience, rather than with business histories of media empires" (Ibid. 213). We may begin to set aside the "male model of journalistic accomplishment" that has "tended to give the greatest recognition to builders of giant journalistic institutions, technological innovators and tough reporters of momentous events, like wars" (Ibid. 218), according to Beasley.

In sum, the circle must be widened to include women who contributed to women's pages; have identified themselves as, or are identified as, literary journalists; left journalism to gain reputations in writing fiction; and championed the feminist press and other alternative media. The women of the lesbian press must also be included. As Beasley writes, "All women who have made use of journalistic techniques—gathering new information of current value and presenting it in various popular formats—have a claim to be studied as journalists, regardless of whether their primary mission has been to advocate, report, comment or entertain" (Ibid. 217).

The Role of Women in American Journalism

Although this study recognizes that news gatherers and news consumers are different groups, it argues that the American women who write news and those who consume it have had similar dreams, goals, and expectations. Newspaper editors in the 1950s and 1960s tried to lure readers with women's pages (chapter 2). To increase circulation, male editors were forced to learn more about women in order to target them as a market. As Myra Macdonald writes, "'Women's material' has often been defined in consumer terms, related to lifestyle and traditional feminine interests. The difficulties of allowing women's voices off the leash in prime-time broadcasting or within the pages of the serious press remain" (*Representing Women* 50).

Since the 1990s, newspapers have been losing women readers. "The 1990s find fewer women reading newspapers, although women continue to purchase more women's magazines and books," wrote Cynthia Lont in 1995. "This trend alarms newspaper publishers because women also purchase more products and more expensive products such as new cars" (*Women and Media* 6). She quotes Mindi Keirnan, former managing editor of the *St. Paul Pioneer Press* and a member of Knight-Ridder's Women Readers Task Force: "The problem is not with women. . . but with newspapers themselves. If editors really want to stem the decline in women's readership, they must look within—and be prepared to make some sweeping reforms" (Ibid. 6). The task force told the industry that women want more information on education, personal safety, health, finances, parenting, and ethics. They also want to read more about successful women (Ibid.).

Although media institutions have been slow to recognize women as consumers of information, much laudable work has been done to uncover stories about important women in American journalism history. I do not presume to do more in this chapter than summarize that work and highlight representative women. Susan Henry has noted that "women's participation in American journalism is as old as the field itself. We know, for example, that the first press in the American colonies (established in Cambridge, Massachusetts, in 1638) was owned by a woman, and that at least seventeen women worked as printers in colonial America before the ratification of the Constitution in 1788. Still more women labored in print shops as compositors, binders, writers, and press workers during this period" ("Changing" 34). Dealing with the lesser-known stories "calls into question the tendency of journalism historians to pay little attention to journalists who worked behind the scenes or lacked official titles. Equally important, it illustrates the importance of better recognizing the collaborative effort—some of it between husbands and wives—that may well have been behind a substantial amount of our journalism" (Ibid. 49).

Between 1865 and 1883 newspapers sought women readers in unprecedented numbers. "The revolution in retailing affected the newspaper in ways in addition to advertising," Ted Curtis Smythe writes. "It stimulated the development of evening editions, which were targeted to women in the home, and spurred the spread of the Sunday newspaper, which carried news directly to the home to reach women and children" ("The Press and Industrial America" 206). The beginning of department store advertising during this time emphasized the importance of women buyers.

In some cases, women made strides because of supportive male editors or those who knew women reporters could draw women readers. During the era of the penny press (1833–80), William Lloyd Garrison, editor of *The Liberator,* created a "ladies department" to allow black women to state their opinions in print. A strong supporter of women, Garrison wrote in *The Liberator* on May 31, 1844, "As our object is universal emancipation to redeem woman as well as man from a servile to an equal condition—we shall go for the RIGHTS OF WOMEN—to their utmost extent" (Sloan and Startt, *The Media in America* 144–45). *New York Tribune* editor Horace Greeley, both an abolitionist and supporter of women's rights, also worked to further the role of women in journalism. (Not surprisingly, Nixola Greeley-Smith, his granddaugher, was hired by Joseph Pulitzer and worked for twenty years as a reporter.)

During the era of yellow journalism, William Randolph Hearst and Pulitzer were known for hiring women to write human interest stories and to per-form publicity stunts, thereby increasing the circulation of their newspapers. One of their competitors, Adolph Ochs of the *New York Times,* maintained a higher quality of news during the yellow journalism era, but he did not believe that women belonged on newspaper staffs. Anne O'Hare McCormick, an international correspondent and columnist for the *New York Times,* was hired in 1921 and became the first woman to serve on the newspaper's edi-torial board, but she had to wait until Ochs died to be appointed (Beasley, "The Emergence of Modern Media" 290). In 1937 McCormick became the first woman to win a Pulitzer Prize for foreign correspondence.

During the 1880s, 288 of a total of 12,308 journalists were women; by 1900, that number had risen to 2,193 of 30,098 (Beasley and Gibbons, *Taking Their Place* 10). By 1920, there were 7,105 women reporters and editors; by 1930, the number was 14,786; and by 1940, 15,890. "Even though the war created an ideology that supported women's work outside the home to help the military effort, women journalists did not receive the respect accorded men. Many editors saw them as either too innocent to cover the unsavory elements of hard news or lacking the physical and mental ability of men" (Ibid. 15).

During Franklin Delano Roosevelt's administration, however, Eleanor Roosevelt organized 348 press conferences in twelve years and limited her press conferences to women, largely because she wanted them to have jobs during the depression (Beasley, "The Emergence of Modern Media" 298).

Doing so "assured coverage of her and the First Family on the women's pages of newspapers and, because men were excluded, motivated editors to hire women" (Folkerts and Teeter, *Voices of a Nation* 405).

By 1960, women made up 37 percent of the total number of editors and reporters in newspapers, magazines, and book publishing (Beasley and Gibbons, *Taking Their Place* 17). Beasley maintains that women were marginal in newspaper work until the Civil Rights Act of 1964 ("The Emergence of Modern Media" 288). Smythe observes that women after the Civil War generally covered meetings, weddings and social events ("The Press and Industrial America" 215). According to one American Society of Newspaper Editors study, fifty-five thousand professionals were employed at 1,600 daily newspapers by 1988, but only 35 percent of them were women (Beasley and Gibbons, *Taking Their Place* 29).

Numbers, however, are only half of the equation. The questions must be, What were the roles of the women in newspaper publishing in the late 1980s, and which stories did editors assign to women reporters? It is important to have reliable figures that would help answer such questions.

Ishbel Ross was one of the women who defied the stereotype of being able to write only lightweight, human interest stories. Ross, author of the first and one of the best-known histories of women in journalism (*Ladies of the Press*, 1936), was hired in 1919 by the *New York Tribune*. She left reporting in 1933 after covering the kidnapping of Anne and Charles Lindbergh's baby. By the time she died in 1975, she had written fifteen more books. Along with Nan Robertson's *The Girls in the Balcony: Women, Men, and the* New York Times (1992), *Ladies of the Press* is an essential supplement to this study.

Fortunately, the stories of more women in American journalism are being told as women historians review correspondence, diaries, and other primary documents that are being released by estates and cataloged in print media archives. Information about the first women in newspaper work is sparse and the reports of historians are sometimes contradictory, but research that does exist is useful in understanding how early—and significant—the role of women in American newspapers was. Before telling the stories that lie on the edges of journalism history, it is perhaps helpful to survey what is already known.

Representative Women in Newspapers

Among the women of early American journalism to whom historians often refer are Ann Franklin, Sarah Goddard, Mary Katherine Goddard (Sarah Goddard's daughter), Anna Catherine Maul Zenger, and Elizabeth Timothy.

More familiar names from subsequent eras include Anne Royall, Sally Joy, Sarah Margaret Fuller, Jane Grey Swisshelm, Jane Cunningham ("Jennie June") Croly, Victoria Woodhull and Tennessee Claflin, Eliza Otis, Ida Tarbell, Ida Wells-Barnett, Elizabeth Cochrane Seaman ("Nellie Bly"), Martha Winifred Black Bonfils ("Annie Laurie"), and Dorothy Thompson. Those often recognized for leaving a mark on the twentieth century include Helen Rogers Reid, Genevieve Forbes Herrick, Eleanor (Cissy) Medill Patterson and Alicia Patterson, Charlotte Murray Curtis, Nan Robertson, Mary Baker Eddy, and Katharine (Kay) Meyer Graham. Although that list is not inclusive, those women represent others whose work has been mentioned in biographies and textbooks on the media.

Some women included in this volume were powerful not only because of their talent but also because of their connections to prominent media families. It is no accident that most who worked on early American newspapers were married to, or sisters of, the men who founded, owned, and published those periodicals or were the mothers of men who inherited them. Others made their mark because they moved determinedly into a male-dominated newspaper domain. Still others were actively recruited by male editors who recognized that their work would draw wider readership. The stories of particular women in journalism history are treated metaphorically in this chapter.

How mainstream the representative stories that follow are is debatable. Women media historians disagree about the centrality of women in media history and the degree to which their names are recognizable. Ultimately, it is important to recognize the contributions of historians who have unearthed the names of significant women in early newspaper work. Donald Avery's chapter "The Colonial Press" in *The Media in America*, for example, contains valuable references to studies on particular women journalists during the colonial period. Studies such as *A Place in the News: From the Women's Pages to the Front Page* by Kay Mills also provide access to brief narratives about notable women, from those of the colonial press to the contemporary media.

Significant resources such as the Washington Press Club Foundation's Oral History Project also are celebrated in this chapter. As Peggy A. Simpson, a former reporter and editor, explains, eleven oral historians conducted 301 interview sessions with fifty-six women for the project. The interviewers generated more than 8,700 pages of primary material and "set a priority on finding minority journalists, knowing that they were doubly invisible" ("The Washington Press Club Foundation's Oral History Project" 293). The contribution of such a resource is obvious.

Although the entries that follow are admittedly appropriate for an encyclopedia, they are also essential for a detailed study of those outside the norm. It is only by learning about these reporters, editors, columnists, and photographers that we can understand the enormous contributions of the women whose work is discussed in chapters 2 through 6.

Ann Franklin

Although some consider Dinah Nuthead of Maryland to be the first colonial woman printer, most historians agree that Ann Franklin was the first to be involved in printing a newspaper. She was married to James Franklin, who founded the *Rhode Island Gazette* in 1732. A typesetter for that publication, she took over the printing house when he died in 1735; twenty-five years later, she and their son, James Jr., began publishing the *Newport Mercury*. When he died in 1762, she published the newspaper until her death in 1763 (Henry, "Ann Franklin"). George H. Douglas notes that Franklin and her two daughters also ran the *Newport Mercury* (*The Golden Age of the Newspaper* 172).

Sarah and Mary Katherine Goddard

Sarah Goodard and her daughter, Mary Katherine Goddard, were printers who published the *Providence Gazette and Country Journal* beginning in 1762. Legally, the newspaper belonged to Sarah Goddard's son, William. After 1765, Mary Katherine Goddard ran two other newspapers that her brother had begun: the *Pennsylvania Chronicle and Universal Advertiser* and the *Maryland Journal.* She also managed several print shops.

Anna Catherine Maul Zenger

At least four women were involved with newspapers before 1765, and more than twelve printed newspapers during the colonial era (Avery, "The Colonial Press" 143; Mills, *A Place in the News* 16). Michael Emery and Edwin Emery bring that number to seventeen (*The Press and America* 58). In addition to Franklin and the Goddards, they include Anna Catherine Maul Zenger, who worked on the *New York Weekly Journal* from 1734 to 1735 while her husband, John Peter Zenger, was confined after being charged with seditious libel. She ran the newspaper again for a few years after he died in 1746 (Douglas, *The Golden Age of the Newspaper* 172).

Elizabeth Timothy

Elizabeth Timothy, touted by some scholars as the first woman publisher, was the wife of a printer, Lewis Timothy, and began publishing Charleston's *South Carolina Gazette* in 1738, after her husband, who founded the newspaper in

1734, died of smallpox. A small notice in the January 4, 1739, issue informed readers that Timothy had taken over the newspaper in her son's name at the time of her husband's death. During her seven-year tenure, Timothy introduced woodcuts and educational, literary, and cultural material into the four-page *Gazette*. Published on Saturdays, it featured speeches by colonial governors, shipping information, advertising, and foreign and local news. In 1746 Timothy turned the newspaper over to her son, Peter, and when he died in 1781, his widow, Ann Timothy, took over.

Anne Royall

The contributions of women in publishing increased and became more obvious to the public after the colonial era. In a few cases, women were able to launch newspapers on their own. Beginning in 1831, Anne Royall published a Washington, D.C., newspaper, *Paul Pry*, which continued for twenty-three years and later became *The Huntress*.

Royall kept the newspaper afloat by writing travel books that gained success. "In a time when reporters never dreamt of approaching the president of the United States for an interview, Royall went down to the banks of the Potomac River where President John Quincy Adams was wont to fight off his clothes and bathe in the nude. Royall sat on his clothes and refused to allow Adams to emerge with presidential dignity until he had answered her questions" (Douglas, *The Golden Age of the Newspaper* 175). Douglas adds that she "attacked political corruption" and "backed sound money, liberal immigration and tariff laws, and better conditions for wage earners." Although these were popular causes, not everyone liked Royall: "One of the victims of her barbed pen whacked her on the head; another threw her down a flight of stairs" (Ibid.).

Sally Joy

Not all of the women in journalism during this time were colorful, but stories remain about many of them. Although other women of the time are now better known than Sally Joy of Vermont, for example, she was only eighteen when the *Boston Post* hired her in the late 1860s. She insisted that "she wanted 'to be treated like a man,'" and, "for the most part she was. If there was any strong resistance on the part of the males in the city room it took the form of overly solicitous behavior. After a matter of weeks the men in the office were lining the floor with papers to keep her white satin gown from picking up dust. Too, on days when Miss Joy had to attend functions after seven o'clock in the evening, the youngest male reporter in the office was assigned to go along as an escort, a humiliating experience that probably brought the lad some good-natured ribbing from his pals" (Ibid. 177). She later became "Penelope Penfeather," a columnist for the *Boston Herald,* where she wrote about fashion, the home, and other topics. Later still, she would be the first president of the New England Woman's Press Association and would help found the General Federation of Women's Clubs (Ibid.).

Sarah Margaret Fuller

Other women of the time are better known than Joy. Sarah Margaret Fuller, whom Greeley praised lavishly as "the most remarkable, and in some respects, the greatest, woman America has yet known" (Hale, *Horace Greeley* 128), was the first woman staff member on a major newspaper and the first woman foreign correspondent. Hired in 1844 as a literary critic, she wrote for the *New York Tribune* in Britain, France, and Italy, beginning in 1846. "Greeley did not hire Fuller to discourse on 'women's' topics or to oversee a woman's page," Douglas notes. "He hired her because he respected her as a thinker, because of her associations with the New England poets and intellectuals he admired, and because she had already been an editor of the transcendentalist magazine *The Dial*" (*The Golden Age of the Newspaper* 174).

A friend of Ralph Waldo Emerson and Robert and Elizabeth Browning, Fuller became the chief editor of *The Dial,* a literary magazine and journal of Transcendental philosophy in 1840. She was known as a crusader and reformer and was celebrated for championing women's equality. During her career as a journalist, Fuller wrote news stories about social issues that included prison conditions on Blackwell's Island, the life of prostitutes, the plight of the mentally ill, politics in Italy and elsewhere, and the quality of patient care in New York hospitals. She died in a well-publicized shipwreck off the coast of Fire Island in 1850.

Jane Grey Swisshelm

Another reporter for Greeley's newspaper was Jane Grey Swisshelm, an abolitionist, suffragist, and founder of the *Pittsburgh Saturday Visiter* in 1848. Swisshelm was the first woman member of the Washington press corps. Four years later, Swisshelm became the associate editor of the *Family Journal and Visiter,* with which the antislavery *Saturday Visiter* merged for financial reasons. In 1857 Swisshelm left her husband, took their six-year-old daughter, and moved to Minnesota. Beginning in 1858, she worked for the *St. Cloud Visiter,* later called the *St. Cloud Democrat.* She also reviewed Union hospitals during the Civil War. As William E. Huntzicker observes, "Some editors like Jane Grey

Swisshelm would not bend from their beliefs; she could not be purchased at any price or intimidated by any threat" ("The Frontier Press" 191).

Jane Cunningham Croly

Another notable woman during this period was Jane Cunningham Croly ("Jennie June"), who began her career with James Gordon Bennett's *New York Herald* in 1855, writing about fashion, beauty, social gatherings, drama, news, advice, and careers for women. During her forty-year tenure, Croly also wrote the first syndicated column for women. One of the most interesting incidents involving Croly occurred in 1868, when British novelist Charles Dickens was scheduled to speak at the New York Press Club, of which Croly was a member. Denied a ticket to Dickens's presentation because she was a woman, Croly founded Sorosis, a women's study club, and in 1889 established the New York Women's Press Club. A professor at Rutgers Women's College, Croly was also the first woman to teach journalism at the college level.

Croly is remembered for supporting abolition and women's ownership of property and other legal rights; teaching journalism and literature; being a reporter, editor, correspondent, and women's section editor; interviewing Louisa May Alcott, Oscar Wilde, and other literary celebrities; receiving an honorary doctorate from Rutgers, where she was honored with a chair of journalism and literature; and writing the *History of the Women's Club Movement*. She was also the first woman to sit in a congressional press gallery.

Victoria Woodhull and Tennessee Claflin

Like Croly, Victoria Woodhull and her sister Tennessee Claflin were known for their courage and activism during a time when women and their talents were undervalued. *Woodhull and Claflin's Weekly,* the New York publication the sisters founded in 1870, argued for open expressions of love, equality for women, and abortion rights. As Douglas writes, the newspaper was a "raucous sheet which gleefully exploited the kind of news for which the penny papers had long been chastised" (*The Golden Age of the Newspaper* 175–76).

Charming and attractive, Woodhull convinced Wall Street financiers to support the newspaper, which was "devoted to topics such as free love, prostitution, social disease, medical malpractice, all subjects that were deemed 'improper,' 'indecent,' and 'unwomanly' at the time" (Ibid. 176). Woodhull ran for president in 1872 against Ulysses S. Grant and Horace Greeley but won no electoral votes although she "considered her campaign for women's suffrage a notable success" (Ibid.). *Woodhull and Claflin's Weekly* lasted until 1876.

Eliza Otis

Other important, but perhaps less colorful, figures also deserve mention. Eliza Otis, wife of *Los Angeles Times* founder Harrison Gray Otis, wrote poetry for the newspaper; did local reporting; and wrote travel columns, editorials, and stories offering household advice. She also ran the *Santa Barbara Press* for her husband when he became a U.S. Treasury agent in 1879. Their daughter, Marion, married Harry Chandler, who subsequently established a media empire.

Ida Minerva Tarbell

Muckraker Ida Minerva Tarbell gained her reputation when she wrote a nineteen-piece exposé on Standard Oil for *McClure's*. The series was published in book form as *The History of the Standard Oil Company* in 1904. She also wrote a two-volume *Life of Abraham Lincoln* (1900). Pejoratively called "muckrakers" by President Theodore Roosevelt (the term alludes to the "Man with the Muckrake" in John Bunyan's *Pilgrim's Progress*), Tarbell, Lincoln Steffens, and others introduced investigative journalism. She worked with Steffens as an editor of *American Magazine* until the publication was sold in 1915. Tarbell is the subject of considerable attention from various media historians.

Ida Bell Wells-Barnett

As well respected but not as well known as Tarbell, Ida Bell Wells-Barnett made her mark as a suffragist who helped found the National Association for the Advancement of Colored People in 1909. When her parents and her brother died of yellow fever, she supported her remaining siblings. Later, while teaching and attending school in Memphis, she joined a reading group composed of public school teachers and began editing the group's newsletter, the *Evening Star.*

In 1884 Wells boarded a Chesapeake and Ohio Railroad train bound for Woodstock, Tennessee, and sat in the ladies car. Three men put her off the train when she refused the conductor's instruction to move to the smoking car with the other black passengers. As Rodger Streitmatter notes, "White passengers stood on their seats and applauded" the men's action (*Raising Her Voice* 51). Wells filed suit against the Chesapeake and Ohio and was awarded $500, although the Tennessee supreme court reversed the decision three years later. The lawsuit was judged "not in good faith" and was considered "an attempt to harass the railroad company" (Rhodes, "Activism through Journalism" 33). Because Wells's courage was obvious, her reputation spread rapidly beyond Memphis, and she began writing for national African American newspapers, including the *New York Age, Indianapolis World, Fisk Herald,* and *Detroit Plaindealer.*

The visibility that resulted from these early events would serve her well. Referred to as the "Princess of the Black Press," Wells would begin in 1889 using her Memphis newspaper, *Free Speech and Headlight,* to support women's right to vote, investigate discrimination, promote education for African Americans, and oppose lynching. With a circulation of four thousand, the Baptist weekly would later include stories about the mutilation and murder of three black Memphis grocery store operators in 1892. When the three tried to defend themselves against armed white men, some of the white men were killed. Soon after, the three were taken from jail and lynched. Wells retaliated by asking black residents of Memphis to move out of the city. The fact that some did resettle in the West and Midwest damaged the Memphis economy (Ibid. 34).

The newspaper's office was closed and Wells's friends feared violence against her after she argued in print against the prevailing belief that black men often rape white women and claimed instead that some white women are attracted to black men and have consensual sex with them. Wells, who was attending a conference in Philadelphia at the time, was warned not to return to Memphis. At the age of thirty, Ida B. Wells "was exiled from the region of her birth, and it would be several decades before she again set foot on southern soil" (Ibid. 35).

After living and working in New York for the *New York Age,* Wells moved to Chicago and married Ferdinand Lee Barnett, a lawyer and founder of *The Conservator,* the first Chicago newspaper for blacks, in 1895. There, she continued her antilynching campaign. One of the two black women to participate in the founding of the NAACP, Wells founded the Negro Fellowship League to help migrant workers; the Alpha Suffrage Club, the first African American women's suffrage organization in Illinois; and the Ida B. Wells Club of Chicago, which worked to establish black cultural and educational institutions. She also led in the formation of various groups through the black women's club movement.

Elizabeth Cochrane Seaman

Another of the most famous women in the journalism of this period was Elizabeth Cochrane Seaman, best known as "Nellie Bly," a pseudonym a Pittsburgh editor borrowed from a song by Stephen Collins Foster, one of the most popular tunes of the nineteenth century. Called by some historians the first woman staff writer, Cochrane worked for $5 a week at the *Pittsburgh Dispatch* beginning in 1885, having gained the position after she read a piece in the *Dispatch* entitled "What Are Girls Good For?" Although her response to that question was not published, it caught the editors' attention, and she was asked to write on the same topic for the Sunday edition. "Originally," Douglas comments, "Cochrane was supposed to write only on society, theater and the arts. . . but industrial Pittsburgh brought out her inquisitional faculties and she tramped through factories and workshops writing exposés of the abuses she found there. Since she developed an emotional style of high indignation it was only natural that her aspirations would eventually be directed to the *New York World,* where Joseph Pulitzer had made his paper famous for its crusades, exposés, and stunts" (*The Golden Age of the Newspaper* 179).

In 1887 the editors of the *New York World* hired Cochrane after she exposed unethical practices at the Blackwell's Island asylum by feigning mental illness and having herself admitted. Four physicians found her to be insane (Ibid.). In addition to patient abuse at the institution, she also discovered poor sanitation and unhealthy food, and the investigation led to broader political discussion and, ultimately, a grand jury investigation and social reforms. "After she got out," Douglas notes, "she wrote a series of articles on her experiences, telling how patients were abused and beaten, describing the hospital as a 'human rat trap, easy to get into, impossible to get out of'" (Ibid). (Douglas draws much of his information about Cochrane from the work of Ishbel Ross.)

In 1889, Cochrane, as "Nellie Bly," captivated the world by imitating the adventures of a fictional character in Jules Verne's *Around the World in Eighty Days* (1872), and her series of travel stories appeared in Joseph Pulitzer's *New York World,* gaining her a reputation as a "stunt girl." The twenty-four-year-old Cochrane traveled 24,899 miles around the globe in seventy-two days, six hours, and eleven minutes. As Elizabeth Burt observes, "Readers and sources alike found Bly a warm and sympathetic champion of those about whom she wrote. In addition to this characteristic part of her success was due to her highly personal and somewhat breathless style of writing and her direct appeal to readers' emotions. But above all, no matter what story she was covering, she always made herself a central character in the drama" (Sloan and Startt, *The Media in America* 232).

Before her career was over, Cochrane had become known as a fearless reformer who wrote about immigrants and the poor; conditions in factories, tenements, mental institutions, health-care facilities, jails, and women's prisons; life in rural areas of America; the Chicago Pullman strike and other labor issues; gambling; prostitution; orphans; sexual harassment; and Wild West shows. She also wrote about anarchist Emma Goldman and covered World War I in Austria between 1914 and 1918. Late in her career, she wrote news stories and a column about abandoned children for the *New York Evening Journal*.

Martha Winifred Sweet Black Bonfils

Another woman who took a nickname and also became known as a reformer was Martha Winifred Sweet Black Bonfils, who was best known as "Annie Laurie," a name she borrowed from a Scottish lullaby. Bonfils gained her reputation during the era of yellow journalism. It was a period when editors emphasized stories about sex and crime and also championed the rights of the average person. As a reporter and managing editor for the *Denver Post* and the newspapers of William Randolph Hearst, Bonfils became famous for stories that exposed political corruption, social injustices, and inefficient government.

Bonfils was Hearst's West Coast answer to the *New York World*'s Cochrane. During a fifty-year career she gained the devotion of the American public for coverage of social issues. She also "developed her own brand of personal, vivid writing," which Douglas describes as "short sentences and paragraphs with hard jolts." The appeal was "extravagantly emotional" (*The Golden Age of the Newspaper* 182).

In 1889 the *San Francisco Examiner* hired Bonfils, and she worked there as a reporter and later a columnist, producing scoops, exposés, and sensational stories about everything from a leper colony on the island of Molokai to a flood in Galveston, Texas. She covered conditions in hospitals; investigated juvenile courts, fruit canneries, cotton mills, and brothels; exposed racketeers; and described the 1906 San Francisco earthquake and its aftermath. She also wrote about the Versailles Peace Conference, polygamy in 1898 Utah, and several murder trials.

Bonfils's techniques for getting stories were as controversial as the stories themselves. After the Galveston tidal wave and flood of 1900, during which six thousand people died, she reported on disaster relief in the city—the only woman to do so—and dressed as a boy to gain access to the destruction. Using funds from the Hearst newspaper chain, she subsequently opened a clinic to help flood victims. While investigating conditions in a public hospital, Bonfils posed as indigent and feigned a fainting spell, and when exposing the treatment of women in factories, she went undercover and pretended to be a worker. It is said that she gained an exclusive interview with President Benjamin Harrison in 1892 by hiding under a railroad dining car table and emerging when he sat down for dinner.

Like Dorothy Dix, Nixola Greeley-Smith, Ada Patterson, and others, Bonfils was considered a "sob sister," meaning that she wrote human interest stories that employed a descriptive, highly emotional style. Beasley and Gibbons define sob sisters as those who wrote "tear-jerking accounts of flamboyant events" (*Taking Their Place* 111). The sob sisters, including Bonfils, were particularly well known for their coverage of the 1907 trial of New York's Harry Thaw, accused of killing Stanford White, an architect, for pursuing his wife, Evelyn Nesbit Thaw.

Bonfils covered celebrated trials and issues of social injustice for newspapers as prestigious as the *San Francisco Examiner* and the *New York Journal* and worked as a foreign correspondent, drama critic, society editor, city editor, and managing editor. Married to Orlow Black in 1892 and divorced five years later, she then married Charles Alden Bonfils, a journalist with the *Denver Post,* in 1901. That marriage, too, ended in divorce.

Bonfils was respected by colleagues as well as readers. In one of her last articles, a 1936 piece for *Good Housekeeping,* she praised Hearst, her former editor and publisher, for having confidence in her. When she died on May 25, 1936, in San Francisco, she was celebrated by the public in an unprecedented way—her casket lay in the rotunda of city hall in San Francisco, and city officials served as pallbearers.

Dorothy Thompson

Dorothy Thompson, author of the syndicated column "On the Record," did not stand in the shadow of any of the women who preceded her. In fact, the column appeared in 196 newspapers, boasting a total readership of 7.5 million (Schilpp and Murphy, *Great Women of the Press* 176). Thompson wrote for the *Philadelphia Public Ledger, New York Post, New York Herald-Tribune,* and *Christian Science Monitor.* One of her three husbands was Sinclair Lewis, the first American to win a Nobel Prize in literature. They divorced in 1942.

A foreign correspondent, Thompson supported suffrage and was the first woman to head an international news bureau. During her career, she covered news in Europe, worked for the Red Cross, freelanced, and served as a correspondent. As chief of the *New York Post's* Berlin office, Thompson interviewed Adolf Hitler in Berlin in 1931 when he was a leader in the Nazi Party. After warning U.S. officials about the spread of Fascism, she argued for U.S. intervention in World War II. Thrown out of Germany in 1934, in 1936 Thompson began writing her syndicated column for Helen Rogers Reid at the *New York Herald-Tribune.*

Helen Rogers Reid

Married to Ogden Reid, the son of the publisher of the *New York Tribune,* Helen Rogers Reid became vice president of the *Tribune* and began hiring women as book reviewers and to write about food. Like other women, Reid married into a newspaper family and used her position to provide jobs for qualified colleagues. In addition to hiring Thompson, she sent Marguerite Higgins to cover Europe during World War II. When her husband died in 1947, Reid became president of the newspaper's parent company for six years and later sold it to millionaire John Hay Whitney.

Genevieve Forbes Herrick

Another important woman in journalism in the early twentieth century is Genevieve Forbes Herrick, who began her career at the *Chicago Tribune* in 1921, covered the police and political beats, investigated problems at Ellis Island, and traveled from Ireland to America to conduct research for a thirteen-part series that led to the investigation of corruption in the U.S. Immigration Service. In 1924 she covered the trial of Nathan Leopold and Richard Loeb in Chicago. Herrick also wrote about Representative Ruth Hanna McCormick, who ran for the Senate in 1930, and was close to Eleanor Roosevelt. She later wrote for magazines.

Eleanor (Cissy) Medill Patterson and Alicia Patterson

It is impossible to underestimate the importance of women who married into or were born into media families. One of them, Eleanor (Cissy) Medill Patterson was the granddaughter of the founder of the *Chicago Tribune* and ran Hearst's *Washington Herald* beginning in 1930; the newspaper was called the *Washington Times-Herald* from 1930 to 1948. Her brother, Joseph Medill Patterson, founded the *New York Daily News,* and his daughter (and her niece), Alicia Patterson, founded *Newsday.* During her career, Cissy Patterson was director of the *New York Daily News* and *Chicago Tribune* companies.

She loved journalism and committed herself to the success of the *Washington Herald.* In less than two years the newspaper boasted the largest morning circulation among Hearst publications, and Hearst made her editor and publisher (Mills, *A Place in the News* 19). By 1943 Patterson was making a profit on the "largest-circulation newspaper in Washington" (Beasley and Gibbons, *Taking Their Place* 158). The newspaper later was consolidated with the *Washington Post.*

Alicia Patterson also made her mark on journalism. Beginning as a cub reporter for the *New York Daily News,* she and her husband, Harry F. Guggenheim, bought the *Nassau Daily Journal* in Hempstead on Long Island, N.Y. Patterson ran the editorial side, and, eventually, the newspaper was renamed *Newsday.* By 1963 the newspaper was reporting a circulation of 375,000.

Charlotte Murray Curtis

One of the women who made her way into journalism without the support of family members in the industry is Charlotte Murray Curtis. She is the subject of many articles and books, including Marilyn S. Greenwald's *A Woman of the Times,* which covers Curtis's journalistic contributions and belief in equality for women. Although Curtis was the first female associate editor of the *New York Times,* she "hesitated to call herself a feminist" (Beasley and Gibbons, *Taking Their Place* 22). Curtis was graduated from Vassar College and took a summer job at the *Columbus Citizen* after her freshman year. Hired full time after graduation, she became society editor but left the newspaper in 1961, the year she was hired to write about home furnishings for the *New York Times.* Two years later she began writing for the society pages, and in 1965 she became editor of women's news. By 1974 she was editor of the op-ed page and became a columnist in 1982.

Nan Robertson

A journalist who acknowledged her debt to the women who came before her, Nan Robertson began writing for *Stars and Stripes* in 1948. She covered Europe for seven years, writing about the Marshall Plan, the Berlin blockade, and the Cold War. She was twenty-eight when she was hired at the *New York Times* as a fashion writer. "The only reason for that was that I had once done public relations for Christian Dior," she stated. The *New York Times* editors "automatically put me on the women's pages as if those seven years in Europe hadn't mattered at all" (Mills, *A Place in the News* 75). She then covered crime, the courts, and fires before becoming a feature writer. "Feature writing," she said later in her career, "is the only semiliterary form in the newspaper" (Ibid. 76).

Mary Baker Eddy

Another major figure in twentieth-century journalism is Mary Baker Eddy, who established the *Christian Science Monitor* in 1908 and dedicated herself to a protest of sensationalism in news coverage. She emphasized international events and downplayed crime reporting. During World War I, with a circulation of 120,000, the *Christian Science Monitor* was distributed more widely in the United States than any other daily (Beasley, "The Emergence of Modern Media" 288).

Katharine (Kay) Meyer Graham

Women journalists in the twentieth century sometimes became national celebrities. One woman in American newspapers who grew into her celebrity and who lived through events such as the release of the Pentagon Papers, the break-in at the Watergate, and the resignation of President Richard M. Nixon is Katharine (Kay) Meyer Graham, longtime publisher of the *Washington Post*. When she died in 2001, her funeral at the National Cathedral in Washington, D.C., was attended by Henry Kissinger, Dick and Lynne Cheney, Rudolph Giuliani, Bill Gates, Oscar de la Renta, Edward Kennedy, Barbara Walters, and Robert McNamara, among others.

The woman who once thought of herself as a housewife—whose father had given the family newspaper to her husband, Philip—became one of Washington's most beloved figures. After Philip Graham committed suicide in 1963, Katherine Graham took control of the Washington Post Company, its television stations, and *Newsweek* magazine. She was known for tenacity and courage, especially in following the *New York Times*'s decision to publish the Pentagon Papers in 1971. Her support of investigative journalists Bob Woodward and Carl Bernstein led to more than four hundred stories about Watergate in the *Washington Post* and also to Nixon's resignation and prosecution of those involved in the break-in and cover-up.

During her career, Graham served as president of the American Newspaper Publishers Association and was the first woman on the Associated Press board of directors. In 1979 Graham's son, Donald, became publisher of the *Washington Post,* and in 1991 he replaced her as chief operating officer although she remained chair of the Washington Post Company. Graham's autobiography, *Personal History,* won a Pulitzer Prize in 1998.

Representative Women Columnists in American Newspapers

One of the issues addressed in this volume is how men in journalism have defined the word *news* according to their own priorities and worldviews. Women in journalism, the inheritors of that definition, could choose to adhere to the priorities of those who hired and trained them, write in a genre other than hard news, or argue for a broader understanding and accept news as providing human interest, entertainment, and practical information about daily life.

Those who edited women's and society news pages and wrote for them as well had to deal with the fact that many senior editors and readers considered the news they provided to be superficial and unimportant in defining political and social norms. Women who became known as literary journalists were attacked by hardline news editors for crossing what, for them, was an obvious line between fact and fiction. Those who founded, edited, or wrote for lesbian publications or other examples of the alternative press broke out of the traditional definitions of news entirely.

Some women who remained in the mainstream press, however, began to redefine the standards of news as provided by major metropolitan dailies. Others became columnists and were well known and part of an entertainment tradition; contemporary women columnists produce well-researched pieces about politics and social issues as well as entertainment and celebrity news. From Elizabeth Meriwether Gilmer ("Dorothy Dix") to Ellen Goodman, women columnists have opened the way for generations of women to move into journalism. Like those who wrote for and edited women's pages, they have been forced to deal with the perception that they have somehow failed to meet the important criteria of real news. Too often, columns by men as well as women are treated as entertainment reporting. In fact, however, they often represent some of the most energetic writing in a newspaper and exemplify the importance of informal, first-person point of view in interpretive news reporting.

Norma M. Schulman has discussed her discomfort with the traditionally male definitions of news, definitions that are particularly important in considering columns by women that address the home, colorful personalities in local politics, the needs of children, and the limitations of social work in a community. Like many other media critics and scholars, Schulman questions the notion that news involves city councils, budgets, and war but not family planning, personal income, parenting, and other issues deemed of particular interest to women. She has traced the development of her concern about definitions of news:

> The detective's voice was patronizing each time he repeated the now-famous line from *Dragnet*: "Just the facts, ma'am." He seemed to say it at least once in every episode of the television show. His intonation never varied. He'd tilt his head down slightly, as if speaking to a younger, smaller, less-focused person—

his hands poised motionlessly above his note pad—while an overwrought female character blurted out what she knew.

The woman the detective admonished was different every week—sometimes a "girl Friday," sometimes a cousin, sometimes a neighbor of the deceased. But one thing remained constant on the *Dragnet* that I remember: She was always too emotional, too illogical, and too unobservant to illuminate much of anything...

Watching this as a girl growing up before the women's movement of the sixties, I thought she seemed to become giddy at the unaccustomed pleasure of being listened to by a serious-looking man who, as he explained by flashing his credentials, was there on official business. Her desire to please came through loud and clear, but her answers to questions were heavily qualified, tentative, or downright vague. When she was specifically asked, on occasion, to describe something concrete, her answers were as flat and unselective as the text of a Sears-Roebuck catalog read aloud. Otherwise she emoted, she free-associated, she wandered far afield of "just the facts."

What bothered me then, and what bothers me more now, both as a journalist and as a woman, is central to the concerns of this chapter on newspaper opinion columns written by women. In the world of my own private *Dragnet,* women seemed to be looked down on as being incapable of separating fact from inference—a separation that somehow proved quite unproblematic to the detective and his (all-male) law enforcement team. In the detective's world, which was the larger, public world, only facts mattered—impressions, opinions, and intuitions merely hindered the pursuit of authoritative and unimpeachable Truth. A single correct version of events existed. Exposing it—with its pristine, unambiguous outlines intact—was Detective Friday's sole function in life. And everything he did—every quizzical arch of his eyebrows—seemed to contribute to achieving this purpose...

It was no accident that when women began entering newspaper journalism in substantial numbers in the late 1960s and early 1970s, they gravitated, or were propelled, toward so-called soft news or human-interest features rather than hard, event-oriented stories on topics of social and political import. It was no accident that the terms used to describe effective prose were then, and are now, perilously close to terms of approbation used to describe the male sex: "lean, dry, terse, powerful, strong, spare, linear, focused, explosive," as [R. B.] DuPlessis (1985) has noted.

A well-written news story is supposed to externalize its point; provide a liberal amount of attributed "proof" in the form of authoritative quotes; employ argument as the preferred mode for discussion; focus on concrete actions, instead of cognitive states or emotion; and offer grounds for objective conclusions, if not outright closure. ("Wrinkling the Fabric of the Press" 56–57)

Schulman praises women columnists such as Mary McGrory, Ellen Goodman, and Anna Quindlen for initiating a "refreshing new trend—one that already shows signs of spreading to their male colleagues: integrating commentary on public affairs with insights into the human condition." She also maintains that a newspaper column allows for "self-reflection, the full range of emotional tones, the distinctive (even idiosyncratic) authorial voice, and the progressive discovery-by-analogy that mark some of the most outstanding examples of women's journalism in the United States today" (Ibid. 58).

The following listing of columnists is intended to be illustrative rather than comprehensive. How the women made their way into newspapers is especially relevant; often, they were sought out and hired by men who espoused a definition of news that defied the prevailing criteria. Especially during the eras of the penny press and yellow journalism, the work of women columnists was far more in keeping with the objectives of mainstream metropolitan newspapers than would be the case by the mid-1900s.

Elizabeth Meriwether Gilmer

Elizabeth Meriwether Gilmer, the first national personal advice columnist, is best known by her pen name, Dorothy Dix. Emery and Emery (*The Press and America*) and Douglas (*The Golden Age of the Newspaper*) spell her real name as *Meriweather Gilmore,* but Mills (*A Place in the News*) and the official Web site dedicated to her work list it as *Meriwether Gilmer*). Gilmer chose the pen name because "alliterative pseudonyms [were] voguish in those days for gentlewomen concealing their real names from the stigma of the sordid newspaper world" (Schilpp and Murphy, *Great Women of the Press* 115). Gilmer began her advice column at the *New Orleans Picayune* and in 1901 went to work for Hearst at the *New York Journal,* writing a regular column called "Dorothy Dix Talks." She published readers' letters and her responses to them three days a week and "homilies or sermonettes" on the other days and described herself as the "mother confessor to millions" (Douglas, *The Golden Age of the Newspaper* 186; Schilpp and Murphy, *Great Women of the Press* 120).

In a career that lasted from 1895 to 1949, Gilmer worked for several newspapers, including *The Picayune, New York Post,* and *New York Journal.* A sob sister, she often covered murder trials, which Schilpp and Murphy describe as "America's real-life soap operas before the advent of television." Gilmer also provided the "lurid details" of the "nation's love triangles" (Ibid. 116).

In addition to the entertainment that her columns provided, Gilmer championed woman suffrage, women's right to equal educations, and women's right to work. Beasley notes that Gilmer often focused upon trials of women charged with murder and wrote about those victimized by men ("The Emergence of Modern Media" 288). By the time of her death at age ninety, she was a millionaire, had sixty million readers, and received between seven hundred and a thousand letters daily (Schilpp and Murphy, *Great Women of the Press* 113).

Louella Parsons

Louella Parsons began her career in Chicago and later moved to New York. In 1923 she was movie editor for the *New York American,* a Hearst publication. Two years later, she became a movie editor for Hearst's Universal News Service and in 1926 moved to Hollywood. Remembered especially for her coverage of two scoops—the divorce of actors Douglas Fairbanks and Mary Pickford in 1935 and the pregnancy that followed Ingrid Bergman's affair with director Roberto Rossellini in 1949—Parsons became a celebrity because of the famous people she covered.

Hedda Hopper

Unlike Parsons, Hedda Hopper longed to act. After finishing the eighth grade, she joined a theatrical troupe. While covering Metro-Goldwyn-Mayer films during the 1920s, she began writing to compete with Parsons. Known for her colorful hats, Hopper wrote about actors and about politicians and government officials—including Richard M. Nixon, J. Edgar Hoover, and Ronald Reagan—and their families. After World War II she became "increasingly conservative and urged a boycott of films by writers, actors, and directors with Communist connections" (Mills, *A Place in the News* 29).

Sheilah Graham

Sheilah Graham, Parsons, and Hopper composed a formidable and often charming trio of Hollywood columnists. By 1964 Graham's work appeared in 178 American newspapers, and her radio and television programs were successful during the 1950s. Graham is also remembered for having had a brief relationship with F. Scott Fitzgerald.

Born Lily Shiel in London on September 15, 1904, Graham was the daughter of a man who died of tuberculosis when she was an infant; her mother was a domestic worker. At the age of six, Graham was placed in an orphanage, and as a young woman she studied drama, worked as a chorus girl, and wrote articles about show business. She married Major John Graham Gillam, renamed herself "Sheilah Graham," and moved to the United States in 1933 to write for the *New York Mirror* and *Evening Journal.*

In 1935 Graham became a syndicated columnist for the North American Newspaper Alliance. Divorced two years later, she moved to California and began writing columns about Hollywood. That same year, she met Fitzgerald at a party given to celebrate her engagement to the Marquis of Donegall. Graham fell in love with Fitzgerald, broke off the engagement, and lived with the writer until his death three years later in December 1940.

After Fitzgerald died, Graham married Trevor Westbrook, an executive for a company that manufactured the Spitfire fighter airplane, in 1941, but they divorced in 1946. Her son, Robert Westbrook, and her daughter, Wendy Westbrook Fairey, have written about their mother's life and relationship with Fitzgerald.

In addition to stories about Hollywood, Graham also wrote columns in 1941 about women's roles in munitions factories and about the London bombings and several books.

Georgie Anne Geyer

Georgie Anne Geyer is best known for books, columns, and news stories on foreign affairs. In the early 1960s and on her first foreign assignment, she traveled with guerrilla fighters through the jungles of Guatemala on a trip funded by a Seymour Berkson Foreign Assignment Grant. Geyer was twenty-seven, and no other American women correspondents were in Latin America at the time. She remained there to write about revolutions for the *Chicago Daily News* for several years, and her courage and tenacity have been rewarded in a long and productive career as a reporter and columnist who traveled the globe to report on people and events. Fascinated by the motivations of world leaders and their ability to retain power, Geyer is also interested in differences among cultures and drawn to understanding varied perspectives on the same issues. She has interviewed world leaders, including Saddam Hussein, Yasser Arafat, the Ayatollah Khomeini, and Fidel Castro, and has also been a columnist for the Universal Press Syndicate, which has distributed her column three times weekly to more than 150 newspapers.

Called prophetic by many colleagues and critics, Geyer went to Yugoslavia in the 1980s and predicted its collapse. She also predicted the breakup of the Soviet Union. Geyer and her counterparts, including Molly Ivins, Ellen Goodman, and Anna Quindlen, have moved into the spotlight since the 1980s and crossed from women's news to the lifestyle sections of American newspapers and then to editorial and op-ed pages.

In 1974 Geyer moved to Washington, D.C., and began writing columns, although she continued to conduct research and read widely. Her books include *The New Latins: Fateful Change in South and Central America; The Young Russians; Buying the Night Flight: The Autobiography of a Woman Foreign Correspondent* (her autobiography); *Guerrilla Prince: The Untold Story of Fidel Castro; Americans No More* (about modern immigrants); and *Waiting for Winter to End: An Extraordinary Journey through Soviet Central Asia.*

Dorothy Gilliam

Dorothy Gilliam began her career at the *Louisville Defender,* a black weekly, while attending Ursiline College. At seventeen she became the society editor. In 1961, Gilliam began writing for the *Washington Post,* for which she covered James Meredith and his controversial admission to the University of Mississippi in Oxford. As she recalled, "In those days, they had to send two reporters if they were going to get to the black community. They knew they couldn't send me to do the white story. I remember a guy named Bill Chapman was covering the campus, and I was covering some of the black community. He stayed at the Sand and Sea Motel and I stayed at the black funeral home because there were no places for black people to stay. . . . In many ways as I look back, I think that was one of the shining hours of the press in terms of really covering an American story that made a difference" (Mills, *A Place in the News* 181). Gilliam became a columnist in 1979 and for seven years was assistant editor of the "Style" section of the *Post,* covering social issues that included race and ethnicity.

Ellen Goodman

"I didn't want to draw lines between private lives and public lives but rather to connect those lives" (Ibid. 264), Ellen Goodman has said. Schulman praises Goodman, who has been a syndicated writer for the *Washington Post* and *Boston Globe* and in 1980 won a Pulitzer Prize for commentary, as having accomplished her goal and describes her as an "architect of a new type of newspaper column that bridges the gap between personal experience and the larger arena of social, cultural, and political analysis" ("Wrinkling the Fabric of the Press" 61).

Goodman became a news reporter and feature writer when the *Detroit Free Press* hired her in 1965. In 1967 she began writing for the women's pages of the *Boston Globe,* where she became a columnist and associate editor. A cum laude graduate of Radcliffe College, Goodman became a Nieman Fellow at Harvard in 1973 and 1974. Among the recognition she has received are the American Society of Newspaper Editors Distinguished Writing Award (1980), the Hubert H. Humphrey Civil Rights Award from the Leadership Conference on Civil Rights (1988), the President's Award from the National Women's Political Caucus (1993), and the American Woman Award from the Women's Research and Education Institute (1994).

Although Goodman refers to images familiar in domestic life and individual experience, she deals with the larger society. In a January 1989 column "Exit Ron Reagan: Stage Right," for example, she refers to the response of the average American watching television and film: "So, as the credits start to roll on his last hours in office, this is the Reagan I take away: A man who followed and recreated a great American story line. A man who thought of us as an audience rather than a citizenry. A man who elicited goose bumps more often than action. He projected an image on the screen to make us feel as good as we did at a Saturday matinee, when everybody knew the good guys from the bad and the good guys always won. The End" (394).

Collections of Goodman's work, such as *Turning Points, Close to Home, At Large, Keeping in Touch,* and *Value Judgments,* reflect her versatility. Her work has appeared in more than 450 newspapers and includes commentary on safe sex, singles clubs, aging, competition, suicide, AIDS, women in the workplace, country music, marriage, divorce, religion, smoking, rape, abortion, and nuclear weapons. Among the celebrities and political figures whom she has interviewed are Barbara Bush, Fred Astaire, Oliver North, Bishop Tutu, Gary Hart, Pat Robertson, Salman Rushdie, Madonna, the Rolling Stones, Elizabeth Taylor, Theodor Geisel (Dr. Seuss), Doris Lessing, Eleanor Roosevelt, Sally Ride, Raisa Gorbachev, Mother Teresa, Pablo Picasso, and John Lennon.

Molly Tyler Ivins

Known as a columnist and political pundit, Molly Ivins was born in Monterey, California, but grew up in Houston, Texas. She received a B.A. degree from Smith College and a master's degree in journalism from Columbia University. A former coeditor of the *Texas Observer* and former Rocky Mountain bureau chief for the *New York Times,* Ivins also worked for the *Houston Chronicle, Minneapolis Star-Tribune, Dallas Times-Herald,* and *Fort Worth Star Telegram.* Her freelance work appeared in *Esquire, Atlantic, The Nation, Harper's,* the *Progressive, Mother Jones, TV Guide,* and other publications.

In 1967 Ivins became the first woman at the *Star-Tribune* to cover the Minneapolis police beat. "They had other good women," she said, "but they sent me because I looked the part. I'm six feet tall. Nobody ever looked at me and said, 'Oh, you poor sweet dainty little thing. We can't send you out to cover a riot.' It was more, 'Ivins, get your ass out there'" (Mills, *A Place in the News* 88). Critics and media scholars agree with Ivins's perception of herself: "Ivins is big and she's brash, like Texas, and if the state fits, wear it" (Ibid. 61).

A three-time Pulitzer Prize finalist, Ivins began writing for the *New York Times* in 1967 and later became nationally known for a political column that appeared in more than 110 newspapers.

Anna Quindlen

Like Goodman, *New York Times* syndicated columnist Anna Quindlen also uses personal anecdotes and description to comment on a range of social issues that include parenting, human rights, media, child care, and family planning. The winner of a 1992 Pulitzer Prize for her *New York Times* column "Public and Private," Quindlen deals with issues involving discrimination against gays, racial and ethnic minorities, children and other groups. In a provocative June 27, 1993, column entitled "Another Kind of Closet," for example, she observes that in America, "Homosexuals will be tolerated as long as they don't homosex" (Schulman, "Wrinkling the Fabric of the Press" 65).

Quindlen and other woman columnists transform images from personal life into the universal. In "The Lightning Bugs Are Back," a 1988 column, she writes that fireflies symbolize a way of life: "This is why I had children: to offer them a perfect dream of childhood that can fill their souls as they grow older. . . . And to fill my own soul, too, so that I can relive the magic of the yellow light without the bright white of hindsight, to see only the glow and not the dark. Mommy, magic, those little flares in the darkness, a distillation of the kind of life we think we had, we wish we had, we want again" (*Living Out Loud* 3–5).

A reporter and columnist for the *New York Times* from 1977 to 1994, Quindlen now writes a regular column for *Newsweek*. Her novel *One True Thing* became a motion picture in 1998; other novels include *Object Lessons* and *Black and Blue*. Her columns have been collected in *Living Out Loud* and *Thinking Out Loud*.

Representative Women Photographers as Social Reformers

Writers are not the only women journalists of note; those who work as photographers have also gained fame. Capturing the "transient moment" (Westling, *Eudora Welty* xv), a phrase borrowed from Welty in a collection of her photographs, describes the contribution of women photographers as they encouraged social reform in America during the nineteenth and twentieth centuries.

Margaret Bourke-White

Originally a freelance architectural and landscape photographer in Cleveland, Ohio, Margaret Bourke-White was hired by Henry Luce in 1929 to take pictures of business and industrial sites for *Fortune* magazine. In order to get her famous images of the Chrysler Building that towered above Manhattan, Bourke-White "perched on a high tower, swaying eight feet in the wind, sometimes in subfreezing temperatures" (Schilpp and Murphy, *Great Women of the Press* 184). She also covered stories in Russia, Africa, India, Korea, Czechoslovakia, Hungary, England, Romania, Turkey, Syria, Egypt, and Pakistan, and her work was published in *Fortune, Life, Time,* and other periodicals.

The first woman to fly on a combat mission, and considered by some to be the first woman war correspondent, Bourke-White was praised for her work as a World War II photographer, covering the war in Italy and the liberation of the concentration camps in Germany. The former Associated Press reporter Tad Bartimus calls her "arguably the most famous female journalist in the world" ("Bullets and Bathrooms" 10).

The colorful and influential Bourke-White has gained praise from women journalists who followed in her footsteps. "She was in Moscow with five cameras, twenty-two lenses, three thousand flashbulbs and four portable developing tanks when the Germans attacked the Soviet Union in 1941," Bartimus writes. "She wore red shoes and a red hair-bow to a rare interview with Joseph Stalin, then worked all night in a U.S. Embassy bathroom to print her historic pictures" (Ibid. 11). Bartimus was particularly impressed when she found a self-photograph of Bourke-White in *Life:* "Shown wearing a sheepskin-lined, high-altitude flight suit, and standing before a B-17 in North Africa in 1943, she was described in the magazine as 'the first woman ever to fly with a U.S. combat crew over enemy soil.' Twenty years later that same picture, spotted in an old magazine in my grandmother's attic, made me exclaim, 'I want to do that!'" (Ibid. 12).

Bourke-White, whose photographs of the Fort Peck, Montana, dam appeared on the November 23, 1936, cover of *Life* magazine, is also known for her pictures of the Dust Bowl and for collaborating with Erskine Caldwell on *You Have Seen Their Faces.* The couple married in 1939. As Schilpp and Murphy write, "Travelling together most of one summer, the two gathered the bitter tales of poor Southerners. His realistic prose and her stark photos made a book still regarded today as a classic documentary against racial injustice" (*Great Women of the Press* 186).

A writer as well as a photographer, Bourke-White also published *Eyes on Russia* and an autobiography, *Portrait of Myself,* that chronicles the story of a woman who began as an industrial photographer and became famous for photographs of sharecroppers in the South and farmers in the Dust Bowl.

Frances Benjamin Johnston

Perhaps less visible to the public than Bourke-White, Frances Benjamin Johnston worked as both a newspaper photo illustrator and a photographer. She considered photography as one of the most accurate of media and did not view herself as a social reformer but rather an objective reporter.

Johnston, who affected the social and political attitudes of newspaper readers for many years, studied art in Paris and at the Art Students League in New York. She is best known for her political photography in Washington, D.C., in 1889 and for her pictures of the Kohinoor coal mines of Pennsylvania, Mesabe iron ore range on Lake Superior, female factory workers in Massachusetts, and black students at the Hampton Institute in Virginia and the Tuskegee Institute in Alabama.

In 1899 Johnston was invited to the Hampton Institute, an industrial school for blacks, to help with public relations and fundraising. She photographed the students and graduates and chronicled their progress. From 1902 to 1906 she photographed students and teachers at the Tuskegee Institute, including Booker T. Washington and George Washington Carver, and poor residents of the rural South.

During her late sixties and early seventies, Johnston took more than six thousand images of historic buildings and gardens from Maryland to Louisiana and also photographed famous people. The survey of southern colonial architecture for the Carnegie Foundation from 1933 to 1940 resulted in two collections: *Plantations of the Carolina Low Country* and *The Early Architecture of North Carolina*. Johnston also became known for her portraits of Susan B. Anthony, Joel Chandler Harris, Theodore Roosevelt, Mark Twain, Andrew Carnegie, Alexander Graham Bell, and others.

Dorothea Lange

Like Bourke-White and Johnston, Dorothea Lange photographed a variety of geographical and personal landscapes and revealed an America few wanted to acknowledge. In particular, she took photographs of strikes, demonstrations, food lines, and migrant and internment camps and was a catalyst for widespread social reform. She also traveled among the Shakers and the Amish, interviewing and photographing members of those communities. One of her most celebrated photographic essays is entitled *The American Country Woman.*

During the 1920s, Lange was a San Francisco portrait photographer, covering parties, weddings, and debutante balls. By 1939, however, she had published *An American Exodus* with her second husband, fellow photographer Paul Taylor, and depicted the strength and character of those most financially devastated by the depression. During her work for the Farm Security Administration (FSA) from 1935 to 1942, she collected more than 270,000 images. Calling herself a "chronicler," she is perhaps best known for photographing the "dispossessed people" of the Dust Bowl era and farmers and their families in the Southwest and Deep South (Marzolf, *Up from the Footnote* 68).

While working for the FSA, Lange gained great sympathy for the migrant workers and tenant farmers of the country. Like Eudora Welty, Walker Evans, and James Agee, she supplied a major sociological record of an important historical period. As Mary Louise Tucker notes, "Photo documentaries of the scope [of the FSA project] will probably never be attempted again. These are major sociological and historical records of the South in rapid transition from an agrarian to an industrialized society, documents of a people witnessing the collapse of social and religious traditions and experiencing the disintegration of the extended family unit" ("Photography and Photographers" 98).

Although a reporter for the Associated Press in 1989 called Lange's pictures a "misery index" ("Welty Photos" 1E), other critics such as Archibald MacLeish cite their poignancy. MacLeish, among those who claimed that Lange preserved the integrity of those she photographed, used much of her work in *Land of the Free* (1938). "Like all great artists in the visual arts, her subject was mankind," he said. "And she was a great artist" (Meltzer, *Dorothea Lange* 185).

Several of Lange's photographs are particularly representative of the land, era, and people she knew well. One, *Ex-Slave, Alabama* (1937), depicts a farm woman engaged in conversation while taking a break from hoeing. Her head in a kerchief, the woman is expressive and determined and appears to be strong and in control as she grips the hoe's handle. Lange's titles are often ironic. In this case, does the word *ex-slave* refer to the woman's poverty and exhaustion from fieldwork, or is the title straightforward, implying that no matter how shabby her attire, she is at least free?

Few can look at *Hoe Culture, Alabama* (1937) without actually feeling the rough wood of the handle. The knuckles, swollen with work, and the blackened fingernails tell their tale more effectively than the absent face ever could. Those who study such photographs must decide for themselves whether Lange exploited grief and poverty or produced a social document that recorded history and revealed the inner strength of those who survived the era.

Eudora Welty

Perhaps Eudora Welty was speaking for Bourke-White, Johnston, Lange, and herself when she wrote that the focus of one of her photographs of a woman during the depression was "not the South, not even the perennially sorry state of the whole world, but the story of her life in her face." Then she added, "And though I did not take these pictures to prove anything, I think they most assuredly do show something—which is to make a far better claim for them. Her face to me is full of meaning more truthful and more terrible and, I think, more noble than any generalization about people could have prepared me for or could describe for me now. I learned from my own pictures, one by one, and had to; for I think we are the breakers of our own hearts" ("One Time One Place" 354).

In some ways, Eudora Welty was the quintessential media professional, although she is best known through short stories and novels. Her work in advertising and journalism and the influence of journalism on her fiction are rarely part of the dominant scholarship in literature or media studies. Few realize that she earned a living in print media, broadcasting, advertising, and public relations before becoming famous for her fiction (chapter 4).

Welty freelanced for Mississippi newspapers, wrote copy for radio station WJDX in Jackson and a Sunday column about Jackson society for the *Memphis Commercial Appeal,* and photographed rural Mississippians for the Works Progress Administration (WPA) in the 1930s. Her brief media career affected her development as a writer of fiction. A study of her work reveals the importance of place and the supremacy of the moment and indicates her desire to stand outside the action to observe rather than interpret. An examination of Welty's fiction reveals the effect of her photographic experience on the ability to isolate and contain the moment; it also indicates the influence that writing society news had on her ability to portray fictional Mississippians with realism and humor. Welty learned to see into the life of things and found what she called "my real subject: human relationships" (*One Writer's Beginnings* 87).

If her work with newspapers contributed significantly to her ability to reproduce dialect and capture regional humor, the time Welty spent with the WPA altered her perspective on art forever. As she recalled, her "first full-time job was rewarding to me in a way I could never have foreseen in those early days of my writing" (Ibid. 84). Established to combat the Great Depression, the WPA needed photographers to travel across the state, write articles for county newspapers, and take photographs. Welty's recollections of that point in her career were vivid:

> With the accretion of years, the hundreds of photographs—life as I found it, all unposed—constitute a record of that desolate period; but most of what I learned for myself came right at the time and directly out of the *taking* of the pictures. The camera was a hand-held auxiliary of wanting-to-know.
>
> It had more than information and accuracy to teach me. I learned in the doing how *ready* I had to be. Life doesn't hold still. A good snapshot stopped a moment from running away. Photography taught me that to be able to capture transience, by being ready to click the shutter at the crucial moment, was the greatest need I had. Making pictures of people in all sorts of situations, I learned that every feeling waits upon its gesture; and I had to be prepared to recognize this moment when I saw it. There were things a story writer needed to know. And I felt the need to hold transient life in *words*—there's so much more of life that only words can convey—strongly enough to last me as long as I lived. (*One Writer's Beginnings* 84–85)

Photography, Louise Westling maintains, "trained Welty's vision, by focusing and fixing information in precise images, teaching her to see human emotion as it is expressed in movement, and helping her understand how to capture the transient moment" (*Eudora Welty* 15).

During her time as a photographer Welty took 1,200 images throughout eighty-two counties of Mississippi, capturing on film the state's cotton pickers, teachers, Baptist deacons, nurses, weavers, storekeepers, farmers, Confederate veterans, children, and washerwomen. She did not see people as "sociological data or political victims" but approached them "with a sense of kinship and admiration for the spirit with which they lived their difficult lives" (Ibid.). When interviewed for the collection *Photographs,* Welty remarked that her "pictures were made in sympathy, not exploitation" (xxvi): "I was never questioned, or avoided. There was no self-consciousness on either side. I just spoke to persons on the street and said, 'Do you mind if I take this picture?' And they didn't care. There was no sense of violation of anything on either side. I don't think it existed; I know it didn't in my attitude, or in theirs. All of that unself-consciousness is gone now. There is no such relationship between a photographer and a subject possible any longer" (xiv).

Her compassion for humanity is evident in the photographs as well as in her novels and short stories. Robert MacNeil contends that Welty's motivation and execution of craft set her apart from professional news photographers:

> Photography in all its forms has made extremes of the human condition a valuable commodity. The news industry gambles on futures in the commodity of human suffering and spends lavishly to record it. Over land and ocean without rest thousands speed at the bidding of networks or newsmagazines to track down the most bloody, the most tragic, the most touching, most sentimental, most patriotic images they can find. And those images become our news, and increasingly our national memory and our history. To supply that commodity lives are risked, privacy is invaded, people are humiliated, or undressed: we are shocked, angered, titillated, embarrassed, and relieved that it is not we who stare so numbly at the world. In the end we are uneasy, because often the pictures come with an odor of exploitation. The person taking the pictures cares only to get an effective picture. He may be totally indifferent to the human condition he witnesses. Indeed if he is a professional he had better be indifferent, or he would be sick with the accumulated suffering he has witnessed. (*Eudora Welty* 9–10)

Of Welty and her photography, however, MacNeil writes, "The person who took these pictures is not indifferent: she is curious but affectionate. I think her pictures are acts of love. I don't mean personal love but the kind of encompassing love that some few people feel for their fellow humanity; a loving sensibility that is not blind to human folly, greed, cruelty—but witnesses it all compassionately" (Ibid.).

As Welty reminds us, a snapshot is a "moment's glimpse" ("One Time, One Place" 354), and that glimpse takes in several important cultural groups often omitted from conversations about media, politics, and society. Among them are women photographers, who did not gain recognition as readily as James Agee or Walker Evans; the determined, strong, intense female subjects of the photographs, women who were also often the poor and the outcasts of their communities; farmers and shopkeepers of the Deep South who populated a diverse region often caricatured and belittled and suffered extreme poverty during the depression; and black Americans, recognized by the photographers in this study as struggling heroically to gain the representation and respect already guaranteed others.

Welty's determination to remain at a distance, an observer of events, may be traced to her early journalistic training: "I wished to be, not effaced, but invisible—actually a powerful position," she said. "Perspective, the line of vision, the frame of vision—these set a distance" (*One Writer's Beginnings*

87). Welty's seeming objectivity should not be confused, however, with unconcern. In every interview about her photographs she expressed great admiration for her subjects. In 1989, for example, she said that her favorite was a picture of a middle-aged woman standing, hands at her side and wearing a tattered sweater: "It shows such a marvelous character. These were taken in the Depression when everybody had absolutely nothing. And she looked so valiant and courageous, dignified and completely self-possessed while she was so poor—and in an old sweater full of holes" ("Welty Photos" 1E). The pictures are not social statements as much as personal photographs of people Welty wanted to remember.

Capturing a moment in fiction or in photography was one of Welty's highest callings. She marveled at the courage of those she met during the depression years and tried to portray them as the heroic people she believed they were. "White and black, really didn't have too much to do with the Depression," she observed about poverty. "It was ongoing. Mississippi was long since poor, long devastated" (*Photographs* xvii). Of her photograph entitled *A Woman of the Thirties, Hinds County,* Welty described its subject as standing strong and stark against a sterile background: "She has a very sensitive face, as you can see; she was well aware of her predicament in poverty, and had good reasons for hopelessness. Well, she *wasn't* hopeless. That was the point. She was courageous. She thought it was a hopeless situation, but she was tackling it" (Ibid. xxvii).

Welty's goal in publishing her photography was not to instruct or startle. Rather, "[My] wish, indeed my continuing passion, would be not to point the finger in judgment but to part a curtain, that invisible shadow that falls between people, the veil of indifference to each other's presence, each other's wonder, each other's human plight" ("One Time, One Place" 355). That sense of compassion and connection with her subjects is evident in Welty's short stories and novels as well (chapter 4), and in the work of Bourke-White, Johnston, and Lange.

It is important to emphasize the contributions of women photographers who are too often overlooked. Their pictures are rarely invasive or manipulative. They are not sensationalistic. They do not chronicle misery, nor are they merely historical documents to be filed so viewers can remember a former time. The faces are those of real humans to whom the photographers were drawn. Those pictured are courageous, determined, and—on film—eternal.

Conclusion

The women described in these pages are representative, and there are important omissions such as Gloria Emerson of the *New York Times,* Sally Quinn of the *Washington Post,* Kate Webb of United Press International, and many others. With the exception of sources such as Tad Bartimus, the chapter necessarily also omits women foreign correspondents, wire-service journalists, and others. Beasley writes that innovative and courageous women reporters "purloined photographs, tracked down gangsters, and charmed murderers into giving them exclusive interviews" ("The Emergence of Modern Media" 286). The story of reporters such as Lorena Hickok, the "front page girl" of the Associated Press, was an exception to the careers of most women reporters and photographers during the first three centuries of American journalism. As Beasley explains, "Relatively few women journalists could ever hope for front page bylines. In most cases the women's and society pages provided their only viable opportunities for newspaper careers" (Ibid.).

It is important to remember the women who made professional reputations in less normative ways, fell into history books purely by chance when a historian unearthed their stories, were discovered by virtue of being related to prominent men, and may have written letters or journal entries that were preserved and collected.

Certainly, much has changed for women in journalism since Ann Franklin presumably became the first to print a newspaper. Working independently and collectively, women have dismantled assumptions about being unable to compete with male counterparts. "It was always the bathroom thing," Bartimus writes. "Women, the men said, couldn't go to war because there was no proper place for them to relieve themselves discreetly. That was The Big Excuse" ("Bullets and Bathrooms" 8). The first three centuries of media history were spent trying to obliterate Big Excuses:

> Women covering wars don't worry about such things. Female journalists, like their male counterparts, worry about getting the facts right, getting the story out, beating the competition and surviving to tell another tale. We are resourceful or we wouldn't be in this business. We don't march in ideological lockstep. We don't want extra attention. We expect to carry our own gear and to pull our own weight. . . . It's commonplace to see front-page bylines and nightly news stand-ups from women reporting from Kosovo, Chechnya, the Middle East and a dozen other hot spots around the globe. (Ibid. 8–9).

Now, Bartimus argues (perhaps correctly, perhaps optimistically), "Women journalists no longer have to plead or finagle their way into combat coverage just because of their gender. They have proved—to soldiers, editors, each other and themselves—that they can go everywhere and do everything. And hardly anybody talks about bathrooms anymore" (Ibid. 15).

Avoiding the stereotype of the male-identified, hard-talking, hard-living reporter, some women journalists began careers by working on women's pages or society pages. They used those pages for news stories of interest to women, especially during the years that Eleanor Roosevelt worked cooperatively with them, or they moved on to other sections of the newspaper and other reporting assignments, including work as war correspondents.

Chapter 2 deals specifically with women's pages and the contributions of women editors and reporters to the broader journalistic spectrum. Many who entered the male-dominated world of newspaper reporting and editing did so successfully only by internalizing the prevailing news values and knowing how to relate to men on the job, or they agreed to work in society news and on women's pages. Some were grateful to women's page editors for hiring them and providing them with the opportunity to work on a newspaper. Others considered working on women's pages and human interest features to be degrading but felt trapped into doing so, did time on women's pages until they could move into the newsroom, or built solid professional reputations as reporters while remaining somewhat ambivalent about writing for women. There were also women who genuinely enjoyed contributing to society news and women's pages.

2

Women of Society News
and Women's Pages

On October 28, 1993, Thomas W. Cutrer, then editor of *Cañon: The Journal of the Rocky Mountain American Studies Association,* returned an article about Katherine Anne Porter to me for revision. As is customary, he included excerpts from the reviewers' comments, and the statements by one particular reviewer caught my eye. Responding to an argument that Porter left the *Rocky Mountain News* (and the profession of journalism) largely because she had been forced to write fashion news for the women's section, the reviewer wrote:

> Male editors are not fiends who spend their time plotting to keep women chained to the stove. Women in Porter's time were consigned to the society pages not because of some malign conspiracy of male editors and publishers, but because of mores and attitudes that were generally accepted by our culture at large. . . Yes, there was (and remains) discrimination against women in journalism. But the fact cannot fairly be used to demonize the men who worked in journalism, many of whom quietly supported and encouraged women writers and photographers. Women were discriminated against across the board—in all trades and professions. . . . But within the context of time and place, these choices were the result of custom (accepted by women as well as men), not of deliberate, malevolent conspiracy.

The reviewer raises important issues that are central to any discussion about the role of women in American newspaper history, particularly the role of female reporters and editors in society news and women's pages. Although I do not discredit the sentiment behind these comments—male newspaper editors were not demons and many were no doubt sensitive to the women who wrote and took photographs for their publications—it is also important to recognize the fallacies in the reviewer's comments. Discrimination against women in journalism is often justified by arguing that it is a "result of custom ... not of deliberate, malevolent conspiracy." Furthermore, women often are blamed for their presumed complicity in their own oppression ("these choices were the result of custom, accepted by women as well as men.")

Practices accepted by the majority have been used to justify discrimination throughout the centuries and across the globe. Many social evils have occurred "because of mores and attitudes that were generally accepted by our culture at large." In some cases, discrimination continued precisely because men of character who occupied influential positions "quietly supported and encouraged" those who were oppressed—instead of championing them loudly and publicly. To those who have been, and continue to be, subjected to unfair salaries and glass ceilings in newsrooms across America it is no solace to know that their oppression is the result of "custom" rather than a "deliberate, malevolent conspiracy," even if that happens to be true.

One of the purposes of this chapter is to highlight the lives and contributions of the women society news reporters and editors who transformed the publications for which they worked. In many cases the women were discriminated against, whether by the men in control of the newspapers or, during the 1960s and 1970s, by some in the women's movement. Women political activists sometimes sought to put an end to women's pages, arguing, quite persuasively, that news of particular interest to women should be on the front pages of America's newspapers. The goal was admirable but ultimately short-sighted.

The History of Women's Pages

Women's pages are a product of the late nineteenth century and were designed to draw a large audience for advertisers interested in marketing to women. Joseph Pulitzer and other editors of the period are credited with increasing the number of women readers by establishing sections designed specifically for them. The success of women's pages "constituted one important factor in the expansion of daily newspaper readership, which doubled in the period from 1892 to 1914" (Sloan and Startt, *The Media in America* 286). Women's pages appeared in larger newspapers during the 1890s and covered fashion, food, relationships, health, etiquette, homemaking, interior decorating, and family issues as well as social news and women's accomplishments. The pages initially were "designed to capitalize on department store advertising aimed at housewives," and "the image of an idyllic home and hearth as a woman's main priority—with career achievements as admirable but secondary pursuits—continued in newspaper women's pages through the 1960s" (Beasley and Gibbons, *Taking Their Place* 175).

Marion Marzolf has provided dates in the history of women's pages and described their development during those years. She suggests that although it is not clear who initiated women's pages, it was Joseph Pulitzer who "popularized" them (*Up from the Footnote* 206). By 1886 the *New York World* carried columns for women, and by 1891 a page in the Sunday *World* featured women's fashion and society issues. In 1894 a page with the headline "For and About Women" appeared in the daily *World*. From 1891 to 1894, the *New York Recorder* advertised itself as "a home paper with a view to pleasing women," claiming more than a hundred thousand female readers and promoting "The Only Woman's Page" that featured society and economic issues as well as advice columns and information on fashion, food, gardening, child rearing, advice columns, and other topics (Ibid.).

By the 1920s women's pages were sometimes called "Home Pages," and "Home Page Journalism" was being taught along with magazine and feature writing (Ibid. 208). By 1943 the *Chicago Tribune* featured columns that had such standing headlines as "White Collar Girl" and "Women Who Work" (Ibid. 209). The *Tribune* also ran a column by Eleanor Roosevelt and, in the 1950s, analysis of the Kinsey Report (Ibid.). Also during the 1950s, Lee Hills, executive editor of the *Miami Herald,* is said to have told women's editor Dorothy Jurney to expand her coverage of political and social issues, including coverage of equal rights and professional women.

Stories about the home and human relationships were segregated from men's ideas, which could, presumably, affect the political and economic landscape. One of the most familiar anecdotes about the conflict between men's and women's news involves an incident on June 6, 1949, at Columbia University. At a "Seminar on Women's Pages" presented by the American Press Institute, the dean of the Columbia University School of Journalism, Carl W. Ackerman, told his audience:

> The front pages of newspapers are filled each day with stories of crises, disaster, tragedies. . . . But the inside of a newspaper is like the inside of a home. . . . The spiritual strength of a nation is safeguarded in the home. In writing about health, schools, the church, food, child care, home living and other similar subjects women as journalists contribute to the uplifting of our national life. There is as much wholesomeness in the inside of a newspaper as there is in

the inside of a home. The newspapers are indebted to women as journalists for this development. (Beasley and Gibbons, *Taking Their Place* 177–78)

Although there is nothing wrong with being known for safeguarding the "spiritual strength of a nation" or contributing to the "uplifting of our national life" or bringing "wholesomeness" into the homes of readers, it is striking that the "stories of crises, disaster, [and] tragedies" were considered the important stories and belonged to men, who presumably were capable of understanding world events and having an active impact on the world outside the home. Also notable in this quotation is that "women as journalists" are celebrated for contributing to women's pages. There is no acknowledgment of their working in any other department of newspapers or covering any other type of news.

It is important to realize that women were often relegated to working on women's pages, and discrimination was so institutionalized that they often did not challenge the status quo or identify the discrimination. Several historians have commented on that fact. Two, Beasley and Gibbons, maintain that "prior to the women's movement, most newspaperwomen were confined to jobs on women's pages and society sections of newspapers. These positions, which routinely paid less than jobs held by men, kept women out of direct competition with males. Women's pages reinforced the idea of separate spheres for men and women. Men ran the world: The news of their conflict, power, and influence dominated the front pages. Women took care of homes and children: The news of noncontroversial domestic and social pursuits appeared on the women's pages" (Ibid. 3). Adding insult to injury, male editors often denigrated women's pages:

> Despite their role in the newspaper organization, the women's pages were barely tolerated by male journalists. Segregated from the main city room in areas given such names as the "hen coop," women's page staff members received even poorer pay than their male counterparts. Often male editors limited the women's pages to a trite formula of fashion, beauty hints, and domestic chitchat. Nevertheless, coverage of women's organizations and community interests served to make these sections into a limited means for women to communicate among themselves. To some degree women's pages showcased women of achievement, although most of the women pictured there were portrayed as wives of prominent men. (Beasley, "The Emergence of Modern Media" 286)

Some women journalists began their careers by writing for women's pages but grew famous after moving into other sections of the newspaper. Marguerite Harrison, for example, began on the society pages of the *Baltimore Sun* but later wrote about camouflage, ship building, labor disputes, immigration before and during World War I and then about postwar Germany. She also covered Russia, interviewing Leon Trotsky and Vladimir Lenin, and was arrested there in April 1920 and released in July 1921. Harrison also wrote for the *New York Evening Post* and the Associated Press. "Throughout her stories," Jean Folkerts and Dwight L. Teeter Jr. comment, "she conveyed an underlying theme of women's competence in heavy industrial jobs" (*Voices of a Nation* 336).

Like other fields in which women worked, journalism underwent a dramatic transition during World War II. With men going to war, women learned trades and moved into professions that had before been closed to them. The content of women's pages continued to change. "By this time," write Beasley and Gibbons, "women's pages were changing from their presentation of weddings, society news, and what one early-twentieth-century critic [Marion Marzolf] called 'glaring drivel'—freckle-removal recipes, fashion 'dots and doings,' and superficial advice to wives and mothers. Before World War II, some papers instituted 'home' pages, which attempted to elevate homemaking into the profession of home economics. During the war, the pages chronicled women's efforts to help the war effort" (*Taking Their Place* 16). Women's pages began to include more substantive issues, including opinion pieces, but the effect was negligible: "Political messages aside, in the eyes of many journalists, male and female, women's pages ranked akin to a newspaper Siberia, covering the Four Fs: food, furnishing, fashion, and family" (Ibid. 17).

When the war ended and men returned home to reclaim their jobs, journalism, like the other trades that drew women, shifted back to business as usual. "When peace came in 1945, women of undisputed competence faced demotion from city desks to women's sections. Dorothy Jurney, who had been acting city editor of the *Washington Daily News,* was told she could not be considered for the position permanently because she was a woman. She was asked to train a male successor before moving to the *Miami Herald* as women's editor" (Ibid. 16). Jurney was not alone.

Twenty years after World War II, the women who wrote for women's pages both did and did not consider themselves on the cutting edge of women's rights. Some who staffed women's sections did, however, consider themselves supporters of women's rights and were proud of their role in introducing important topics to women readers.

The Washington Press Club Foundation's Oral History Project features several women who edited women's pages after World War II. The project, an eight-year effort to document the contributions of fifty-four women journalists, provides generational, ethnic, geographic, professional, and topical diversity. Among its contributors are Marie Anderson, women's page editor at the *Miami Herald* in the late 1950s to early 1970s; Vivian Castleberry, women's page editor at the *Dallas Times-Herald,* beginning in 1956; Mary Garber, society reporter from 1940 to 1944 for the *Winston-Salem Journal;* Jurney, assistant women's editor of the *Miami News,* women's editor of the *Miami Herald,* and women's editor and assistant managing editor of the *Detroit Free Press;* and Marjorie Paxson, who changed the concept of women's pages in Houston and Miami.

These journalists contributed both hard work and a new ideological perspective to coverage of news for and about women. Anderson abandoned the traditional focus on society news at the *Miami Herald,* and her section won four prestigious J. C. Penney–University of Missouri journalism awards. Castleberry, a women's page editor for twenty-eight years, provided exposés of a county foster home and stories about battered women, child abuse, and incest. Jurney, too, emphasized substantive news and influenced a generation of women's page editors.

An important supplement to the oral history interviews is Rodger Streitmatter's "Transforming the Women's Pages: Strategies that Worked" in which he details the contributions of Anderson, Castleberry, and Jurney. "Together," Streitmatter writes, "these three women edited the women's pages of half a dozen metropolitan daily newspapers for an aggregate of eighty years" (74).

> By 1900 many metropolitan newspapers were publishing women's pages filled with society news and advice on fashion, homemaking, manners, and romance. Such material continued to dominate women's pages for half a century. The male editors and publishers who controlled American journalism paid scant attention to the quality of the stories, fully satisfied to fill the space with flowery prose describing debutante balls, superficial advice to wives and mothers, and frivolous stories on the latest trends in fashion. . . . Various scholars of American journalism have studied the changes in women's pages, finding that during the late 1960s and early 1970s society and homemaking news shrank to make room for coverage of such hard-hitting topics as sex-based job discrimination and women's reproductive rights, as well as stories highlighting women who were expanding their lives beyond the four walls of the home. (Ibid. 72)

Women's page editors kept in touch with one another, read one another's work, and shared stories by adapting them for their own publications. Castleberry, Streitmatter notes, "read Anderson's section religiously" and traveled to Jurney's newspaper to learn what she was doing (Ibid. 77). Anderson was, for Castleberry, on the "cutting edge of women's issues" (Ibid.), and major newspapers such as the *New York Times* lagged far behind. Throughout the 1960s, for example, the *Times*'s women's section was called "Food, Fashion, Furnishings and Family," leading Streitmatter to maintain that credit for the development of content on the women's pages does not belong exclusively to large metropolitan newspapers—the "journalistic giants"—but to smaller, community-based metropolitan newspapers as well (Ibid. 79).

During the 1960s, some editors attempted to make women's pages more contemporary and increase their focus on lifestyle, culture, family living, and social problems. The names of the pages were changed to "Style" at the *Washington Post,* "View" at the *Los Angeles Times,* "Living Today" at the *Miami Herald,* and "Day" at the *St. Petersburg Times.* At some newspapers the name of the section changed but content did not. Small-town dailies and weeklies often opted to "wait and see" (Marzolf, *Up from the Footnote* 200–201). "Even some of the smaller newspapers," however, "included articles on the Equal Rights Amendment and abortion reform in traditional women's pages" (Ibid. 201). Still other editors took the middle road and included more lifestyle stories but retained the standard features of women's pages.

It is tempting to celebrate the news value of stories about the women's movement and the various achievements of women editors, although the role of women's pages began to be questioned. "The newsroom debate over what a woman's section should be, or even if it should be published at all, reached a crescendo in the newsrooms of the late 1960s," Beasley and Gibbons comment. "By then, the women's movement and the civil rights movement were developing broad bases of support, and the content of many women's pages looked anachronistic in light of the public debate for equal rights, pay equity, reproductive choice, and career advancement" (*Taking Their Place* 179).

The 1960s and 1970s were a time of conflict not only between male and female journalists but also between women editors and readers and women editors and leaders of the women's movement. "Some women in the mainstream media. . . found themselves caught between conflicting interests," Beasley and Gibbons maintain. "On the one hand, the movement spoke to many of their personal concerns. On the other, their emotional involvement ran counter to adherence to accustomed professional values" (Ibid. 2).

Betty Friedan and Gloria Steinem had extensive experience in journalism, but women editors of society news sections often found them, and other activists in the women's movement, to be unsympathetic to their efforts. Paxson—who worked for the *Houston Post* (1948–52), *Houston Chronicle*

(1952–56), *Miami Herald* (1956–68), *St. Petersburg Times* (1968–70), *Philadelphia Bulletin,* (1970–76), and *Idaho Statesman* (1976–78)— shared the movement's goals but believed she lacked its leaders' support:

> I still have not quite forgiven women's movement activists for turning against women's editors. In the early days of the movement in the sixties, most substantive newspaper coverage of the movement was on the women's pages. I considered myself a part of the movement and so did many other women's editors I knew across the country.
>
> But the activists wanted the movement news off our pages and in their eyes, we women's editors were traitors.
>
> When editors responded by changing women's sections to general interest feature sections, women's editors paid the price. We were not considered capable of directing this new kind of feature section. That was man's work.
>
> I shuddered every time I read another story in *Editor & Publisher* about a paper making the switch and the former women's editor either being demoted or given the lateral two-step.
>
> I know how they felt because it happened to me—not once, but twice.
>
> On the *St. Pete Times,* the change was made the Tuesday after Labor Day, 1969, and I ended up as the No. 3 person in the new setup. In December the *Times* was notified that I had won a Penney-Missouri award for general excellence of the now-defunct women's pages. In May 1970, six weeks after I went to Columbia, Missouri, to accept that award, I was fired.
>
> I landed on my feet as women's editor of the *Philadelphia Bulletin.* But... in 1973, again on the Tuesday after Labor Day, the *Bulletin* abolished its women's section for a Focus section with a male editor and I was exiled to the Sunday magazine as associate editor. ("Marjorie Paxson" 125–26)

In spite of losing two positions as editor of a women's section, Paxson became a Gannett News Service executive and publisher. At the time of her retirement she was the publisher of the *Muskogee* (Oklahoma) *Phoenix.*

Janet Sanford, who became publisher of the *Visalia Times-Delta* outside Fresno, California, also took issue with feminists who denigrated the work of women's page editors. While editor of "Today's Living," the women's section of the *Phoenix Gazette* in 1970, she interviewed Steinem, who "peered over her granny glasses and asked who I was." When Sanford introduced herself, Steinem replied, "That shows what your paper thinks about women's issues." Sanford admits, "That made me think. I mean, newsside hadn't sent a reporter, but at least I was there" (Mills, *A Place in the News* 117–18).

The anecdote represents the heart of the controversy. If women's page editors did not cover issues of particular interest to women, would those issues appear in the newspaper at all? The answer is inconsistent from region to region, newspaper to newspaper, or editor to editor. What is clear is that the source of the dispute concerns the definition of news and how the media machine often arbitrarily categorizes men and women.

Gender and Definitions of News

A heated debate about the prevailing definitions of news lies at the heart of the development, demise, and short-term contemporary rebirth of women's pages. The initial placement of the announcement of the National Organization for Women's formation in 1965 is a case in point. Women media scholars have been amused as well as enraged by the fact that the *New York Times* ran the first story describing the event between a recipe for turkey stuffing and an article about Saks Fifth Avenue.

The development of the tenets of news in American newspapers cannot be depicted as a steady line that has moved determinedly upward. In the colonial period, news was defined, constructed, and disseminated by those in power. Owner-publishers were educated males and members of the landowning elite, invested in building a country through strong government and healthy commerce. Logically enough, their understanding of what constituted news became codified.

Women did not contribute significantly to the prevailing definition of news during the colonial era, nor were they well represented in newspaper work until the radical shift in readership during the penny press era. The perceived role of women changed, and definitions of news became more inclusive when Benjamin Day and others began to understand the importance of local news for an increasingly literate audience, Horace Greeley began addressing women's issues, and other editors acknowledged the untapped reservoir of women readers. Legitimate news began to include human interest and local stories, presumably of more interest to women, as well as accounts of government and commerce, traditionally understood as the domain of male readers.

Joseph Pulitzer, William Randolph Hearst, and other editors at the turn of the century not only began to recognize women as newsmakers and invested readers but also hired women as correspondents and investigative reporters. Pulitzer and Hearst waged a circulation war, and newspapers across the nation competed for readers as well. Male editors realized that many of those readers were female and instituted what they considered to be news of particular interest to them. The desire for higher circulation, however, did not necessarily indicate commitment to the advancement of women.

News directors and professors of journalism continue to teach established characteristics of news that include timeliness; impact, consequence, or importance; prominence of the people involved; proximity to readers and listeners; conflict; the unusual nature of the event; and currency. Most scholars, however, acknowledge that news is relative and definitions of it are fluid and historically determined. Moreover, the role of gender in determining definitions of news cannot be exaggerated. As Kay Mills writes, "Hard news? Soft news? Where did these terms come from? Their sexual implications fairly leap from the page. Hard news is about foreign policy, the federal deficit, bank robberies. Historically, men's stuff. . . . Soft news is about. . . family, food, fashion and furnishings. . . . Plays, movies, books. Lifestyle. The things I like to read" (*A Place in the News* 110).

In 1978, Cynthia Fuchs Epstein argued that there is a serious problem with the "mix" of information on women's pages, where "news on women astronauts, the Equal Rights Amendment, recipes for lobster newburg, and the length of skirts [appears]. I suggest that the mix of news about women and the women's movement with food, fashion, and furniture news violates the very notion of news" ("The Women's Movement" 217–18). She also maintains that "news of the women's movement does not belong on the women's page": "Just by appearing there, the stories maintain the status quo, for they tell both women and men that news of the women's movement is not of general concern. . . . Furthermore, relegation of the women's movement to the ghetto of the women's pages means that the movement news will receive the same treatment as society news" (Tuchman, Daniels, and Benet, eds., *Hearth and Home* 145–46).

G. William Domhoff takes a different perspective: "Whatever feminists may think of the women's page, and I know their opinions vary, it is one of the most valuable pages in the newspaper when it comes to understanding power in America." Domhoff calls women's pages "one of the few parts of the paper—perhaps the only part of the paper—that reveals to us how fully and deeply our rulers meld together and form an authentic ruling class" ("The Woman's Page" 161). He concludes, "It is on the women's page we learn that our business, cultural, and government leaders, for all their public differences on specific issues, share in a deeper social community that keeps them as one on essential questions concerning the distribution of wealth and the system of property, questions that seldom become issues, questions that rarely receive attention on the straight news page. Only on the women's page does the newspaper tell us each and every day that there is a ruling class in America" (Ibid. 175).

Domhoff may be correct, but his premise is a dismaying one for women to confront in their daily newspapers. Although women might agree with his central argument, they would presumably want to break down the power structure rather than have its reality reinforced on the pages of local newspapers. Whatever the case made about the value of women's pages as a social diary, scholars such as Gaye Tuchman understand that defining events as "news" confirms their importance. Leaders of the women's movement understood how thoroughly "standard reportorial practice favors those with institutional power" and how often those with institutional power are male (Tuchman, "The Newspaper as a Social Movement's Response" 196).

One of the most potent statements about the institutionalization of male views about "real news" appears in Harvey L. Molotch's "The News of Women and the Work of Men": "The formal news business is not only the powerful talking to the less powerful. It is essentially men talking to men. The women's pages are a deliberate exception: Here it is the case that women who work for men talk to women. But in terms of the important information, the news pages, women are not ordinarily present. . . . News is a man's world" (180).

Epstein argues that putting women's news on women's pages "suggests, among other things, that men don't have families or love affairs with their attendant problems. Ghettoizing discussions of such matters on women's pages reinforces outmoded views that men should not be concerned with families and their own and others' emotional needs" ("The Women's Movement" 221).

Epstein is correct, but she begs the question of where news of particular importance to women should appear. If that news did not (and does not) appear on the front pages of American newspapers, will it appear elsewhere, and would terminating women's pages guarantee that news for women will make its way onto the front page? The answer to both questions is a resounding no.

Nowhere is the conflict about the definition of news and the appropriate home for issues of particular importance to women more evident than on the women's pages of the 1950s to the 1970s. As Tuchman has summarized the debate:

> Some. . . noted that using the women's page as a resource may be detrimental to the women's movement. General reporters, as well as New York City feminists. . . objected that women were being shunted into a ghetto or reservation; all aspects of women's life should not be segregated as the responsibility of one department or one general or beat reporter. Rather, they insisted, stories

about women should be integrated into all aspects of the world of news just as women should be integrated into all aspects of the world. Such integration, however, cuts off the power and autonomy of those women who run the "women's news reservation," the women's page. ("The Newspaper as a Social Movement's Resource" 211)

The integration of news of particular importance to women has never occurred. Furthermore, when women's sections disappeared, some women editors were considered incapable of heading the new, lifestyle sections and were either reassigned or fired. Others resigned to take positions at other newspapers.

Scholarly reaction to the issue is mixed, although the majority share Epstein's view that "placing news about women on the women's page even reinforces the still-current view that the material is only appropriate for women and that it is less serious and important than news highlighted as general news":

> Even if men read the women's page (and what men wish to be seen by work or traveling companions peering down on that section?) they may well decide the material to be outside their acknowledged sphere of competence. They are therefore not accountable for knowing the information available from reading those pages. And they are not provoked to discuss those stories. For women, the positioning of news about women only reinforces other messages they receive from society: that if a woman demonstrates competence in some important sphere, it is an idiosyncratic event, not worthy of general notice and not to be judged by a universal standard—that is, a male standard. ("The Women's Movement" 217)

M. Junior Bridge also addresses the "male standard" that has become reified in American newspapers and comments, "Traditionally, females have not been considered newsworthy." She adds:

> Even today, despite the many legal and cultural strides forward made by women, media coverage and media images of females are woefully inadequate and often misleading.
>
> When the front page of a newspaper contains not one reference to a female, not one female byline, and not one photo of a female, what is the message sent about females? When major stories about war, the economy, social issues, or other topics of great import appear day after day devoid of female references and images, what is the message sent about females?
>
> When females are described primarily by their physical appearance, their

clothes and hairstyles, and their marital and parental status whereas males are described by their accomplishments and status, what is the message sent?

The message sent is a misleading, erroneous one: Females are saying and doing nothing of importance, nothing worth reporting. Their intellect, their skills, their perspective, their ideas, their accomplishments are devalued by underrepresentation and invisibility in the news. ("What's News?" 16)

Beginning in 1989, Bridge, who served as president of Unabridged Communications, a research and education company in Alexandria, Virginia, published annual reports on women and media. One of her more startling discoveries occurred when data indicated that references to women on the *New York Times*'s front page had risen from 5 percent in 1989 to only 13 percent in 1993. Questioned about the absence of women in the study, *Times* executive editor Max Frankel suggested that more women would appear on the front page if the newspaper were "covering local teas." Bridge observes that "in this one testy comment, Frankel belittled and insulted the wisdom, talents, and contributions of women, ranging from unpaid mothers to highly salaried Pulitzer prize–winning scientists, from local politicians to world leaders. Yet the attitude expressed by Frankel is not uncommon in the news world and in society in general" (Ibid. 18–19).

Given (at best) the general disinterest in and (at worst) the denigration of news of importance to women, it is important to remember that there were distinct advantages to having news about the women's movement and other important issues displayed on women's pages. The women's page of the *New York Times* became an ideal home for news of the women's movement and other information of particular interest to women:

1. Women's sections typically did not cover "breaking news" (Tuchman, "The Newspaper as a Social Movement's Resource" 201). Since deadlines were less important, reporters for women's sections could cover events that occurred on weekends and at night. Those times allowed for women with families to participate more fully in political action.

2. There was less competition on the women's pages with other breaking news. As [Joan] Whitman explains, stories about the women's movement didn't have to compete with stories about issues such as the Watergate scandal. *New York Times* reporter Judy Klemesrud said succinctly, "If the feminist stories didn't run on our page, they wouldn't run anywhere" (Ibid. 203).

3. The stories on the women's pages gained better display and larger, more dramatic photography. "'I always get flack from women in the movement' who

think stories about their activities should be run on the general news pages. I just think they're wrong. It's better to have lots of space and good display . . . than to be in a four-paragraph story'" (Ibid. 204).

The underlying questions remain: What constitutes news? Is news gender-less, or is it invested with values and attitudes that have become identified with men or women? In light of the appearance of women's pages, the debate about what stories should appear there, and the eventual transformation of those pages into lifestyle sections, the answer seems obvious. Conversations about what constitutes news should be ongoing, and part of those conversations must be acknowledgment of the gendered aspects of news-gathering and making.

The Controversial Women's Pages

Although women are divided about the importance of women's pages and their content, there is no doubt that issues involving women's pages are resurfacing in the early twenty-first century. Some women journalists continue to celebrate the fact that they were never part of the staff of a women's section, whereas others readily discuss what they learned from their time there.

As journalist-turned-novelist Anna Quindlen describes women's pages during the controversial days of the 1970s, "We were all ghettoized—the bright writers, the feature writers, the back-of-the-book writers—in what we called the style sections, but what we all really knew, with a wink and a nudge, were the women's sections. As late as 1978 I was assigned to cover all women's issues, from battered wives to day care. Child care wasn't a congressional issue, it was a women's issue. Abortion wasn't a political issue, it was a women's issue" (Kurtz, *Media Circus* 357). Beasley and Gibbons concur: "The bland orientation of lifestyle pages hardly served for serious discussion of these political issues. Lesbian issues, alternatives to conventional marriage, and feminism as it affected women of color fit poorly, if at all, within the confines of lifestyle/women's pages" (*Taking Their Place* 23).

Nellie Revell, Judith Brimberg, and Molly Ivins have also discounted women's pages. Revell, who wrote for newspapers in Chicago, Denver, San Francisco, and New York for thirty years, bragged that she "had never written a single line for a 'woman's page' or a line of society news." Instead, she covered "prizefights, murder trials, [and] everything else that would come to a general duty reporter" (Douglas, *The Golden Age of the Newspaper* 187). When Brimberg, a *Denver Post* reporter, died in 1996, the news story that accompanied her obituary read: "The newspaper business operated by different rules in 1957, when male reporters picked off plum assignments and most women toiled on the 'ladies page' chronicling tea parties and such." The story then related a portion of Brimberg's letter of application: "I should make it clear . . . that I do not handle woman's news coverage" ("Death Claims Tough, Witty Post Reporter" 1B). Ivins was conflicted about the existence of women's pages but never wanted to work for a women's section. In *Women on Deadline,* she is quoted as saying that "a generation of older women" had been "stuck in women's sections, which were always called the snake pit. I determined very early that I was going to be on the city desk. I was never going to be assigned to the women's section, God forbid!" (Ricchiardi and Young, *Women on Deadline* 141–42). In hindsight, however, Ivins commented:

> It took me years to notice a remarkable phenomenon. For a long time, the best journalism about women, family issues, and social issues came out of those sections. These reporters were writing about abortion, wife and child abuse, incest—stories far out on the cutting edge. Their stories got into the paper because nobody was paying attention to what they did. . .
>
> There's no question about it. If women ran newspapers, the toxic shock syndrome stories instantly would have been on Page 1. As it was, it took quite awhile for that to happen.
>
> If an after-shave lotion was killing men, you better believe it would have been front page news. But, writing about menstruation and tampons was taboo. The handling of those stories truly revealed male squeamishness and the blindness of sexism.
>
> Wife abuse, family violence, divorce, incest—those topics never made the newspapers until women began covering them. Now, we see them on the front page. (Ibid. 142, 144)

As historians and other media scholars are discovering, the question of women's pages is so complex that issues related to them were revisited in the 1990s and continue to be discussed. As readership among women continues to decline, newspapers are reexamining the role of news for women and, in some cases, returning to a kind of refurbished women's section. As partial explanation for this phenomenon, Mills ends *A Place in the News* by stating, "The march from the women's page to the front page is hardly complete" (349).

Perhaps the front page did not turn out to be a worthy destination, or, as is more likely the case, perhaps topics of particular interest to women readers never reached that part of the newspaper in any discernible way. Whatever the case, editors and writers at several American newspapers occasionally have opted to march back. It is too early to determine the outcome of their experiment, but their reasons for the attempt are worth exploring.

Prototypes of women's sections reappeared in the most unlikely places in the 1990s; raised predictable issues, especially for feminist publishers, editors, reporters, readers, and critics; and made it imperative to analyze readership and reexamine the accepted definitions of "serious" news. The *Chicago Tribune* was one of the largest metropolitan daily newspapers to resurrect women's pages in order to remake and revitalize them, but it was not alone.

During the same period in which *The Tribune* launched the experimental "WomaNews"—editors added another *n* in 2000, changing the title of the section to "WomanNews"—the *Charlotte Observer* created a section that dealt with relationships ("Connect"). In addition, the *Cleveland Plain Dealer* revived its women's section, editors of the *Arizona Republic* decided to establish a stand-alone section called "AZW" ("Arizona Women"), and the *Lexington* (Kentucky) *Herald-Leader* followed suit. A women's magazine was tucked into the *Santa Barbara News-Press* in 2002 and also was published on line. The thirty-six-page "Woman Magazine" provided information on health, fitness, education, career, financial issues, travel, food, and relationships with family and friends. The idea of executive editor Allen Parsons, the section also featured an events calendar and list of local resources.

Small newspapers published by women and of interest to women readers also sprang up around the country. One, a tabloid called *HERS: Not Just for Women,* gained popularity in 1993 in Longboat Key, Florida. Susan Fernandez and Diane Mason, coeditors and publishers, included information about domestic violence, global overpopulation, the lack of representation of women on sports pages, women in public office, menopause, breastfeeding, women's health care, breast cancer, and other issues. The *Palm Beach Post* initiated a section called "Charm" that boasted the slogan "for women of all ages and stages." Edited by Pat Morgan, Ann Rogers, and Amy Royster, "Charm" featured stories about fashion, motherhood, shopping, women confronting their forties, and other topics.

Because women's pages were considered a thing of the past, few were prepared for the reappearance of women's news, and they were especially surprised by the prototype presented by the editors of the major metropolitan daily in Chicago. The *Chicago Tribune* is an important focus for this study because of its tradition of seeking out women readers and the radical decision of self-avowed feminist and associate editor Colleen Dishon to reintroduce a women's section before her retirement (she died in 2004). When it appeared, "WomanNews" sparked a predictably intense and mixed reaction.

"WomanNews"

After presenting a prototype of a women's section at the 1990 meeting of the American Society of Newspaper Editors, representatives of the *Chicago Tribune* reappropriated a symbol of the stereotyped American woman and transformed it. In spite of differences of opinion among editors, reporters, and focus groups, senior editors eventually agreed to launch a new type of women's section and try to regain the loyalty of women readers. The first issue of "WomanNews" appeared April 28, 1991, and soon became a popular weekly section.

The first issues were startlingly different from women's sections of the 1960s. In 1994, the women on the cover of the weekly "WomanNews" were black, Asian, Latino, Native American, and white. In the section, women were not always models, nor were they standing in the shadow of powerful men or even necessarily assumed to be heterosexual. They were representative and distinguished, average and extraordinary. They looked, therefore, like the women of metropolitan Chicago.

The August 28, 1994, edition was my first encounter with the new section. Featuring a story about those who have been killed in an abortion war in Pensacola, Florida, the staff presented news not exclusively of interest to women but undeniably news. Using traditional definitions of news, the staff clearly separated "WomanNews" from early women's pages and—assuming the superiority of hard news over soft—made it an improvement over other contemporary feature sections.

The surprises in the August 28, 1994, women's news section continued below the fold with a story about Mmatshilo Motsei, a woman battling domestic violence in South Africa. Instead of seeing ten male faces and an occasional woman—the case when women readers look at the front pages of many current metropolitan dailies—readers saw twelve women, and all but one were newsmakers not models. Also included were stories about a woman actor; a female psychotherapist renovating a Frank Lloyd Wright cottage; a column on domestic violence; a traditional two-page spread on fashion; a column entitled "Miss Manners"; a column on relationships; examples of the "first-female" syndrome (this time the "first female" was the new president of the American Bar Association and the first brigadier general in the Israeli Defense Forces); a column on professional success; a collection of quotations and short articles by celebrities and readers; and stories on sexual harassment, adoption, and summer camps.

The next week, a page-one story described using humor to teach children desired behaviors, and stories in the righthand column dealt with the *Encyclopedia of Chicago Women* and a local summit on economic parity for women. Inside the section were stories on women artists; a Latino victim of polio who helped design shoes for those with disabilities; fashion news (this time, shoes); a column on women in the international sphere alongside stories on Cairo and India; stories on women's health, networking, and Gena Rowlands; a column on women and their workplaces; and information about childbirth and the women of Generation X.

Later, "WomanNews" editors featured career self-reliance, divorce, Japanese women who chose death rather than capture at the end of World War II, female priests, women's rights in Egypt, rape, charter schools, the impact of new babies on fathers, doctor-patient relationships, poverty among children in Chile, and other international, national, and local topics.

Dishon and Marla Krause were two of the women responsible for the preliminary success of "WomanNews." In 1991 the section's creators relied upon a long-time *Chicago Tribune* tradition of seeking out women readers and serving them, Dishon commented during a series of telephone interviews in 1994 and again between 2000 and 2004. At the time of the women's movement, for example, "Women became their own role models." That necessitated a section in which "women shared information so they knew they weren't alone."

A women's pages editor for fifteen years at the *Chicago Daily News* and *Milwaukee Sentinel,* Dishon had worked as an editor for the Features and News Service, an organization founded in 1968 to provide "diversified content" for women's pages (Marzolf, *Up from the Footnote* 203). "I see an unmistakable opportunity for women's pages to report in depth the changes in women's world and the problems women face," she said. "We can use our space to report on discrimination, women in poverty, infant deaths, politics—all of the things that are vital to women and to everyone in society" (Ibid.). In 1970, the University of Chicago's Center for Policy Study examined seven hundred women's sections, and Dishon employed that study's conclusions in 1976 to redesign the *Chicago Tribune*'s "Tempo" section (Ibid. 210).

Another factor in the formation of the contemporary women's news section was Dishon's experience with women reporters during her tenure at the *Chicago Tribune.* "Women at the paper often came in to talk with me," she recalls, "and they told me that when they watched TV, they thought they should be happy now that they could have it all. They thought they were the only ones who weren't happy. We do have an opportunity to have it all, but we need to appreciate how hard that is. There is a price to be paid. Sharing that philosophy empowers us to make decisions. Then, it's all a matter of choices."

Dishon, who had been at the *Chicago Tribune* for nineteen years at that point, listened to her colleagues and others in the community and "got rid of society news and got rid of weddings." What she created instead was "WomanNews" to replace the Sunday edition's "TempoWoman." She added a column about international women and made a commitment to run news on page one of the section. Profiles in one issue included everything from stories about Margaret Thatcher to women in India who worked on population control. "The idea was to use stories from everywhere to show ordinary women having an impact on their world," she says. "A lot was going on, but it hadn't been reported, so we didn't know about it."

Dishon disagrees vehemently with those who have criticized the name "WomanNews." "It's about women and it's about news. Why not say so?" she asks. "Some implied, 'How dare you call it women's news. Real news is not about women.' I agree that men and women read the same things. For me, though, 'WomanNews' was like having a sports section, but this time everyone was committed and dedicated to women instead of sports. We ran information you'd never get if it were a part of the whole."

Dishon was the first woman to be listed on the masthead of the *Chicago Tribune*. During her career, she created seventeen new sections. In her opinion, a story's placement does matter, and those about women should be well-written, long enough to cover the topic, and laid out effectively. "Woman-News," she maintains, allowed such placement.

Founding "WomanNews" was different from running it, and Krause, who had been at the *Chicago Tribune* for sixteen years, writing sports, working on the news desk, and serving as associate metro assignment editor, became its editor in 1994. The Sunday section, she said soon after her appointment, "is a paper within a paper. . . . We run stories I care about. We are always reacting to the news." In August 1994, for example, she sent a reporter to Pensacola, Florida, to profile volunteer escorts at abortion clinics and then ran a series about the violence surrounding abortion in the Florida community.

The writing in "WomanNews," Krause contends, was often better than that in the rest of the newspaper; the stories could be longer, staffers had more time to write and edit, and topics were varied. Krause emphasized "colorful, anecdotal" writing; wedding announcements and club news appeared in other sections. The information in "WomanNews" emphasized women in sports and business, family and health issues, and relationships. It was important to Krause that men wrote more than 35 percent of the copy; letters and telephone calls indicated a regular male readership.

The *Chicago Tribune* carried teasers on its front page to highlight provocative stories in the "Perspective," "Arts and Entertainment," "WomanNews," and "Sports" sections. During its early years "WomanNews" carried stories about prominent governors who promoted women's issues (Christine Todd Whitman of New Jersey, William F. Weld of Massachusetts, Ann Richards of Texas, and others); job success; girls in Chile; women in Missouri who played football; the computer use of men and women; singers; welfare; safe toys; doctor-patient relationships; new-baby blues; political leaders; men who are accused of sexual harassment but fight back and win; Buddhism; female abusers; rape; education; contraceptives; abducted children; women physicians; birth control; divorce; investing; and weight control. The section also included profiles of sharecroppers, priests, and sports, television, and political celebrities. There were features about books, collectibles, pets, the YWCA, and smoking, as well as traditional women's page fare that included two-page spreads on fashion, furniture, gardening, and fundraising.

In 1995, Melinda D. Hawley, then assistant director of the James M. Cox Jr. Institute for Newspaper Management Studies at the University of Georgia, conducted a study entitled "Is the 'Women's Section' an Anachronism?" The results of the study were, understandably enough, contradictory. Since 1990, when the ASNE tested the prototype of "WomanNews," Hawley learned that "women's sections can help to retain women readers and increase the visibility of women in newspapers." Through interviews with staff of the "Woman-News" section and reader focus groups, however, she also learned that the name of the section appeared to "exclude men from coverage of substantive issues affecting women," "reinforce stereotypes of women," "create a 'women's news ghetto,'" and attract advertising that may conflict with editorial content (introduction, n.p.).

Referring to a 1994 Knight-Ridder Task Force Report indicating that women, a "once-loyal readership group," have stopped reading newspapers "at a significantly accelerated rate compared to men," Hawley suggested that newspapers have responded to this phenomenon in various ways: "Some newspapers increased coverage of so-called 'women's issues'—health, parenting, careers and relationships—and thus, 'mainstreamed' women's news in regular sections. Other papers, guided by research that indicates women are more likely than men to focus on relationships, changed reporting and packaging of their content to highlight the people behind the news" (Ibid. 1). At least two newspapers "took the relatively risky and potentially politically incorrect step of reviving the women's section" (Ibid. 2). It was a decision made in part as a reaction to research that indicates "women are alienated by 'male' characteristics of mainstream daily newspaper coverage shaped by news values that emphasize conflict and hierarchy rather than connection and consensus" (Ibid. 3).

Hawley's conclusions are essential to a consideration of the contemporary role of women's pages in American newspapers. As she reported, "Many women journalists and readers in this study voiced opposition—in some cases, strong—to the concept of a women's section, yet, they reported regularly reading and enjoying WomanNews. Similarly, several women readers expressed concern that the inclusion of that section in their newspaper could offend men or preclude their exposure to its content—yet, they believed it played an important role at the *Chicago Tribune,* saying they doubted this content would appear at all, were it not for the existence of WomanNews" (Ibid. 22). Although members of the focus groups expressed concerns, they were "enthusiastic" about the product (Ibid. 3). Both Krause, then editor of "WomanNews," and Barbara Brotman, staff columnist, however, opposed the creation of "WomanNews" and "were initially reluctant" to join it (Ibid. 11).

For several decades the *Chicago Tribune* described itself on its nameplate as the "World's Greatest Newspaper." How have editors and publishers of the "world's greatest newspaper" viewed women readers since the publication's founding in 1847? What did they hope to accomplish by returning in the 1990s to a women's section called "WomanNews"? And was "Tempo," which appeared during the week, a feature, family news, or women's section? Did its emphasis change with the advent of "WomanNews?"

One of those charged with addressing these and other questions was "WomanNews" editor Cassandra West, who took over the section in 2002 after becoming an assistant editor in 1997. In consultation with other editors and with readers, West changed the focus of the section from "female firsts and empowerment" to stories that dealt with women's "everyday issues and concerns." The section also emphasized local women rather than international issues. Topics that were particularly controversial for "WomanNews" were those involving gay-lesbian-bisexual-and transgender issues and abortion, West reported.

The section continues to be popular. "I have hope," West says, "that the section still has life, relevancy. Our readers continue to tell us they think so, but we are challenged to continue to evolve and remain topical and fresh. Our ad base has strengthened, and we recently got expanded color on our inside pages." She is most proud of the fact that men read the section: "I've seen men on the commuter train and in coffee shops reading the section. Many of our letters come from male readers" (West, September 29, 2005).

Certainly, media scholars remain interested in the decision by some publications to reinstitute women's pages (or a section that appeals primarily to women). Therese L. Lueck's "'Her Say' in the Media Mainstream: A Cultural Feminist Manifesto" was published as a monograph in 2004. She discusses the "Her Say" column in "WomanNews," which "articulated the terms of a separate women's culture, the bounds of which continued to be defined by newspapers across the nation as they introduced their own women's sections." Lueck adds, "As the mouthpiece for the 'WomanNews' section, 'Her Say' heralded a revaluing of 'woman,' and challenged the industry to hasten its redefinition of 'news' for twenty-first-century relevancy" (61).

Dishon addressed these and other issues throughout her career in news. An ardent feminist until and after retirement, Dishon believed that women deserve more from their news sources and understood why women readers had fallen away from regularly subscribing to and reading newspapers. "When women tell newspaper editors they do not see themselves in the newspaper," she observes, "they suggest that the newspaper does not see life complete and whole, the way they see it, live it" (Beasley and Gibbons, *Taking Their Place* 181).

In 2007, the *Tribune*'s editors continued to evaluate the benefits and drawbacks of "WomanNews," which by December 2005 had become a few pages in the weekly "Tempo" section. West accepted a buyout—a common practice in newspapers nationwide—and as of June 2007 was teaching, writing, and enjoying having time to consider her career options.

Ultimately, the history of "WomanNews" is important in a study of women in journalism because it illustrates the sociological shifts in readership among women and provides a text for scholars who will undoubtedly continue to analyze women as a demographic and speculate about what will happen next in the print media industry.

Conclusion

Answers to the following questions and others as well go to the heart of understanding women as news consumers and savvy readers whose definitions of what constitutes news may differ from what is considered to be the norm:

What becomes of gender-based distinctions between hard and soft news on newer versions of women's pages? Is news now genderless?

Do women enjoy having women's pages in their local newspapers?

Do issues of interest to women appear regularly on page one and in news magazines? If not, why not? If so, do women need yet another forum for news by and for them?

Will more and more newspapers move toward shorter, more formulaic news coverage, as *USA Today* has done? If so, could women's pages—with their emphasis on the news-feature and extended feature—become home to the best writing in a newspaper? If not, what will give the pages (assuming they continue to exist in some form) long-term quality and distinctiveness?

What are the deeper implications of a return to women's sections? Will women's issues, for example, be devalued by being relegated to a separate part of the newspaper, will women's page editors gain more column inches with which to address topics of importance to women, or will both be true?

Is one reason for the return to women's pages in newspapers the desire to compete with successful women's magazines in both style and content?

What kind of assumed audience or "ideal reader" is evolving in the minds of newspaper publishers and editors? Indeed, who were the readers of the women's section at the *Chicago Tribune* and elsewhere?

What about "ghettoizing" women's news, separating it from the "serious" news in the rest of the newspaper? Would having a separate section appear to release a newspaper's establishment from the responsibility of including women's events and women's faces on the front page?

The *Chicago Tribune*—like other American newspapers—has made significant strides in its portrayal of women. It has been common, however, to open the newspaper and find photographs of, for example, eleven men (three National Hockey League commissioners, two football players, five Haitian gunmen, and one pumpkin grower) on a page that carries no images of women and no women mentioned in a story. That is true even though the stories were varied and would have allowed for women to be presented as sources; they involved sports, war, teens and drinking, a new local expressway, and healthcare costs.

The financial, ethical, and cultural cost of making more than half of the American population nearly invisible on a front page should be evident. At minimum, readership among women will continue to drop when they and their interests and concerns are not represented. More subtle but perhaps more pervasive is the fact that when women do not see themselves portrayed equally in newspapers, they may begin to internalize a false definition of news. For young women journalists to alter the culture of the newsroom and expand the understanding of news, they will need to address the ways in which male definitions of news have been reified.

At least two things are certain. First, with the advent of "WomanNews," the *Chicago Tribune* made history; less certain is whether the decision broke new ground or rebuilt old fences. Second, women deserve and are demanding more attention from media outlets, including newspapers.

> Whether the story is about war, social conflict, the economy, science, agriculture, the environment, or any other issues, female voices and strong images are frequently absent or minimal. Women play major roles in all these arenas, and they are certainly affected by actions taken on such subjects. Women constitute 45 percent of the paid labor force, and that number is growing. Women make most of the consumer decisions. There are more female voters than male. Women own most of the agricultural land in this country. By 1993, women-owned small businesses employed more people than the Fortune 500 companies combined. Females are the majority of the U.S. population. Why, then, is the face of the news male? (Bridge, "What's News?" 23)

It is impossible to overexaggerate the contribution of women in changing the prevailing definitions of news. One touchstone is a 1989 comment by Carol Richards of *Newsday* (then of Gannett News Service), who began covering social issues—considered the special province of women—in 1976: "It was like shooting ducks in a barrel. It was the greatest beat in the world. Nobody was covering it that way. Papers were putting my stories on the front page. My bosses were surprised I had thought of it. I was surprised that nobody else had thought of it. Perhaps that was a woman-y thing: to look at the way people live rather than at government institutions" (Mills, *A Place in the News* 237).

Laurily Keir Epstein maintains that "there is a relationship between what is reported as news and what individuals and groups think of as socially and politically important" (*Women and the News* ix). If she is correct, then women in media bear some responsibility for helping shift attitudes about news. Women reporters and editors, too, absorb prevailing definitions of "real" news. Do they conform to those definitions, build their careers, develop a reputation as hard-hitting investigative journalists, and then alter the news structure? It's not likely. Epstein wrote in 1978 that the media may have "moved away from describing a leading nuclear physicist as a 'petite grandmother of five'" (Ibid. x). Institutionalized discrimination exists, however, and women as well as men often find themselves relying on previously unrecognized stereotypes.

Utimately, Suzanne Pingree and Robert P. Hawkins are correct: "With the basic fact in mind that there are *not* more men than women in the world, an audience confronted with the disproportion in news media attention to men might conclude that men are more important, more worthy of attention than women; or they might conclude that men are more involved in the significant events of the world; or simply that men's activities are news and women's are not" ("News Definitions and Their Effects on Women" 125–26). Although acknowledging that a women's section is an effort by editors of a particular newspaper to equalize news coverage, Pingree and Hawkins remind us that "the fact that there is a 'women's' section may be the most powerful message of all that the news is for and about men: how odd to think of one separate section for half the population, while the rest of the paper is for the other half" (Ibid. 126).

Much of the enthusiasm that accompanied the second wave of women's pages in the 1990s has subsided, and it is too early to predict the longevity of these experiments in the newspaper world or measure their impact. It is not too early, however, to reconsider the role of women reporters and editors at American newspapers, reassess the prevailing definitions of news, and pay more attention to the expressed desires of women readers. The history of women's pages is a reminder that the industry has not yet leveled the playing field for women in newspaper work and for women consumers of news.

3

Women in Contemporary
American Literary Journalism

While some media scholars address definitions of news as they affect women, others explore differences between and purposes of traditional news and literary journalism. One literary journalist, Sara Davidson, is among those who write extended nonfiction, emphasize thematic over chronological organization, and have interest in definitions of "news," "objectivity," "fairness," and "truth" in news-gathering and dissemination.

In both *Real Property* and *Loose Change: Three Women of the Sixties*, Davidson establishes authorial voice immediately. More important, her work relies on allegory, a multilayered symbolic system, and phenomenology, a search for meaning. It is surprising that allegory and phenomenology remain relatively unexplored in appraisals of literary journalists such as Joan Didion, Jon Krakauer, Jane Kramer, Adrian Nicole LeBlanc, Norman Mailer, Hunter S. Thompson, Tom Wolfe, and others. This chapter focuses on the work of three women journalists, Davidson, Didion, and Susan Orlean, and explores allegorical significance and meaning-making in their work.

Davidson's essay "Real Property" in a book by the same title begins with a polemic:

> "Who is the rich man?" asks the Talmud. The question has never seemed more relevant. The answer of the sages is: "He who is satisfied with what he has."
>
> I live in a house by the ocean with an outdoor Jacuzzi. I owned, until an embarrassing little accident, a pair of roller skates. I still own a volleyball, Frisbee, tennis racket, backpack, hiking boots, running shoes, a Mercedes 240 Diesel and a home burglar alarm system. But I cannot say that I am satisfied. (3)

By questioning her own values, Davidson accomplishes two things: She introduces herself as the central character in her morality play and encourages readers to identify with her in her quest. In *Loose Change,* Davidson employs the same technique. Here, too, her self-effacing tone suggests to readers that it is all right if they, too, are unsure about who they are and how they fit into the social order:

> It is the summer of '76 and I am living by the ocean in Southern California. I have fixed up my house as if I intend to stay. I've planted a cactus garden and furnished the rooms with wicker and Mexican tile. People tell me I speak like the natives. They say I look "laid back."
> I don't know. (366)

Davidson's foray into self-discovery is also a foray into the heart of American culture. Joan Didion and Susan Orlean are powerful social critics as well, and they blend the desire for purpose in life with a critique of contemporary attitudes and events.

As scholars have understood since at least the publication of Norman Sims's 1990 landmark book *Literary Journalism in the Twentieth Century,* literary journalism is a borderland between literature and journalism, and it is a borderland that makes some academicians in both English departments and schools and departments of journalism and mass communication uncomfortable. Because literary journalists acknowledge writing a type of nonfiction that puts the mainstream journalism establishment on edge, media and literary scholars must be honest enough to admit that critical study of their work puts some of them on edge as well.

Literary journalism is not fiction—the people are real and the events occurred—nor is it journalism in a traditional sense. There is interpretation, a personal point of view, and (often) experimentation with structure and chronology. Another essential element of literary journalism is its focus. Rather than emphasizing institutions, literary journalism explores the lives of those who are affected by those institutions. "Rather than hanging around the edges of powerful institutions," Sims writes, "literary journalists attempt to penetrate the cultures that make institutions work" ("The Literary Journalists" 3).

The debate about the virtues of literary journalism explodes again with the publication of every example of the genre that the public embraces. When Truman Capote's *In Cold Blood* appeared in 1965, he called it the first nonfiction novel. Journalists accused him of having gambled with the integrity of news by employing literary techniques such as stream of consciousness, and literary critics accused him of glorifying sensationalism and violating the high calling of fiction writing.

The controversy that followed *In Cold Blood* erupted again with the 1994 publication of *Midnight in the Garden of Good and Evil*. In an author's note, John Berendt acknowledges taking "certain storytelling liberties" but maintains that the story remains "faithful to the characters and to the essential drift of events as they really happened" (n.p.). The nonfiction novels of Capote and Berendt are catalysts for what former United Press International reporter Norman Sims calls an exploration of the "borderlands" between fact and fiction (*Literary Journalism in the Twentieth Century* v).

Literary journalism does not gain its name or identity from being the only lyrical or creative prose in journalism. It does, however, differ significantly from everyday journalistic stories published in newspapers and magazines. It requires immersion in an event; presumes a point of view; and employs literary techniques unapologetically, making rich use of stream of consciousness, metaphor, symbolism, description, point of view, narration, dialog, and other conventions considered by many to lie within the province of literature.

Some literary journalists experiment with chronology and/or change the names of characters, but most adhere to rigid journalistic practices while writing an extended narrative that captures the reader's interest and builds suspense and an investment in the development of complex characters. Literary journalism also is often interdisciplinary and combines genres. As Sims maintains, "The liveliness of literary journalism, which critics compare to fiction, comes from combining this personal engagement with perspectives from sociology and anthropology, memoir writing, fiction, history, and standard reporting. . . . Literary journalists are boundary crossers in search of a deeper perspective on our lives and times" ("The Art of Literary Journalism" 19).

Tracy Kidder defends literary journalism against the charge that its practitioners use literary techniques (and, presumably, violate journalistic ethics) with the following comment: "Some people criticize nonfiction writers for 'appropriating' the techniques and devices of fiction writing. Those techniques, except for invention of character and detail, never belonged to fiction. They belong to storytelling. In nonfiction you can create a tone and a point of view. Point of view affects everything that follows" (Sims, ed., *Literary Journalism* 19).

Since the 1960s and 1970s, the orthodoxy of news—especially the concept of objectivity—has been under fire. Literary journalists challenge the notion that traditional inverted-pyramid, "just-the-facts-ma'am" journalism can meet readers' deeper needs and intellectual demands. For literary journalists, "understanding begins with emotional connection" and "quickly leads to immersion" (Sims, "The Literary Journalists" 10). John Hartsock has also highlighted the point of view essential to a literary journalist: "It should come as no surprise then that narrative literary journalists who did not 'leave' their material but instead engaged their subjectivities in it found themselves having to take sides" (*A History of American Literary Journalism* 79).

Rather than distancing themselves from the subjects of their stories and striving to maintain objectivity, literary journalists immerse themselves in the lives and environments of their subjects and, although they may strive for balance and fairness, they trust readers to realize that their stories are bounded by time, space, and human limitation. There is no place for omniscient point of view in literary journalism. Hartsock is helpful in understanding these concepts but rightly refuses to privilege literary journalism over traditional objective journalism:

> In addition, we can see at work in the two strains of journalism the kinds of ideological concerns that would eventually be reflected in the development of objective objectified news and narrative literary journalism, and that raise a fundamental epistemological question, How best can one account for the phenomenal world? In principle, objective news would seem to serve the purpose better because of its announced intention to exclude partisanship. But as several critics have noted, objective news paradoxically disempowers readers by excluding their participation in such discourse. Narrative literary journalism offers more of an opportunity for reader engagement precisely because its purpose is to narrow the distance between subjectivity and the object, not divorce them. . .
>
> Nor is this to suggest that one form of journalism is superior to the other.
> That has been precisely the problem in the historic privileging of the information or discursive model over the story model, and more specifically of objective news over narrative literary journalism in our own century. Rather, given that the strengths of both are also their liabilities, such a conclusion argues in favor of a diversity of journalisms in the problematic attempt to interpret the phenomenal world. (Ibid. 132–33)

The stories of Davidson, Didion, Kramer, John McPhee, Orlean, Gay Talese, Wolfe and others dance along the border between nonfiction and fiction; provide the context often missing in straight news stories; and suggest the role of perception, vantage point, and authorial voice in all storytelling. Perhaps more important, their narratives are reminders that the lives of average people engaged in uncommon events are often the most compelling stories of all.

Susan Orlean has said that she rejected news for features, acknowledging that feature writing is often demeaned. "I just wanted to write what are usually called 'features'—a term that I hate because it sounds so fluffy and lightweight, like pillow stuffing, but that is used to describe stories that move at their own pace, rather than the news stories that race to keep time with events. The subjects I was drawn to were often completely ordinary, but I was confident that I could find something extraordinary in their ordinariness" (Introduction x–xi). Defining literary journalism as the "poetry of facts and the art in ordinary life," Orlean describes her quest to bring an average ten-year-old boy to life on the page by saying, "An ordinary life examined closely reveals itself to be exquisite and complicated and exceptional, somehow managing to be both heroic and plain" (Ibid. xi, xii).

News is not a collection of facts, no matter how finely arranged, and news-gathering is not merely the recording of a source's words or a description of chronological events. Within human events are meanings that sometimes propel those involved toward other events, a governing philosophy, or a re-lationship with the characters who drive the action. External events contain images and symbols that participants and observers transform into interior reality. If the events and people with whom we come in contact transform us, then they also transform those who cover the news.

Certainly, some characteristics of literary journalism concern traditional literary critics, especially what they consider to be the secondary nature of nonfiction in literary studies—never mind the place of daily journalism in their estimation. Neither journalists nor professors of English are likely to be reassured by the argument in this chapter that the work of at least three women literary journalists—Davidson, Didion, and Orlean—qualifies for serious critical attention not only as nonfiction but also as allegory. Like lit-erary journalism, allegory is in disrepute in some academic circles because it is misunderstood and often misdefined.

Allegory and Literary Journalism

Like the fictional figures in John Bunyan's allegory *Pilgrim's Progress,* a literary journalist's characters may be flesh and blood, grounded in place and time, and still richly representative and suggestive. Literary journalism is often allegorical in the sense that it makes an extended symbolic system tangible. As John J. Pauly suggests, literary journalism helped resurrect the "romantic vision of the writer" ("The Politics of Journalism" 119). Like William Carlos Williams, who wrote that "it is difficult / to get the news from poems, / yet men die miserably every day / for lack / of what is found there" (*Asphodel, That Greeny Flower and Other Love Poems* 19), Pauly allows nonfiction writers their place in a literary tradition that explores the depths and heights of experience.

What is found in poetry is, of course, acknowledgement of the complexity of life and human society and a vivid, lyrical language with which to communicate it. Joseph Webb employs the term *romantic reporter* in his discussion of literary journalists and their focus on "internal, rather than external, human processes" ("Historical Perspective" 43). What Webb suggests is that literary journalists aspire to a purpose higher than entertainment or even the dissemination of facts in their work; he also may be suggesting that the language used by literary journalists approaches poetry.

Sims, Hartsock, and Ronald Weber acknowledge the importance of underlying meaning in literary journalism texts. Weber discusses "nonfiction with a literary purpose" (*The Literature of Fact* 1) and writes of a kind of cultural allegory. During the 1960s and 1970s in particular, he maintains, the "only hope of making literary sense of such a society was through indirect, nonrealistic means," what he calls "irrealism" (Ibid. 11, 7–15). Citing Wolfe's concept of "saturation reporting," Weber refers to literary journalism as "reporting that went to the bottom depths of the material and sought out not only what was said and done but what was thought and felt, reporting that got inside character and scene the way novelists did but without the invention they employed" (Ibid. 19). To his list of characteristics of literary journalism, Sims adds "a search for the underlying meaning," also described as "symbolic realities" and "resonance" ("The Literary Journalists" 21–25).

Hartsock, too, suggests that the result of what he calls "narrative journalism" is "social or cultural allegory, with potential meanings beyond the literal in the broadest sense of allegory's meaning. Largely, although not exclusively, that allegory is about embracing an understanding of the social or cultural Other" (*A History of American Literary Jouurnalism* 22). For him, classics of literary journalism such as *In Cold Blood* and Norman Mailer's *The Executioner's Song* might be considered "allegories about the dark side of the American experience" because of "their attempts to understand the subjectivities of convicted murderers" in a new and dramatic way (Ibid. 78).

Allegory has been disparaged as being a too-blatant system of correspondences that reduces what is mysterious and profound to something concrete and simplistic. In American literature, allegory is not reductive but expansive. Although we may speak of an "allegorical system," allegory does not provide tidy systems but is a product of oppositions and tensions that must be held in balance. To understand that fact is to begin to confront the violence or conflict inherent in allegory. One writes allegory after learning the limits of realism in dealing with the metaphysical. Allegory has rich symbolic potential. When writers such as Franz Kafka or Jorge Luis Borges either change men into insects or set up hopelessly forking paths, they have entered a realm that defies realism and tapped into what the Transcendentalists knew as the unified world of Spirit behind the "thing." To create an allegory is to move into the realm of faith.

Yet it is not necessary to read solely for the moral or message within allegory or even parable. Allegory is rich with signification and builds on contradiction and surprising reversals. By employing symbols, allegory approaches myth. Allegories point toward as well as away from themselves and often point outside plot and character to a higher truth. To salvage allegory from the waste bin of second-rate fictional method, one must recognize that it can be broadly suggestive as well as specifically didactic.

Literary scholars usually agree that allegory is extended metaphor, equates persons and actions with meanings that lie outside the text, and has characters that are often personifications and events and settings that may be either historical or fictitious. What may be lost, however, is that allegory operates as much through tension and concealment as through equations and correspondences. Writers move into allegory when they have set out on a metaphysical quest and when their meaning lies beyond the familiar, common, and recognizable patterns of reality.

Critics have been reluctant to discuss news as allegory—in part because such a discussion suggests that news has a fictive element—but they have addressed in great depth mythology's role in news-gathering and reporting. At least one issue of *Journalism and Mass Communication Quarterly* has been devoted to the topic. In that special issue, Jack Lule summarizes the role of myth in American culture by saying that "myth has provided the stories that make sense of a society, for a society" and "is essential social narrative" ("Myth and Terror" 276, 277). He also highlights the role of myth in news by connecting mythology with storytelling and alluding to the history of news ("with roots in drama, folktale, and myth") until it was reconceptualized in the late nineteenth century to be "objective and scientific" rather than "dramatic and mythic" (Ibid. 277).

Allegory is more didactic and less universal than mythology, but both derive from society's need for stories that explain the inexplicable, rely on symbols for impact and cohesiveness, and have a role in nonfiction, a genre that purports to be "true" while acknowledging absolute reliance on the storyteller's point of view.

A quest is at the center of many successful allegories. Hartsock discusses authors whose "mock heroic in the picaresque tradition" leads the readers on a long pilgrimage in which they identify with the hero or anti-hero. At the end of many examples of literary journalism that incorporate a journey, however, "the American dream is found to be empty" (*A History of American Literary Journalism* 163). That conclusion is true for both Davidson and Didion, two formidable contemporary literary journalists.

Sara Davidson

One secret sharer in the literary journalism community is no secret to readers who have been introduced to Sara Davidson's bestsellers *Loose Change: Three Women of the Sixties* and *Cowboy: A Novel. LEAP! What Will We Do with the Rest of Our Lives?* (2007) was featured in *Newsweek* and provides a humorous, insightful, and provocative look at Baby Boomers at mid-life. Featuring celebrities such as Carly Simon, Jane Fonda, and Tom Hayden, *LEAP!* provides a glimpse into the everyday and addresses issues such as retirement, new careers, family, love, sexuality, and spirituality.

Davidson has not received her just due as an equal to Mailer, Thompson, Wolfe, and other males who have written literary journalism. The essay "Real Property," one of Davidson's most compelling literary achievements, is an example of the allegorical power and poetic energy of literary journalism as several scholars, including Thomas Connery, Hartsock, Pauly, Sims, and Weber, allude to it.

Davidson said that when she first began writing for magazines, Lillian Ross, the celebrated writer for *The New Yorker,* was her literary role model: "I was going to do what Lillian Ross had done. She never used the word 'I' and yet it was so clear there was an orienting consciousness guiding you" (Sims, "The Literary Journalists" 7). She also learned from the narrative strategies of Didion, Wolfe, and Peter Matthiessen (*The Snow Leopard*).

A reporter and national correspondent for the *Boston Globe* from 1965 to 1969, Davidson has published more than seventy articles and essays in *The Atlantic, Esquire, Harper's, Life, Los Angeles Times Magazine, McCall's, Mirabella, Ms., New York Times Magazine, New Woman, O: The Oprah Magazine, Spirituality and Health,* and other publications. She is best known for the international bestseller *Loose Change,* a social history of the 1960s told through the lives of three young women who meet at Berkeley; *Real Property,* a collection of her early essays; and *Cowboy,* a memoir of a relationship. She is also the author of *Friends of the Opposite Sex* and *Rock Hudson: His Story* and several scripts for television shows such as *Heartbeat,* which ran from 1988 to 1989 on ABC, and *Dr. Quinn, Medicine Woman,* which ran from 1992 to 1996 on CBS. The topics that draw Davidson are as rich and varied as the venues in which her work has appeared.

Davidson, a Phi Beta Kappa graduate of the University of California at Berkeley with a degree in English, also holds a master's degree in journalism from Columbia University. By the age of twenty-six she was a freelance magazine writer. Like many literary journalists trained in the study of English and journalism, she is self-conscious about her craft and deeply invested in conversations about the nature of artistic nonfiction, creative nonfiction, literary journalism, the new reportage, personal journalism, parajournalism, art-journalism, essay-fiction, factual fiction, journalit, or intimate journalism (whatever term the literary critics prefer).

One of her essays, "The Gray Zone," addresses the role of memoir, a particularly rich and problematic category of nonfiction. In that work, Davidson deals generally with the complexity of nonfiction, in particular with the difficulties she has encountered in writing a memoir. She begins with a reference to Patrick Hemingway, editor of his father's *True at First Light,* and his decision to publish the work as "fictionalized memoir." "When a story has its wellspring in life—in actual events and real people," she asks, "what constitutes a fictional rendering and what constitutes memoir?" ("The Gray Zone" 49). The answer matters "absolutely" in journalism, she says, because reporters have a responsibility not to "invent, change or embellish the smallest detail" (Ibid.). The answer is not always as clear in the "gray zone" in which she writes:

> When a writer sets out to tell a true story, he immediately finds himself constrained by the fallibility of memory. No one can recall the exact words of a conversation that took place a few days ago, let alone years, even if the writer attempts to recreate that conversation faithfully. In addition, the very process of translating mood, nonverbal signals and emotions into words creates a reality on the page that does not exactly mirror the event in life. But beyond this, the writer makes a deliberate choice as to how much he will permit himself to take liberties. (Ibid.)

Ultimately, Davidson argues for what she calls "not a better system of classification" for works of nonfiction but for "full disclosure" by authors (Ibid. 50).

Discussing the difference between fiction and nonfiction and novel and memoir, Davidson writes in her introduction to *Cowboy* that "at one end of the spectrum are works that are entirely imagined, and at the other end, works that purport to be fact. Most, however, are a blend of fact and imagination, and yet a line has been drawn to separate one from the other" (xi). She adds:

> I have long worked in what I perceive as the slippery slope between the two poles, the terrain where we find such entities as the nonfiction novel and the imagined autobiography. In *Loose Change*, published as nonfiction, I wrote about real people and historical events, yet I used fictional techniques—inventing dialogue, rearranging time, and combining scenes for dramatic purpose.
>
> Then it came to me to write the story in my own voice, as I remembered it, which is not the same as the way it occurred. I tried to convey the experience as strongly as I could, and to that end, I began to add elements and imagine things I could not have known by any other means. To protect the privacy of my children and ex-husbands, I created fictional characters to stand in their stead and speak and act in ways they hadn't. What has resulted is a book that defies categories—a hybrid—and if that sounds like an elaborate dodge, what I can say is that I'm telling you this story in the best and perhaps the only way I can. (*Cowboy* xii–xiii)

Davidson knows the difficulties of writing a memoir firsthand; in *Loose Change*, she discusses intimate aspects of her life. The other two women and her former husband, central characters, read drafts of the work. Although Davidson changed the names of many characters and those of the two women, people knew who they were. "Suddenly, something that was all right as a manuscript was not all right when it was being read widely and people were responding to it," Davidson comments.

> There's one scene where I had a fight with my husband and he slapped me. Well, he started getting crank calls from people who accused him of being a wife beater. It's true, he did slap me. But suddenly he was being vilified, publicly. There were people who read it and thought he was a monster. One of the women would be walking down the street and someone would come up to her and say, "My God, I didn't know you had an abortion in your father's office when you were 16!" Relatives of the family would call in horror that she had exposed this kind of thing about herself and her family. The man she had lived with for seven years thought it was a major violation of confidence and trust. He said, "I wasn't living with you to have it become public knowledge. We weren't living our life as a research project." (Ibid. 19–20)

Because *Loose Change* was hurtful to those portrayed in the novel (even though they knew they would appear and had consented to do so), Davidson moved into a kind of disguised memoir when she wrote *Cowboy*. Of *Loose Change,* she says, "What bothered me was that I had caused pain to other people, to my husband, to the women, who went through hell. People say knowing it was about real people heightened their appreciation and relationship to it. They preferred that it was nonfiction. But I do know I would never, never write again so intimately about my life because I can't separate my life from the people who have been in it." The fact that the women in *Loose Change* had signed releases made it legal for her to use the material, but "emotionally and morally, it's not always so clear cut" (Ibid. 20–21).

Davidson altered her point of view (and disguised characters' identities) in *Cowboy*. She also changed names and altered events to protect individuals. and included an author's note: "This book is based on a true story—a love affair I've had with the character whom I call Zack. For reasons of privacy, however, I have placed this story in a fictional context. I've created imaginary characters for the heroine's extended family. . . . No relationship should be inferred between these characters in the book and any living persons, nor should incidents about them be taken as fact" (*Cowboy* n.p.).

Loose Change and *Cowboy* are better known, but Davidson's most provocative book is *Real Property,* which became a Literary Guild selection and bestseller. Richly allegorical, the first essay, "Real Property," is drawn from diaries Davidson kept while living in Venice, California, in 1967. By camouflaging the identities of many of the people she interviews, Davidson is able to suggest their representative natures; by juxtaposing the golden paradise of California legend with daily reality, she is able to set up political, social, psychological and religious correspondences. The twelve vignettes that compose the work can then be understood on multiple levels.

The episodic structure of "Real Property" suggests the fragmentation of the lives she describes. Vignettes include descriptions of Venice, Marina del Rey, a man who seems not to have been affected by the pain of those around him, Davidson's mother and sister and the ironic legacy of real estate, the symbolic nature of buying and selling real estate as a parable of American priorities, a man who represents the new southern Californian, college women, dating rituals, Israel, financial success, a skating accident, and Davidson's running over a drunken man with her car.

Davidson's allegory is suggestive, not heavily didactic, although there is no doubt about her opinion of American excess and greed. She knows she is writing about the "decaying social order" ("Notes from the Land of the Cobra" 213), and she tells the reader in the same essay—a morality play about the Symbionese Liberation Army, Patricia Hearst, and California—

that she is writing an allegory that is truer than reality: "What I have come up with are fragments, shards of pathos and humor, and a suspicion that the symbols in this drama may be more potent and meaningful than the reality" (Ibid. 200).

Davidson's tone remains consistent throughout *Real Property* and *Loose Change,* and the conclusion of the latter summarizes issues raised in the nonfiction novel and makes them problematic. The anguish of the narrator as she surveys her world is evident when she explains the title of the book: "We had predicted that the center would not hold but it had, and now we were in pieces. 'Loose change,' I told a friend" (366). When she admits confusion about drugs, the sexual revolution, the civil rights movement, and other phenomena of the 1960s, she says, "I'm afraid I will be criticized for copping out. ('We want to know what you *make* of it all, what this period meant in terms of a society, a culture.') But the truth is, I have not found answers and I'm not sure I remember the questions" (367). Here as elsewhere Davidson defies narrative closure, recognizing that a tidy conclusion to the book suggests a tidy resolution to issues shaking the foundation of the society.

In "Real Property," Davidson invites readers into a world defined by real estate sales and shallowness of spirit and in doing so deftly employs clichés and familiar images and symbols. "What does it mean that everyone I know is looking to make some kind of 'killing?'" she asks. "It means, I think, that we are in far deeper than we know" (6). Of a man who embodies the cultural attitudes that concern her she writes:

> He did not want to hear about frustration. He did not want to know about writer's block. He did not think I should feel jealous if he dated other women, and he did not believe a relationship should be work.
> "I think we do too much talking," he said.
> "That's funny. I think we don't do enough." (Ibid. 9)

Like Didion in *Slouching Towards Bethlehem: Essays,* Davidson writes of a world in which the core values are unraveling and faith is dissipating, and, like Didion and poet William Butler Yeats, she fears that the center will not hold: "Rolling, rolling. The wind is blowing, the palms are blowing and people are blowing every which way. I cannot walk on the boardwalk these days without feeling it in my stomach: something is wrong. There are too many people on wheels. The skaters will fall, the bikers will crash, they will fly out of control and there is nothing to hold onto" (*Slouching Towards Bethlehem* 5).

Against this tableau of commercialism and empty social connections lies Davidson's essay about Israel, "Last Days in Sinai." A teaser for that essay appears in "Real Property," in which Davidson observes that "life in Israel is in diametric contrast to life in Southern California" and that "Israelis are reminded, almost daily, that human life is transient and relationships are not replaceable" ("Real Property" 27, 28). At the end of the essay "Real Property," she expands her description of the real estate boom and hedonism of southern California into commentary on the nation and her generation. Literary journalists rarely if ever provide closure. There is a sense of an ending but not a resolution:

> It is a cliché, a joke, something we are past feeling anguished about, but the fact is that a considerable number of people have passed through a door and come out wearing different clothes, and this transformation has taken place almost without comment. People who, in the flowering of the Sixties, gave their children names like Blackberry and Veda-Rama have changed them to Suzy and John. The parents are "getting our money trip together." If they are successful, they are buying homes, Calvin Klein suits and Porsches and sending their kids to private schools to avoid busing.
>
> Not all have come through the door, of course. There are still groups of New Age people in places like Berkeley, Oregon, Hawaii and Vermont. They are still dedicated to social change, still wearing beards and flowing shawls, still holding symposiums where they talk about holistic health care, living closer to the earth and creating communities where people can love each other and share and cooperate. But their numbers are dwindling and few young recruits come along.
>
> Those who have crossed the line cannot help but feel some irony and bafflement about "the people we've become." They retain an awareness, however faintly it is pulsing, that the acquisition of material wealth does not necessarily bring satisfaction, but that awareness is fading rapidly into unconsciousness. (Ibid. 14)

Davidson's concerns about the essential values of society and her interest in the manner in which a journalist employs literary techniques raise several questions. Is there room for various "journalisms"? Is it possible for the academy—whether departments and schools of journalism and departments of English—to acknowledge what Davidson calls the "gray zone" and embrace it as journalism, literature, and a symbolic genre of its own? Will it be possible to address and redefine the practices of news reporting and writing during this century? What does our understanding of literary journalism suggest about fact and fiction as they are traditionally understood and about the nature of truth? Is there a place in daily news reporting for stories that do not end with a description of our worst selves but challenge people to exemplify courage, commitment, and concern for others? And, finally, can news consumers and media scholars begin to address the profoundly allegorical nature of news?

Joan Didion

One of Davidson's friends and intellectual and literary soulmates is Joan Didion. Like Davidson, Didion is also facing transitions in her life. After more than thirty years of marriage, she lost her nearly constant companion, editor, and best friend, the playwright John Gregory Dunne in 2003. Didion described the experience in *The Year of Magical Thinking* (2005), which in 2007 became a Broadway play starring Vanessa Redgrave.

Didion is a fifth-generation Californian, one reason that she and Davidson connect personally and professionally. Although many American writers, including Samuel Clemens and John Steinbeck, have written about California, it has taken literary journalists such as Davidson and Didion to round out the wonders of sandy beaches, endless sunshine, Yosemite, and San Francisco. They have added depth and perspective to the American myth of western expansion and California dreaming. It is impossible not to recognize the similarity in themes in "Real Property" and "Some Dreamers of a Golden Dream," an essay from Didion's *Slouching Towards Bethlehem: Essays* (1977).

At the heart of the genre of literary journalism, Didion writes as a participant-observer about growing up in California in the 1950s, the tumult in America in the 1960s, and more recent political and cultural events. Critics describe her work as highly personal and profoundly apocalyptic. She writes of spiritual disintegration, and her narrators, although wise, are never quite omniscient. She also concerns herself with media's role in creating reality for readers and viewers. In *The Last Thing He Wanted,* she discusses news as fact, fiction, and tales. Of one of her characters, she writes, "It occurred to her that possibly what was misleading was the concept of 'news' itself, a liberating thought" (30).

At the center of Didion's work is the dread and despair of individuals who sense an unpredictable universe. A master of journalistic detail, she discusses natural disasters such as Santa Ana winds, mud slides, wildfires, and earthquakes; employs a sometimes wry but always biting tone to describe a changing and often frightening political landscape; and comments on existential loneliness, true love, tragedy, and human destiny.

Didion, always a self-conscious writer committed to perfecting her art, credits Ernest Hemingway, Joseph Conrad, and Henry James as literary ancestors. She received a B.A. degree in English from the University of California at Berkeley and was twenty-two when *Vogue* magazine hired her and she began work in New York. The job was the result of a literary award she won at Berkeley.

Her credits are rich and varied. Didion and Dunne wrote the screenplays for the 1976 version of *A Star Is Born* and *Up Close and Personal*. Didion is also well known for columns and essays in *The Saturday Evening Post, Esquire,* and other magazines. Although she has written several novels and collections of essays, she is perhaps most famous for *Run River, Slouching Towards Bethlehem, Play It as It Lays, A Book of Common Prayer, The White Album, Salvador, Democracy, Joan Didion: Essays and Conversations, Miami, After Henry,* and *The Last Thing He Wanted.*

Among Didion's themes are objective reality, felt experience, social dislocations, disintegration of family, and need for order. She fuses the personal with the public; believes that American society is nostalgic, romantic, and deluded; and argues against the idea that economic growth equals progress. In fact, no human institutions can form the center for a society in a downward spiral. To support her central thesis, Didion borrows "The Second Coming" by William Butler Yeats for the title of one of her books (*Slouching Towards Bethlehem*) and as the theme around which her narratives revolve.

Slouching Towards Bethlehem illuminates the San Francisco drug culture of the 1960s. Hartsock has commented, "Didion cultivates such incongruities in her writing precisely because they demonstrate how impossible it is to reduce phenomenal experience into a tidy package or, in other words, to critical closure. In the face of such evidence she records, she is reflecting how she feels, or 'what it was to be me' when she confronted the evidence, in this case a kind of disbelief about the circumstances she found" (*A History of American Literary Journalism* 199).

It is clear why Didion chose a poem by an author enchanted by—and committed to—order, form, and civilization yet found himself in a world characterized by soulessness and chaos. Yeats wrote in January 1919 about the conflict between the British and the Irish, "Turning and turning in the widening gyre / The falcon cannot hear the falconer; / Things fall apart; the centre cannot hold; / Mere anarchy is loosed upon the world. . . / And what rough beast, its hour come round at last, / Slouches towards Bethlehem to be born?" ("The Second Coming" 158). He borrowed images of the Second Coming in Matthew 24 and the appearance of the Antichrist (Beast of the Apocalypse) in I John 2:18. Through the use of disruptive, disquieting images, Didion describes California as a land of terror and site of humanity's end rather than a place of enchantment, sun worship, and hedonism.

"In the end," Hartsock observes, "she [Didion] resists critical closure if she is true to her points of reference" (*A History of American Literary Journalism* 153). Referring again to a literary journalist's refusal to be embarrassed by subjectivity, he adds, "Subjectivity alone undoes the lie, and in undoing it literary journalists resist coming to critical closure" (Ibid. 203). Presumably, the "lie" is the implication by traditional journalists that they have understood and encapsulated an event for a reader. There is no presumption of knowing in literary journalism; thus there are no absolutes and no conclusions.

In *Political Fictions* (2001), Didion deals with the allegorical nature of American political systems and reveals that her essays are designed to show "the ways in which the political process did not reflect but increasingly proceeded from a series of fables about American experience" (7). Her powerful narratives combine scathing political commentary with an allegorist's desire to leave no symbol unturned. When she unveils who actually voted in the 2000 election, the message is a damning one for powerbrokers:

> Fifty-three percent of voters in the 2000 election. . . had. . . incomes above $50,000. Forty-three percent were suburban. Seventy-four percent had some higher education; forty-two percent had actual college degrees. Seventy percent said that they invested in the stock market. That this was not a demographic profile of the country at large, that half the nation's citizens had only a vassal relationship to the government under which they lived, that the democracy we spoke of spreading throughout the world was now in our own country only an ideality, had come to be seen, against the higher priority of keeping the process in the hands of those who already held it, as facts without application. (Ibid. 17–18)

Her concerns with the American political process do not stop with politicians but involve those in the shadows who describe and deliver the status quo to the American public—journalists. "American reporters 'like' covering a presidential campaign (it gets them out on the road, it has balloons, it has music, it is viewed as a big story, one that leads to the respect of one's peers, to the Sunday shows, to lecture fees and often to Washington), which is why there has developed among those who do it so arresting an enthusiasm for overlooking the contradictions inherent in reporting that which occurs only in order to be reported" (Ibid. 30).

Allegory depends upon the creation of character, and Didion is quick to point out that the American political tableau is home to some of the best narratives of conflict and some of the most compelling characters. "All stories, of course, depend for their popular interest upon the invention of personality, or 'character,'" she writes, "but in the political narrative, designed as it is to maintain the illusion of consensus by obscuring rather than addressing actual issues, this invention served a further purpose" (Ibid. 41–42). She also notes:

> In other words, what it "came down to," what it was "about," what was wrong or right with America, was not an historical shift largely unaffected by the actions of individual citizens but "character," and if "character" could be seen to count, then every citizen—since everyone was a judge of character, an expert in the field of personality—could be seen to count. This notion, that the citizen's choice among determinedly centrist candidates makes a "difference," is in fact the narrative's most central element, and its most fictive. (Ibid. 44)

Whether or not one agrees with Didion's cynical view of the political process, there can be no doubt that her vision derives from understanding that invented narratives produce intense social reaction. As she explains, "The entire attention of those inside the process was directed toward the invention of this story in which they themselves were the principal players, and for which they themselves were the principal audience" (Ibid. 47). In the 1980s, for example, Americans elected a former actor, Ronald Reagan, as president. The public's enchantment with that particular character was not lost on Didion:

> For the "President," a man whose most practiced instincts had trained him to find the strongest possible narrative line in the scenes he was given, to clean out those extraneous elements that undermined character clarity, a man for whom historical truth had all his life run at twenty-four frames a second, Iran-contra would have been irresistible, a go project from concept, a script with two strong characters, the young marine officer with no aim but to serve his president, the aging president with no aim but to free the tyrannized (whether the tyrants were Nicaraguans or Iranians or some other nationality altogether was just a plot point, a detail to work out later), a story about male bonding, a story about a father who found the son he never (in this "cleaned out" draft of the script) had, a buddy movie, and better still than a buddy movie: a mentor buddy movie, with action. (Ibid. 117)

A full reading of Didion's fiction reveals layer upon layer of allegorical method and characters employed as metaphor. The memoir *The Year of Magical Thinking* is too starkly realistic to be allegorical other than in the way grief affects everyone. "Some Dreamers of the Golden Dream" from *Slouching Towards Bethlehem* has similarities to Davidson's "Real Property"; allegory and phenomenology are both part of it.

Didion is a cultural allegorist, a prophet of the modern day. In "Some Dreamers of the Golden Dream," which was originally published in the *Saturday Evening Post,* she "sets her sights on the shallow promise and Gothic nature of the California dream" (Hartsock, *A History of American Literary Journalism* 199). Dennis Russell also recognizes that Didion documents an America that is "socially, politically, and spiritually adrift" ("Baudrillardesque Impulses" 20). He provides a helpful study of Didion as an allegorist in which he also maintains that she uncovers the "counterfeit nature of the American narrative" (Ibid. 25). "Her subjects nostalgically and desperately cling to lifestyles, norms, values, and beliefs that long since have crumbled under the weight of their own mythologies," Russell adds, "and in so doing are systematically replicating an America that may never have existed" (Ibid. 28).

Once again, the setting for the complex tale of American values is southern California, this time the San Bernardino Valley. As Orlean writes in an interview with Didion, the author of "taut, chilling" essays for *Vogue,* the *National Review, Saturday Evening Post,* and *New York Times Magazine* describes California "as a world both real and imagined, at once the bedrock of familiarity to her as a native and a place that was then fracturing into strange, disordered pieces" ("Straight and Narrow" 282).

The first line of "Some Dreamers of the Golden Dream"—"This is a story about love and death in the golden land"—signals symbolic intent. The allegorical expectation is heightened with: "There has been no rain since April. Every voice seems a scream. It is the season of suicide and divorce and prickly dread, wherever the wind blows" ("Some Dreamers" 3). Readers have little doubt that the tale of Lucille Maxwell Miller, her husband Gordon "Cork" Miller, and Banyan Street will be ominous. Those familiar with Didion will suspect that the story about the Millers is about the couple and yet not about them: "Unhappy marriages so resemble one another that we do not need to know too much about the course of this one" (Ibid. 8).

Arrested for the murder of her husband, Miller becomes an ironic symbol of a world gone mad. Again, the center will not hold. As detectives begin their investigation, so do Didion and the reader. Crimes are nothing if not puzzles, but Didion's crimes inevitably take on cultural significance. She writes of her lost protagonist and the search for a motive for her crime:

> They set out to find it in accountants' ledgers and double-indemnity clauses and motel registers, set out to determine what might move a woman who believed in all the promises of the middle class—a woman who had been chairman of the Heart Fund and who always knew a reasonable little dressmaker

and who had come out of the bleak wild of prairie fundamentalism to find what she imagined to be the good life—what should drive such a woman to sit on a street called Bella Vista and look out her new picture window into the empty California sun and calculate how to burn her husband alive in a Volkswagen. (Ibid. 15)

The motive, an affair with the husband of one of her friends, explains the crime and yet does not explain it. Detectives look for simple causes and effects; Didion, as always, looks for clues to human nature and madness in the "golden land" (Ibid. 28). In fact, California becomes a character in Didion's story, a location that seems to have its own terrible energy. Miller's trial opens in a land where "the air smells of orange blossoms" and a sixteen-year-old tries to kill himself:

> January 11, 1965, was a bright warm day in Southern California, the kind of day when Catalina floats on the Pacific horizon and the air smells of orange blossoms and it is a long way from the bleak and difficult East, a long way from the cold, a long way from the past. A woman in Hollywood staged an all-night sit-in on the hood of her car to prevent repossession by a finance company. A seventy-year-old pensioner drove his station wagon at five miles an hour past three Gardena poker parlors and emptied three pistols and a twelve-gauge shotgun through their windows, wounding twenty-nine people. "Many young women become prostitutes just to have enough money to play cards," he explained in a note. Mrs. Nick Adams said that she was "not surprised" to hear her husband announce his divorce plans on the Les Crane Show, and, farther north, a sixteen-year-old jumped off the Golden Gate Bridge and lived.
>
> And, in the San Bernardino County Courthouse, the Miller trial opened. The crowds were so bad that the glass courtroom doors were shattered in the crush, and from then on identification disks were issued to the first forty-three spectators in line. (Ibid. 19–20)

Miller was sentenced to life in prison with the possibility of parole and incarcerated at the California Institution for Women at Frontera, near a field where cattle graze and where a sprinkler system irrigates the alfalfa. "A lot of California murderesses live here, a lot of girls who somehow misunderstood the promise" (Ibid. 25). At the end of the narrative she mentions "the golden land where every day the world is born anew" (Ibid. 28). What she suggests, of course, is not that innocence returns to California (or America) but that there are few consequences and no moments of epiphany in a world in which "time past is not believed to have any bearing upon time present or future" (Ibid.) and no moments of epiphany. Troubling and prophetic, "Some Dreamers of the Golden Dream" is Didion's critique of human nature and her scathing commentary on American life.

Didion is the best-known woman literary journalist, and talented writers such as Davidson and Orlean have paid tribute to her both directly and indirectly. In the April 2002 issue of *Vogue*, Orlean describes Didion as a "person who will visit El Salvadoran body dumps but is also easily frightened, not by concrete horrors but by abstractions like failure and loneliness and dislocation." Along with Wolfe and Mailer, she observes, Didion invented a "new kind of journalism that slipped into and out of anthropology, politics, and autobiography" ("Straight and Narrow" 281–82, 283).

Susan Orlean

Although Susan Orlean—like all contemporary women writers in America— owes something to Didion and has been called one of her disciples, she is very much her own person and possesses a compelling style and thematic interests of her own. The best-selling author of *The Orchid Thief* and *Saturday Night*, Orlean has been a staff writer at *The New Yorker*, and her articles also have appeared in *Outside*, *Rolling Stone*, *Vogue*, and *Esquire*. A discussion of *The Orchid Thief: A True Story of Beauty and Obsession* is appropriate for a discussion of allegory in literary journalism, if for no other reason than the fact that the nonfiction novel demonstrates how literary journalists weave character and didacticism into an extended symbolic system.

Much of Orlean's work falls into the more traditional category of news features. It is objective in the sense that it is fair, even-handed reporting about an event. It is biased in the sense that it relies upon personal vantage point. An example, "Rough Diamonds: Fidel's Little Leagues," appeared in the August 5, 2002, issue of *The New Yorker*. Although it is a descriptive narrative about Juan Cruz, eleven and a "slip of a kid. . . with dark, dreamy eyes, long arms, big feet, and musculature of a grasshopper" ("Rough Diamonds" 34), it also tells the story of sports in Cuba under the watchful eye of Fidel Castro. Clearly more a feature article with a long shelf life, "Rough Diamonds" is like *The Orchid Thief* in that it reveals the underside of a society while entertaining readers with dialog, description, and narration.

"I didn't want to be a newspaper reporter," Orlean admits, "because I have never cared about knowing something first, and I didn't want to write only about things that were considered 'important' and newsworthy; I wanted to write about things that intrigued me, and to write about them in a way that would surprise readers who might not have expected to find these things intriguing" (Introduction ix). Some of the people she finds intriguing are featured in a collection entitled *The Bullfighter Checks Her Makeup: My Encounters with Extraordinary People.* They include a ten-year-old boy named Colin Duffy, surfer girls in Maui, a New York real estate broker, the controversial ice-skater Tonya Harding, and a woman bullfighter.

"The American Man, Age Ten" is both vintage Orlean and a gem of provocative literary journalism. Asked to write a profile about then-child actor Macauley Culkin, she convinced her editors to let her write an essay about an average young American male. What resulted is a riveting description of what it is like to be a young boy growing up in America, from his love of video games, candy, and pizza to his attitudes about marriage, recycling, money, and girls. There is no attempt on Orlean's part to detach herself from her subject, Colin. She acknowledges in the last line of the essay that she has been captured by the child she describes. Wrapping fishing line around various objects in his back yard, Colin goes into the house after dark, leaving Orlean to admit, "He dropped the spool, skipped up the stairs of the deck, threw open the screen door, and then bounded into the house, leaving me and Sally the dog trapped in his web" ("The American Man" 14).

Informative, "The American Man, Age Ten" also represents the understated tone that many literary journalists employ to undercut the formal tone of reporters, who are interested in establishing themselves as experts on a particular issue. She writes, for example, that "psychologists identify ten as roughly the age at which many boys experience the gender-linked normative developmental trauma that leaves them, as adult men, at risk for specific psychological sequelae often manifest as deficits in the arenas of intimacy, empathy, and struggles with commitment in relationships. In other words, this is around the age when guys get screwed up about girls" (Ibid. 10).

The tone of *The Orchid Thief* is consistent with her earlier work. In addition to being a character in the story, she makes clear that she is telling the stories of others in order to better understand herself and her quest for passion and joy. She uses other people's obsession with orchids to explain her pilgrimage to Florida, and in the end she understands her own obsession with telling their stories and deconstructing their fascination with the unique flowers: "Orchids seem to drive people crazy," she notes. "Those who love them love them madly. Orchids arouse passion more than romance. They are the sexiest flowers on earth" (Ibid. 50).

The Orchid Thief is based on a newspaper article Orlean read about John Laroche and three Seminoles—Russell Bowers, Dennis Osceola, and Vinson Osceola—who had been arrested with rare orchids they stole from the Fakahatchee Strand State Preserve in Florida. "I wanted to know more about the incident," she comments (Ibid. 6). Knowing more became a 284-page novel. The working title of *The Orchid Thief* was *Passion,* and a novel about rare and beautiful flowers became an internal pilgrimage.

"Obviously at the end of the book, I realize I do have a single-minded passion," she admits in an interview included at the end of *The Orchid Thief.* "It is the passion to be a writer and a reporter. But I think the detachment was to my advantage. I don't like writing about things I am too invested in initially. For me, part of the process of writing is the journey to understanding" (Readers Guide n.p.).

Although Orlean's freelance work is provocative and revelatory, her self-discovery in the act of writing becomes clearer in her longer work. Wondering about her potential to be passionate about life and work, she says of her central character, "Laroche's passions arrived unannounced and ended explosively, like car bombs" (Ibid. 4). She also acknowledges being drawn to his ability to transform the day: "One of his greatest assets is optimism—that is, he sees a profitable outcome in practically every life situation, including disastrous ones" (Ibid. 5).

Florida is as evocative for Orlean as California is for Davidson and Didion. Of her journey of self-discovery, she writes:

> I was of a mixed mind about Florida. I loved walking past the Art Deco hotels on Ocean Drive and Collins Road, loved the huge delis, loved my first flush of sunburn, but dreaded jellyfish and hated how my hair looked in the humidity. Heat unsettles me, and the Florida landscape of warm wideness is as alien to me as Mars. I do not consider myself a Florida person. But there is something about Florida more seductive and inescapable than almost anywhere else I've ever been. It can look brand-new and man-made, but as soon as you see a place like the Everglades or the Big Cypress Swamp or the Loxahatchee you realize that Florida is also the last of the American frontier. . . . The developed places are just little clearings in the jungle, but since jungle is unstoppably fertile, it tries to reclaim a piece of developed Florida every day. At the same time the wilderness disappears before your eyes: fifty acres of Everglades dry up each day, new houses sprout on sand dunes, every year a welt of new highways rises. Nothing seems hard or permanent; everything is always changing or washing away. (Ibid. 9)

Searching for permanence and understanding in a semiological jungle, Orlean focuses on setting and character and weaves a tale of growing self-awareness. To make sense of "incongruity and paradox," she asks a park ranger, Tony, to guide her through the swamp. Her critical gaze is both external and internal, and when she asks Tony about his work, he explains his fascination with orchids by connecting them to a phenomenological quest. When asked why he loves orchids, he responds, "Oh, mystery, beauty, unknowability, I suppose. Besides," he shrugs, "I think the real reason is that life has no meaning. I mean, no *obvious* meaning. You wake up, you go to work, you do stuff. I think everybody's always looking for something a little unusual that can preoccupy them and help pass the time" (Ibid. 38).

The "lovely papery white" ghost orchid (Ibid. 39) becomes the book's quintessential symbol of perfection and beauty in a flawed universe: "The whiteness of the flower is as startling as a spotlight in the grayness and greenness of a swamp. Because the plant has no foliage and its roots are almost invisible against tree bark, the flower looks magically suspended in midair" (Ibid.). The purpose of Orlean's quest becomes clear to readers as it does to her: "If the ghost orchid was really only a phantom it was still such a bewitching one that it could seduce people to pursue it year after year and mile after miserable mile. If it was a real flower I wanted to keep coming back to Florida until I could see one. The reason was not that I love orchids. I don't even especially *like* orchids. What I wanted was to see this thing that people were drawn to in such a singular and powerful way" (Ibid. 40).

What Orlean and the reader discover is the commitment that a few followers of the religion of orchids express about their life's work. Searching for orchids is not a hobby or a weekend distraction. It is a pilgrimage. As Orlean observes of their single-minded focus and her own longing, "It was religion. I *wanted* to want something as much as people wanted these plants, but it isn't part of my constitution. I think people my age are embarrassed by too much enthusiasm and believe that too much passion about anything is naïve. I suppose I do have one unembarrassing passion—I want to know what it feels like to care about something passionately" (Ibid. 40–41).

Throughout the nonfiction novel Orlean reminds readers why they are on a quest to see the ghost orchid. The journey, both literal and in the pages of a book, is to discover an explanation for their passions—or at least to discover why other people have passions. One explanation is that obsession provides focus:

> The world is so huge that people are always getting lost in it. There are too many ideas and things and people, too many directions to go. I was starting to believe that the reason it matters to care passionately about something is that it whittles the world down to a more manageable size. It makes the world

seem not huge and empty but full of possibility. If I had been an orchid hunter I wouldn't have seen this space as sad-making and vacant—I think I would have seen it as acres of opportunity where the things I loved were waiting to be found. (Ibid. 109)

Orlean also suggests that the quest provides belief in something greater than ourselves, in this case a perfect, albeit fragile, creation: "They sincerely loved something, trusted in the perfectibility of some living thing, lived for a myth about themselves and the idea of adventure, were convinced that certain things were really worth dying for, believed that they could make their lives into whatever they dreamed" (Ibid. 201).

John Laroche becomes the quintessential pilgrim characterized by "benign derangement" and the "oddball ultimate of those people who are enthralled by non-human living things and who pursue them like lovers" (Ibid. 268, 136). Ultimately, it is her difference from him that she finds reassuring. Orlean and the reader both discover that the point of the quest has been to see, to possess in some form, a ghost orchid. When Orlean fails to do so she learns the ultimate lesson in the quest and uses it to comfort the reader:

In the universe there are only a few absolutes of value; something is valuable because it can be eaten for nourishment or used as a weapon or made into clothes or it is valuable if you want it and you believe it will make you happy. Then it is worth anything as well as nothing, worth as much as you will give to have something you think you want. It saved all sorts of trouble knowing I wouldn't find a ghost orchid here, since then I didn't even need to look. It was a relief to have no hope because then I had no fear; looking for something you want is a comfort in the clutter of the universe, but knowing you don't have to look means you can't be disappointed. (Ibid. 258)

The essential nature of longing and unrequited love for a person or an object becomes the purpose of Orlean's quest. In the end, she acknowledges being sad "for anyone who ever cared about something that didn't work out." She writes that she has "realized it was just as well that I never saw a ghost orchid, so that it could never disappoint me, and so it would remain forever something I wanted to see" (Ibid. 281).

The power of Orlean's allegory lies in what it teaches readers about themselves during a meandering journey through the sweltering, humid heat of the Florida swamps in search of an appropriately named ghost orchid. The quest is a religious experience in a world skeptical of religious zeal; we discover that the impossible quest to know ourselves is a worthy pilgrimage.

For Orlean, literary journalism is the lens by which news—several men are arrested for stealing orchids—becomes an extended examination of the human psyche, the universal truths of being human. For her, literary journalism is an art form. Her commitment to her work is revealed when she writes of those she has interviewed, who have transformed her and shown her what is permanent in a transitory world: "So what I have of them, and always will have, is just that moment we spent together—now preserved on paper, bound between covers, cast out into the world—and they will never get any older, their faces will never fade, their dreams will still be within reach, and I will forever still be listening as hard as I can" (Introduction, *The Bullfighter* xv).

Davidson, Didion, and Orlean remain writers of nonfiction, but other women—even those who might have chosen to remain newspaper reporters and editors or write extended nonfiction—left journalism and built substantial reputations by writing fiction. A few, such as Carson McCullers, author of *The Heart Is a Lonely Hunter, The Member of the Wedding,* and *The Ballad of the Sad Café,* worked in journalism only a short time and discovered they did not enjoy writing news and features. Others, such as Katherine Anne Porter, might have remained in the field had newspapers been more welcoming to and affirming of women reporters and editors. Still others, such as Eudora Welty, had rewarding media careers but found that the themes they wanted to convey were more appropriate for fiction.

4

Women Journalists
Who Chose Fiction

Literary journalism draws on studies in media, literature, sociology, communication, American history and culture, and journalism. It encompasses those who left newspapers and wrote fiction, such as Willa Cather, Samuel Clemens, Stephen Crane, Theodore Dreiser, Ernest Hemingway, Katherine Anne Porter, Upton Sinclair, John Steinbeck, and Eudora Welty; those known for writing creative nonfiction, such as Truman Capote, Sara Davidson, Joan Didion, Norman Mailer, Susan Orlean, Hunter S. Thompson, and Tom Wolfe; and those who write critically about the field, such as David Abrahamson, Thomas Connery, Shelley Fisher Fishkin, John Hartsock, John J. Pauly, Nancy Roberts, and Norman Sims.[1]

Women are often omitted from scholarly texts and collections that deal with literary journalism. The majority of contemporary literary journalists listed are male, and often authors and editors refer to reporters as "he." It is impossible to imagine a contemporary literary journalism text that would, for example, exclude Joan Didion, but that is sometimes the case. Adding insult to injury, theoretical discussions of the development of literary journalism continue to employ sexist language.[2]

As is true with the majority of fiction writers selected for American literature anthologies, most of the journalists who have made names for themselves in news and as fiction writers are men.[3] Often excluded are women such as Willa Cather, Edna Ferber, Harper Lee, Margaret Mitchell, Lillian Ross, Eudora Welty, Rebecca West, and others. Although their media involvement is noted in biographies, their nonfiction is not commonly analyzed along with Capote's, Crane's, Hemingway's, or Upton Sinclair's. Even more startling is the fact that a few—Welty, for example—had rich media careers. Her work spanned radio, print media, advertising, and photography.

Willa Cather

Although it is true that Cather's journalism career has been a focus of scholarly inquiry only since the 1990s, historians and literary critics have been diligent in their research on the Nebraska native and drawn important connections between journalism and her fiction writing.

James Woodress provides the thesis for three others: William Curtin, Carolyn Kitch, and Pamela C. Laucella: Although Cather and some of her peers disparaged it, her time in the newspaper industry was well spent and contributed to her prose style and choice of topics.[4] "When she died in 1947," Woodress writes, "her public was virtually unaware of this foreground as a newspaper and magazine writer. . . it is the long apprenticeship that led to her mature artistry" (*Willa Cather* 88). Laucella maintains that "Cather's journalism clearly reflected an artist in waiting. She embodied not only a talented journalist with her eye for objectivity and detail, but her writings clearly exhibited her potential as an artist" (*"McClure's"* 23). Surprisingly, given Cather's lack of respect for the hack writing she believed permeated American journalism, in a 1915 interview in the *Lincoln Sunday Star* she was quoted as valuing the real-life experience that journalism afforded: "If I hadn't again grasped the thrills of life, I would have been too literary and academic to ever write anything worthwhile" (Bohlke, ed., *Willa Cather in Person* 15).

Curtin, who collected Cather's work from several newspapers and magazines, believes that journalism allowed her to take on the personas of a variety of people, which makes her fiction more compelling. Volumes 1 and 2 of Curtin's *The World and the Parish* (1893–1902) are collections of Cather's work from the *Nebraska State Journal, Lincoln Courier, Home Monthly, Index of Pittsburgh Life,* and *Pittsburgh Gazette.* She was, he says, "a chameleon journalist who assumes many roles and speaks many voices" (*The World and the Parish* 1:xiii).

In "The Work That Came Before the Art: Willa Cather as Journalist (1893–1912)," Carolyn Kitch discusses Cather's transformation from a journalist to a writer of fiction. Kitch also details Cather's two-decade career as a journalist and her work as a newspaper and magazine writer and editor (for five newspapers in all) in Lincoln, Pittsburgh, and New York.

Since 1995, scholars regularly have referred to Cather's early years in newspapers, but more research on the impact of journalism on her fiction is overdue. According to files at the *Omaha World-Herald,* she was introduced to newspaper work early in life, less than a year before she moved to Lincoln to attend college. According to a resume she sent to the *World-Herald* in 1925, her father, Charles Cather, purchased the *Red Cloud* (Nebraska) *Republican,* and she worked there as an editor and business manager.

Cather's interest in journalism continued into and beyond her college years. A professor at the University of Nebraska, for example, submitted a paper she wrote on Thomas Carlyle to the *Nebraska State Journal.* When she was a junior, she began writing for the *Journal* and the *Lincoln Courier,* producing nearly three hundred articles, many of them about the arts. Cather also contributed to a student magazine, *The Hesperian,* and was literary editor for *The Sombrero,* the university's yearbook. By the time Cather was invited to talk to the women of the Nebraska Press Association, she was well established as a journalist (Kitch, "The Work That Came Before the Art" 428).

Cather had already begun writing short stories and poetry before living in Pittsburgh from 1896 to 1906, but she supported herself through journalism. "For the first time she demonstrated her true range in the field. She worked as an editor for two publications and a reporter for at least eight. Wanting a break from the demands of daily journalism as well as time to concentrate on her fiction, Cather taught English in a high school for five years, but still managed to freelance newspaper and magazine articles" (Ibid. 429). Originally, Cather moved to Pittsburgh to accept the editorship of the *Home Monthly,* a women's magazine. Her salary was $100 a month, and she was hired because she was a "hard-working, prolific, eager professional" (Ibid.). Cather wrote features and criticism for three publications: the *Pittsburg [sic] Leader, The Home Monthly,* and newspapers in Lincoln.

One of Cather's most significant contributions was her work for *McClure's.* In 1903 she met S. S. McClure, and five years later he trusted her enough to promote her to managing editor and give her partial responsibility over the magazine's content and direction. He wrote to his wife in 1921 that the "best magazine executive I know is Miss Cather" (Lyon, *Success Story* 390).

Cather was a "magazine executive" but also invested in journalism that transformed society. One article, similar in style to the muckraking journalism familiar to reporters and editors at *McClure's,* followed an 1892 strike in Homestead, Pennsylvania, near Pittsburgh, and a July 1901 steelworkers' strike against the U.S. Steel Corporation. Ironically, Cather "found social reformers very dull people," Woodress maintains. She contributed to activist journalism and "did not despise the expert investigative reporting that *McClure's* published, but her eye was always on art" (*Willa Cather* 188).

In addition to a twenty-year career in journalism, Cather wrote twelve works of fiction, ten collections of short stories, six nonfiction books, and a volume of poetry. She is best known for *My Antonia, O Pioneers!, Song of the Lark, One of Ours, A Lost Lady, The Professor's House, My Mortal Enemy, Death Comes for the Archbishop,* and *Lucy Grayheart.*

Edna Ferber

Edna Ferber also began her career in newspapers; indeed, one of the protagonists in her novels is a newspaperwoman. Born in Kalamazoo, Michigan, she spent her early years in Chicago and Ottumwa, Iowa. When she was twelve, the Ferber family moved to Appleton, Wisconsin, where she went to high school and edited the school newspaper, the *Ryan Clarion.*

Ferber went from high school to a job at the *Appleton Daily Crescent,* due largely to the fact that her senior essay impressed its editor. At seventeen she accepted her first job as a reporter for $3 per week but was fired eighteen months later because a new city editor was "unhappy with the Girl Reporter who dramatized herself and embellished her stories" (Steiner, "Stories of Quitting" 104). The *Milwaukee Journal* then hired her as a court and police reporter.

After spending six months in bed because of health problems, Ferber was turned down for a job at the *Chicago Tribune,* which would, she was told, not hire women (Ibid. 105). The novel *Dawn O'Hara,* the story of a Milwaukee newspaperwoman, was published in 1911, and her first play, *Our Mrs. McChesney,* was produced in 1915 and starred Ethel Barrymore.

Ferber was a popular novelist and won the Pulitzer Prize in 1924 for *So Big,* the story of a woman who raises a child on a truck farm near Chicago. Her other books include *Showboat, Cimarron, Giant,* and *Ice Palace. Giant,* a story about life in Texas, was made into a film starring Elizabeth Taylor and Rock Hudson. Two autobiographies—*A Peculiar Treasure* and *A Kind of Magic*—were published in 1939 and 1963, respectively.

Ferber also reported hard news. As a correspondent for the Air Force, she wrote about concentration camps and European air bases during World War II but did not return to daily journalism. She did, however, attribute the success of her career in fiction to her experiences on newspapers (Ibid. 110).

Margaret Mitchell

Margaret Munnerlyn Mitchell began her career in newsrooms but made her fortune writing fiction, in particular the Civil War epic *Gone with the Wind.* Patrick Allen's *Margaret Mitchell: Reporter* is an edited collection of sixty-four of her columns written between 1922 and 1926. The prolific Mitchell also wrote features, news stories, interviews, sketches, book reviews, and advice columns published in the *Atlanta Journal Sunday Magazine.*

Allen's collection is organized into eight chapters with titles that summarize Mitchell's journalistic work. "Mode and Manners" includes articles about the social graces and appropriate behavior at formal events such as beauty pageants, weddings, and funerals; "The Debutante and the 'New Woman'" provides her work on "society girls," business women, and women voters; and "In and Out of Wedlock" includes pieces on men, divorce, working women, marriage, and elopement. Other chapters are "Personality Sketches," which includes interviews with a policewoman, novelist, woman treasurer, a 102–year-old grandmother, and an Atlanta physician; "Flappers and Sheiks"; "About Atlanta and Georgia," which describes springtime, camp meetings, and Georgia generals; "Bunko Gangs and Rum Runners"; and "News of Books and Writers," the reviews of books by Aldous Huxley, William Faulkner, and others.

After the death of her mother, Mitchell left college to return to Atlanta and was interviewed for a newsroom position in 1922 by the *Atlanta Journal's* city editor, Harlee Branch. He refused to hire her, however, because there were no openings for reporters in society news.

Mitchell then applied for a job with Angus Perkerson, editor of the *Atlanta Journal Sunday Magazine.* In a letter to a friend years later, she explained, "I had had no newspaper experience and had never had my hands on a typewriter, but by telling poor Angus Perkerson outrageous lies . . . and swearing I was a speed demon on a Remington, I got the job" (Allen, ed., *Margaret Mitchell* ix).

Mitchell sparked controversy in 1923 with a four-part series that profiled women in Georgia history: Rebecca Latimer Felton, the first woman U.S. senator; Lucy Mathilde Kenney, who dressed as a man to serve in the Civil War; Mary Musgrove, a Creek Indian; and Mary Hart, who killed a British soldier in the Revolutionary War. Readers applauded a 1925 series on Georgia's Civil War generals, profiles included in Allen's collection.

Gone with the Wind, published in 1936, sold one million copies and earned Mitchell a Pulitzer Prize, a National Book Award, and an American Booksellers Association Award. The 1939 film based on the novel won ten Academy Awards, including the one for best picture.

Mitchell remained a member of the Atlanta Women's Press Club and was proud of her career in journalism. "Being a reporter was a liberal education," she said in 1945 of her years in newspaper work. "It is not so much that people are cold-hearted and selfish, it is just that they have not seen. And what eye has not seen, heart cannot feel" (Ibid. xvi–xvii). She died in 1949 after being struck by an automobile.

Katherine Anne Porter

The path between Porter's work as an objective reporter and her recognition as a fiction writer is rarely acknowledged. A study of her work reveals the importance of place and the supremacy of the moment and—with the exception of the extended essay *The Never-Ending Wrong*—indicates a desire to observe without passing judgment on the events she describes.

It is true that Porter broke the bounds of conventional journalism and turned to a genre that better used her talents. It is also true that having been relegated to "women's" news by the editors of her day, Porter may have left journalism to avoid the rampant sexism present in that work. Certainly, she was not the only woman to be shuffled to the women's pages or sent to cover theater or fashion simply because of gender. It is difficult to separate the harsh words of a Cather or Porter about journalism as a profession from the treatment they received at the hands of male editors. Joan Givner acknowledges Porter's rejection of her work as a journalist and calls it "unfortunate" because it "deflected attention from material which is crucial to the understanding of Porter's life and art." Late in her career Porter said, "I forgive [one] critic here and now, and forever, for calling me a 'newspaper woman' in the public prints. I consider it an actionable libel, but, as is too often the case in these incidents, he has a small patch of solid ground under him. . . . Fifty-odd years ago, for eight short months of my ever-lengthening (or shortening?) life, I did have a kind of a job on a newspaper, *The Rocky Mountain News*" (Givner, "Katherine Anne Porter" 69).

Porter was nevertheless a dedicated reporter during the short time she spent in the field. Instinctively, she understood the importance of careful observation and was skilled in writing newspaper stories as well as fiction. A strong journalistic influence—not an obvious part of her memoirs or the published conversations with her—emerges in an analysis of *Pale Horse, Pale Rider* and *The Never-Ending Wrong*.

Porter's career in journalism began several years before her often-chronicled time at the *Rocky Mountain News*. She moved to Chicago when she was twenty-one and worked as a reporter there for a short time (distracted by watching a film in production, she did not return to the newspaper for five days, only to be paid $18 and summarily fired). She also worked for the *The Critic,* a friend's newspaper in Fort Worth, before moving from Texas to Colorado in 1917 with a fellow journalist, Kitty Barry Crawford.

Porter later moved to Denver and became a reporter for the *Rocky Mountain News*, earning approximately $20 a week reviewing books, plays and concerts; interviewing celebrities; and rewriting crime stories.[5] According to Enrique Hank Lopez, Porter's "incorruptible tell-it-like-it-is attitude"— presumably developed during this time at the *Rocky Mountain News*—was later adopted by Miranda in *Pale Horse, Pale Rider* (*Conversations with Katherine Anne Porter* 46).

In *Pale Horse, Pale Rider* Miranda seeks assurance that she can discern truth, but that desire is consistently undercut. Her colleague Mary (Towney) Townsend, the society editor, says with sarcasm, "I read it in a New York newspaper, so it's bound to be true" (Porter, *The Collected Stories* 284). As a journalist familiar with the William Randolph Hearst–Joseph Pulitzer–Adolph Ochs newspaper wars from the early 1880s to 1900, the fictional Towney would understand the irony of her words even as she reveals a desire for a newspaper's account to be reliable. Instead, yellow journalists were said to tell the truth only when it was sensational enough to sell newspapers. Only Ochs, editor of the *New York Times,* succeeded in providing reliable information because he promised to provide "all the news that's fit to print" and then followed through.

In spite of her disdain for everyday journalism, Porter's short media career affected her development as a writer of fiction. The importance of newspaper work in the fictional references to editors and newsrooms is obvious; less perceptible is the influence of journalism on Porter's understanding of the significance of perception as reality, interest in historical event, and devotion to detail. Furthermore, Porter had the single most important trait for any successful journalist: obsession with those around her. As she admitted, "I have a personal and instant interest in every human being that comes within ten feet of me, and I have never seen any two alike, but I discover the most marvelous differences" (Kunitz, ed., *Authors Today* 539).

Pale Horse, Pale Rider is a description of Porter's journalistic experiences. The title of the short novel comes from a spiritual quoted by Miranda, its heroine: "Pale horse, pale rider, done taken my lover away" (Porter, *The Collected Stories* 303). Miranda and her friend Towney are banished to routine jobs at a newspaper—one to a theater beat, the other to a society beat. The book is a fictionalization of two events in the author's life: her work as a reporter for the *Rocky Mountain News* from 1918 to 1919 (between February 8, 1919, and August 17, 1919, she wrote eighty-one stories that carried bylines) and her near-fatal illness during the flu pandemic that struck Denver and the rest of the country in the fall of 1918. Porter's new love, Adam in the novel, also contracted the flu and later died.

Articles in the *Rocky Mountain News* attest to the seriousness of the flu epidemic in Denver. By October 6, public places were closed to help contain the virus. By November 12, however, the "flu ban was lifted, and theaters and places of amusement were again opened" (Sexton, "Katherine Anne Porter's Years" 103).

The pale rider of the text is Death, and during her illness Porter believed she was dying; her hair turned white, and she became crippled when one leg swelled from phlebitis. Quoted in an article in the *Denver Post* on March 22, 1956 (an interview precipitated by a planned television adaptation of *Pale Horse, Pale Rider*), she described the experience: "I was taken ill with the flu. They gave me up. The paper had my obit set in type" (Hendrick, *Katherine Anne Porter* 76). Asked about her lover, Porter—fighting back tears—said, "It's in the story. He died. The last I remember seeing him. . . . It's a true story. . . . It seems to me true that I died then, I died once, and I have never feared death since" (Lopez, *Conversations with Katherine Anne Porter* 223). Porter also wrote of that period of her life: "My mood for several years thereafter was that it was not a world worth living in" (Ibid. 48). She treats the experience fictionally by describing Miranda's "lost rapture": "There was no escape. Dr. Hildesheim, Miss Tanner, the nurses in the diet kitchen, the chemist, the surgeon, the precise machine of the hospital, the whole humane conviction and custom of society, conspired to pull her inseparable rack of bones and wasted flesh to its feet, to put in order her disordered mind, and to set her once more safely in the road that would lead her again to death" (*The Collected Stories* 314).

In the novel, Miranda's experiences and salary reflect the amounts Porter earned during her early days as a reporter. Asked for money to support the war effort, Miranda replies, "I have eighteen dollars a week and not another cent in the world. I simply cannot buy anything" (Ibid. 273). She also describes the exhaustion and recurring deadlines of newspaper work: "After working for three years on a morning newspaper she had an illusion of maturity and experience; but it was fatigue merely, she decided, from keeping what she had been brought up to believe were unnatural hours, eating casually at dirty little restaurants, drinking bad coffee all night, and smoking too much" (Ibid. 280).

Porter humorously describes Miranda's conflicts with irate readers and impatient editors. The descriptions of the newsroom where people sat on her desk and she heard the incessant "rattle of typewriters" and "steady rumble of presses" are realistic, as are her memories of rigid stylistic principles: "They lolled away, past the Society Editor's desk, past Bill the City Editor's desk, past the long copydesk where old man Gibbons sat all night shouting at intervals, 'Jarge! Jarge!' and the copyboy would come flying. 'Never say *people* when you mean *persons*,' old man Gibbons had instructed Miranda, 'and never say *practically*, say *virtually*, and don't for God's sake ever so long as I am at this desk use the barbarism *inasmuch* under any circumstances whatsoever. Now you're educated, you may go'" (Ibid. 274).

Kathryn Adams Sexton has documented Porter's co-workers. Bill the city editor was actually William C. Shanklin; Old Man Gibbons, Frank McClelland; Jarge, George Day, the copyboy who was to become the Rev. George T. Day; Mary Townsend, Porter's friend Eva Chappell; and Charles E. Lounsbury, Chuck Rouncivale, a sports editor ("Katherine Anne Porter's Years in Denver" 89). One of Sexton's sources also remembers Adam as a "tall, blonde, debonair, and young lieutenant who called for Miss Porter at the *News* office during their short acquaintance" (Ibid. 95).

After her experiences in Chicago, Fort Worth, and Denver, Porter moved to New York in 1919, Mexico in 1920, and back to Fort Worth in 1921 to write for a trade magazine. In a 1963 interview for the *Paris Review*, she "indicated that it was better for a writer to work as a waitress than as a newspaper-woman; it was better to take dull jobs that would not take all her mind or time" (Hendrick, *Katherine Anne Porter* 22). Porter's career as a journalist may have been prompted by a need to support herself, but she left journalism not primarily because of its low salaries and long days but because she valued the act of writing fiction more than writing news and features.

In addition to long hours and poor pay, the women who worked in newsrooms during the early 1900s also struggled with sexism. Porter was often given stories considered the domain of women. Chicago "was a huge brawling city, seething with surface excitements, particularly so for a young convent girl. . . . But the articles she wrote had nothing to do with that aspect of Chicago; her assignments were those generally given to female reporters— wedding notices, obituaries and cultural activities, plus filling in as a coffee-maker and sandwich-getter for the editorial staff. Crime stories and political scandals were the exclusive province of male reporters" (Lopez, *Conversations with Katherine Anne Porter* 39).

During her brief stint at *The Critic* in Fort Worth in 1917, Porter wrote society columns, fashion news, and drama reviews for the weekly newspaper that was devoted to politics, drama, and local events. The woman who would win a Pulitzer Prize and the National Book Award (in 1966) was assigned to stories about music clubs. One critic includes a particularly poor excerpt from a *Rocky Mountain News* story: "The music club is organizing Sing Songs, where our soldier boys may harmonize together quite chummily" (Ibid. 44).

When Porter applied for the job at the *Rocky Mountain News,* the editor cited her lack of experience (a fair claim) and was "shocked to find that the applicant, K. Porter, was a woman" (Givner, *Katherine Anne Porter* 117). From her experience with the *Rocky Mountain News* Porter created the *Blue Mountain News* of *Pale Horse, Pale Rider.* In the novel Miranda strikes up a friendship with Townsend, the society editor, at the *News.* The compassion with which Porter writes of the two women reporters is born of experience:

> [Mary Townsend's] column was called Ye Towne Gossyp, so of course everybody called her Towney. Miranda and Towney had a great deal in common, and liked each other. They had both been real reporters once, and had been sent together to "cover" a scandalous elopement in which no marriage had taken place, after all, and the recaptured girl, her face swollen, had sat with her mother who was moaning steadily under a mound of blankets. They had both wept painfully and implored the young reporters to suppress the worst of the story. They had suppressed it, and the rival newspaper printed it all the next day. Miranda and Towney had then taken their punishment together, and had been degraded publicly to routine female jobs, one to the theaters, the other to society. (*Collected Stories* 274–75)

The implication is that male editors viewed concern for the objects of the news story as weakness and disdained it as "female" failure or poor judgment. Their "punishment" was to be relegated to female news beats—often considered frivolous and undemanding.[6]

Porter's belief in the equality of women is clear. In a May 4, 1919, column in the *Rocky Mountain News,* she describes the stereotypically virtuous and insipid women in dramatic productions of the day: "We are deadly weary of the women who kneel, in song and story, at the feet of the world asking forgiveness for problematical errors. Why don't they stand on their feet and say: 'Yes, I did it. What are you going to do about it, my friends?'" (Sexton, "Katherine Anne Porter's Years in Denver" 33). Porter believed in the equality of professional women and challenged herself never to "kneel. . . at the feet of the world."

What made life "pleasant and interesting" for Porter were human relationships and the wonder and intricacy of human growth and change, but as Givner notes, "Porter herself never acknowledged and probably never realized how much she gained at this time from her journalistic experience" (*Katherine Anne Porter* 137). What she gained was in part awareness that no event is isolated or unimportant and events are part of a web that has a profound affect on many. The simplest occurrence covered by a newspaper reporter or a short story writer may reverberate through time.

Radically different from much of Porter's other work in theme and intent is the extended, didactic essay *The Never-Ending Wrong*. The nonfiction piece is an example of personal investment in event and longing to believe in society and the judicial system. The essay is too biased to be reputable journalism but remains a testament to Porter's courage. In the foreword, she comments:

> This book is not for the popular or best-selling list for a few weeks or months. It is a plain, full record of a crime that belongs to history.
>
> When a reporter from a newspaper here in Maryland asked to talk to me, he said he had heard that I was writing another book. . . . what about? . . . I gave him the title and the names of Sacco and Vanzetti. There was a wavering pause . . . then: "Well, I don't really know anything about them . . . for me it's just history."
>
> It is my conviction that when events are forgotten, buried in the cellar of the page—they are no longer even history. (*The Never-Ending Wrong* vii)

Ironically, by compromising the focus and style of *The Never-Ending Wrong*—by denying it placement in the "popular or best-selling list for a few weeks or months"—Porter relegated the arrest, trial, and execution of Nicola Sacco and Bartolomeo Vanzetti to the place she dreaded, the unpopular and unread "cellar of the page."

Porter became interested in the trial of the shoemaker and the fisherman, both of whom were accused of a violent robbery and murder on April 15, 1920, in South Braintree, Massachusetts. The Italians were political activists, and Porter and her group, which boasted such literary notables as John Dos Passos and Edna St. Vincent Millay, suspected the motives of those who arrested and sentenced the two. Those who opposed the verdict believed that Sacco and Vanzetti had been found guilty primarily because they had been called "foreigners" and "anarchists" throughout the trial. The period after World War I was characterized by heavy pressure toward ethnic unification, Americanization, and forced culturalization. It also was the end of an era of massive immigration and a time of economic turmoil. Documenting the hatred the public felt toward Sacco and Vanzetti, Porter wrote, "Judge Webster Thayer, during the Sacco-Vanzetti episode, was heard to boast while playing golf, 'Did you see what I did to those anarchistic bastards?' and the grim little person named Rosa Baron. . . who was head of my particular group during the Sacco-Vanzetti demonstrations in Boston snapped at me when I expressed the wish that we might save the lives of Sacco and Vanzetti: 'Alive—what for? They are no earthly good to us alive'" (Ibid. 5–6).

Modern reporters have abandoned the notion that objectivity is possible in news coverage, but Porter became overly involved in the case and is thus especially suspect as a reliable witness. The same accusations leveled against Capote (as he both describes and creates the character Perry Smith of *In Cold Blood*) can be leveled against Porter and her treatment of Sacco and Vanzetti. "They were," she reports, "put to death in the electric chair at Charlestown Prison at midnight on the 23rd of August, 1927, a desolate dark midnight, a night for perpetual remembrance and mourning. I was one of the many hundreds who stood in anxious vigil watching the light in the prison tower, which we had been told would fail at the moment of death; it was a moment of strange heartbreak" (Ibid. 8).

The melodrama in the passage is unlike Porter's carefully crafted tales of a young female reporter in Denver. The narrative becomes an essay, personal and occasionally compelling, but it is not straight news, a feature, an editorial, or even an example of commentary. Read as if it were a journal, *The Never-Ending Wrong* chronicles Porter's political development more effectively than it addresses the charges against Sacco and Vanzetti. Explaining her disillusionment with communism, for example, she notes, "I flew off Lenin's locomotive and his vision of history in a wide arc in Boston, Massachusetts, on August 21, 1927; it was two days before the putting to death of Sacco and Vanzetti, to the great ideological satisfaction of the Communist-headed group with which I had gone up to Boston. It was exactly what they had hoped for and predicted from the first: another injustice of the iniquitous capitalistic system against the working class" (Ibid. 20).

Porter's canon was relatively small at the time of her death on September 18, 1980, at the Carriage Hill Nursing Home in Silver Spring, Maryland. Her works include *Flowering Judas and Other Stories; Pale Horse, Pale Rider; The Leaning Tower and Other Stories; The Days Before;* and *The Ship of Fools*. She won great literary acclaim for the short stories and novellas she wrote primarily between 1922 and 1940, however, and *The Ship of Fools* was a popular and financial success. *The Collected Stories of Katherine Anne Porter* won her both the Pulitzer Prize and the National Book Award for Fiction in 1966; in 1967 she received the Gold Medal for Fiction of the National Institute of Arts and Letters. (The award is given only once every five years and had previously gone to William Faulkner.) In addition to yet more awards from other institutions, Howard Payne University in Brownwood, Texas, bestowed an honorary doctorate on Porter during the first symposium on her works in 1976.

Porter never acknowledged the debt she owed to her training and experience as a journalist, and most critics have avoided assessing it. In an article in the *Denver Post* on January 31, 1937, an unnamed writer ventured, "After cultivating an unusual gift for word arrangements, which captivated a large reading public when she was a Denver newspaper reporter, Katherine Anne Porter has been designated to receive one of the four $2500 fellowship awards by the Book of the Month Club to "writers whose works are insufficiently read" (Sexton, "Katherine Anne Porter's Years in Denver" 71).

Perhaps much of her work was and is "insufficiently read," but Porter is an example of a woman who began her career in a newsroom and developed a broad repertoire of writing skills—newspaper stories, essays, short stories, and novels—for which she is now receiving praise. It is left to contemporary scholars to pay tribute to her contributions to literature and continue to critique her newspaper stories, fiction, and extended nonfiction.

Eudora Welty

A friend and valued colleague of Porter's, Eudora Welty enjoyed a career in newspapers, radio, advertising, and photography. She was sixteen when she began college at the Mississippi State College for Women in Columbus. As she recalled, at the beginning of her writing career, "I was lucky enough to have found for myself, at the very beginning, an outside shell, that of freshman reporter on our college newspaper, *The Spectator*. I became a wit and humorist of the parochial kind, and the amount I was able to show off in print must have been a great comfort to me" (*One Writer's Beginnings* 79).

After two years, Welty transferred to the University of Wisconsin and in 1929 graduated with a bachelor's degree in English. She then entered the School of Business at Columbia University, where she studied advertising and wrote and sold advertising as well. In addition, Welty also freelanced for local newspapers and wrote the society column for Jackson, Mississippi, which appeared in print in the Sunday editions of the *Memphis Commercial Appeal*. For a short time, she worked in radio at WJDX, a station her father established in Jackson, and she spent a year with the Mississippi Advertising Commission, writing copy and taking photographs for state tourism publications.

In 1938, Welty accepted a job with the Works Progress Administration and became a junior publicity agent.[7] She took pictures of depression-era places and people, which taught her a deep respect for the importance of the moment as it is captured on film. Whatever motivated Welty to become an experienced photographer, little question exists concerning her true vocation. In *Photographs*, a 1989 collection of her work, Welty says that although she continued taking pictures, she never lost her literary direction: "The new jobs I had all had to do with journalism, not pictures. And fiction writing was my real work all along. That never let up" (xviii).

Welty's journalistic experience contributed to her short stories in innumerable ways and remained a central influence, whether in the importance of a newspaper article in attesting to the significance of a person's life ("A Piece of News"), the importance of society columns in depicting southern families with humor and insight ("Why I Live at the P.O."), the importance of newswriting in creating a sustained and detailed narrative ("Death of a Traveling Salesman"), or the importance of photography in portraits of the Mississippi poor ("A Worn Path").

Ruby Fisher in "A Piece of News" is a lonely woman whose husband beats her each time she commits adultery, which occurs with regularity: "When Clyde would make her blue, she would go out onto the road, some car would slow down, and if it had a Tennessee license, the lucky kind, the chances were that she would spend the afternoon in the shed of the empty gin" (*The Collected Stories* 14). Isolated and escaping more and more often into fantasy, Ruby one day brings home a bag of coffee wrapped in a newspaper. Lying in front of the fire, she opens the paper, an act that takes on sacred importance: "Presently she stirred and reached under her back for the newspaper. Then she squatted there, touching the printed page as if it were fragile. She did not merely look at it—she watched it, as if it were unpredictable, like a young girl watching a baby" (Ibid. 12–13).

In horrible and startling irony, the newspaper contains a short news story about another woman named Ruby Fisher, who "had the misfortune to be shot in the leg by her husband this week." For a few moments, Ruby imagines that it is she who is being described and fantasizes about being "beautiful, desirable, and dead" (Ibid. 14). The woman who has no real place and no real significance in her world now feels important: "She kept looking out the window, suffused with the warmth from the fire and with the pity and beauty and power of her death" (Ibid. 15). Ruby, of course, realizes that the article is either false or about someone else, but when her husband tells her that "it's a lie," she exclaims, "That's what's in the newspaper about me" (Ibid. 16).

Welty the journalist understands the woman's desire to believe the "truth," the facts as printed in the newspaper. Welty the fiction writer realizes the dramatic potential of a woman's psychological need to create her own fantasy as protection from reality. And Welty the observer of humanity understands longing for identity and wholeness. With precision, Welty describes Ruby after her husband explains that the Ruby Fisher mentioned in the newspaper lives in another state:

Ruby folded her still trembling hands into her skirt. She stood stooping by the window until everything, outside and in, was quieted before she went to her supper.

It was dark and vague outside. The storm had rolled away to faintness like a wagon crossing a bridge. (Ibid.)

The newspaper, a reliable record of truth, has tricked Ruby Fisher. Once again, she is unimportant, "dark," "vague," and drifting away to "faintness."

In tone and style "Why I Live at the P.O." is as different as possible from "A Piece of News." When reading the humorous short story—full of exaggeration and dramatic monolog—one must recognize that Welty wrote society news in Jackson. The family saga of Mama, Papa-Daddy, Uncle Rondo, Stella-Rondo, Shirley T., and Sister begins and ends explosively. Sister, the postmistress of the smallest post office in Mississippi, is overwhelmed by her sense of importance and jealous of her sister's arrival (reminiscent, of course, of the parable of the prodigal son in the New Testament). Humor derives from the speaker's inability to see herself clearly: "I was getting along fine with Mama, Papa-Daddy and Uncle Rondo until my sister Stella-Rondo just separated from her husband and came back home again. Mr. Whitaker! Of course I went with Mr. Whitaker first, when he first appeared here in China Grove, taking 'Pose Yourself' photos, and Stella-Rondo broke us up. Told him I was one-sided. Bigger on one side than the other, which is a deliberate, calculated falsehood: I'm the same. Stella-Rondo is exactly twelve months to the day younger than I am and for that reason she's spoiled" (Ibid. 46).

Growing up in Mississippi and having the ability to observe her community critically provided plenty of subject matter, but writing society news and understanding its seriousness for some readers perhaps also explains Welty's finely honed humor. Southerners are stereotyped as being willfully ignorant of family skeletons, for example, and Welty has Sister challenge that taboo:

"Why, Sister," said Mama. "Here I thought we were going to have a pleasant Fourth of July, and you start right out not believing a word your own baby sister tells you!"

"Just like Cousin Annie Flo. Went to her grave denying the facts of life," I remind Mama.

"I told you if you ever mentioned Annie Flo's name I'd slap your face," says Mama, and slaps my face. (Ibid. 50)

Welty makes playful fun of southern double names (Annie Flo) and pokes even more fun at local notions of masculinity by describing Uncle Rondo wearing a pink kimono as he parades around in private.. When Sister ridicules him, Uncle Rondo retaliates: "But at 6:30 a.m. the next morning, he threw a whole five-cent package of some unsold one-inch firecrackers from the store as hard as he could into my bedroom and they every one went off. Not one bad one in the string. Anybody else, there'd be one that wouldn't go off" (Ibid. 53).

Welty's first published story, "Death of a Traveling Salesman," testifies to her ability to sustain narrative and suggests an attachment to realism found often in news stories characterized by tragedy. In the story, R. J. Bowman, who for fourteen years sold shoes in Mississippi, suffers a heart attack and dies. The facts are simple, but Welty explores his death and seems to conclude that Bowman died because he was lonely, became lost, and abandoned his will to live. Bowman, who "distrusted the road without signposts" (Ibid. 199), literally becomes lost one afternoon while driving his Ford across Mississippi. . His life has been marked by nothing but steady work, as the "stares of . . . distant people had followed him solidly like a wall, impenetrable" (Ibid. 120). After Bowman wrecks his car, he is taken in and cared for by a couple who are expecting a baby and are very much in love. They remind him of the emptiness of his own life:

> But he wanted to leap up, to say to [the woman], I have been sick and I found out then, only then, how lonely I am. Is it too late? My heart puts up a struggle inside me, and you may have heard it, protesting against emptiness . . . It should be flooded with love. . .
>
> But he moved a trembling hand across his eyes, and looked at the placid crouching woman across the room. . . . He felt ashamed and exhausted by the thought that he might, in one more moment, have tried by simple words and embraces to communicate some strange thing—something which seemed always to have just escaped him. (Ibid. 125)

Before running to his car, terrified at being lost, Bowman thinks, "A marriage, a fruitful marriage. That simple thing. Anyone could have had that" (Ibid. 129). An artist, Welty, thus transforms a simple news story into a universal tale with which all who have lost a dream can identify.

Welty the photographer depicts characters such as Bowman with finesse and insight, never missing a detail. Her portrait of Phoenix Jackson in "A Worn Path" is perhaps her finest characterization. Named for the bird who rises from the ashes and for Welty's hometown, Jackson, Mississippi, Phoenix Jackson makes an annual pilgrimage to town to buy a gift for her grandson. The old black woman must have reminded Welty of many such figures photographed during her work for the WPA:

She wore a dark striped dress reaching down to her shoe tops, and an equally long apron of bleached sugar sacks, with a full pocket: all neat and tidy, but every time she took a step she might have fallen over her shoelaces, which dragged from her unlaced shoes. She looked straight ahead. Her eyes were blue with age. Her skin had a pattern all its own of numberless branching wrinkles and as though a whole little tree stood in the middle of her forehead, but a golden color ran underneath, and the two knobs of her cheeks were illuminated by a yellow burning under the dark. Under the red rag her hair came down on her neck in the frailest of ringlets, still black, and with an odor like copper. (Ibid. 142)

Welty celebrates Phoenix Jackson's courage and strength, as Phoenix picks her way with a thin cane through treacherous country rife with objects to deceive an elderly traveler: "Thorns, you doing your appointed work. Never want to let folks pass, no sir. Old eyes thought you was a pretty little *green* bush" (Ibid. 143). She accomplishes her mission and returns to her cabin, slowly and deliberately.

Omitting references to Welty's academic training and early media employment is a costly oversight, for she—like Didion, Wolfe, and others—often drew from her experiences with media. Knowing that Welty once wrote society news makes "Why I Live at the P.O" even richer, given that the story relies on her understanding of southern society and the comedic value of gossip. Similarly, the vivid description of Phoenix Jackson in "A Worn Path" is more startling when one knows that Welty was an enthusiastic photographer.

The interviews, autobiographical documents, letters, brochures, newsletters and unpublished photographs collected by the Mississippi Department of Archives and History in Jackson are the best illustrations of Welty's understanding of the impact of her media work on her fiction. Two factors have contributed to the lack of critical attention to Welty's media training and experience. First, in spite of her willingness to be interviewed, Welty rarely spoke about her interest in journalism, advertising, and public relations. Second, she is better understood alongside Carson McCullers, Flannery O'Connor, Katherine Anne Porter and other southern women fiction writers than alongside writers of jingles, radio copy, features, or society news.

Welty did address media careers during a 1971 interview with Charlotte Capers and said she was never tempted to pursue journalism as her life's work: "I never did take journalism. And I instinctively shied away from it, although later on I took some jobs in it, but I think my instinct was right, and I still say that to people who invite my opinion, students, that I think you should take a job, if you want to be a writer, a serious writer, you should take a job that does not use words in a way that is not imaginative" (n.p.). It is thus tempting to place Welty in the company of Stephen Crane, Willa Cather, and others who disparaged journalism as hack writing, but she never denied the value of newspapers in relaying information. For her, editorials and news stories should persuade and inform. She should employ her talents in another genre and toward other objectives.

Welty told Don Lee Keith in 1973 that "fiction is one thing: journalism's another. The distinguishing factor is that in the novel, there is the possibility that both writer and reader may share an act of imagination" ("Eudora Welty" 151). She longed to use her imagination—not to transmit real events in writing but to recreate them. "Whatever our theme in writing," she commented, "it is old and tried. Whatever our place, it has been visited by the stranger, it will never be new again. Some day it may not even be. It is only the vision that can be new, but this is enough" (*Three Papers on Fiction* 15).

Welty made another comparison in 1986, this time between literature and the didactic forms of journalism: "I don't think literature—I'm talking about fiction now—I don't think it can exhort. . . I think it speaks to what is more deeply within, that is, the personal, and conveys its meaning that way. . . I wouldn't like to read a work of fiction that I thought had an ulterior motive, to persuade me politically. . . I think things should be written to persuade, but openly as a column or an editorial or a speech. . . . This is not to say that I condescend to such writing or think of it as less important" (Devlin and Prenshaw, eds., *Welty* 25).

Given that Welty's statements about the differences between journalism and fiction are few and brief, critics are left to speculate about why she turned her back on a career in media. Elizabeth A. Meese, for example, has observed that journalism "was not easily done in conjunction with fiction writing. Doubtless she felt a diffusion rather than a concentration of her energies in simultaneously pursuing varieties of self-expression" ("Constructing Time and Place" 409). Others make their own connections without Welty's confirmation or denial. Peter Schmidt, for example, links a piece Welty called a "witty piece of journalism" for the *Junior League Magazine* ("Women!! Make Turban in Own Home!") with the humor in "Why I Live at the P.O." (*The Heart of the Story* 109).

It is possible that Welty's short career in media affected her development as a writer of fiction. A study of her work reveals the importance of place, the supremacy of the moment, and a desire to stand outside the action as an observer instead of an interpreter. Further, Welty's awareness of the ambiguity of life can be traced to a journalist's sense of realism. A fiction writer may manipulate characters in order to make their reactions reasonable or to frame a narrative, but Welty resists that impulse. She understood that unmediated life is rarely well ordered, and in her fiction she celebrates those who live exuberantly in spite of having unanswered questions.

For Welty, fictional events could be more true than real ones, but she believed places in her fiction must communicate "actuality" in much the same manner that journalists rely on clear and accurate description of place to recreate an event:

> This makes it the business of writing, and the responsibility of the writer, to disentangle the significant—in character, incident, setting, mood, everything—from the random and meaningless and irrelevant that in real life surround and beset it. . . . Actuality, it's true, is an even bigger risk to the novel than fancy writing is, being frequently even more confusing, irrelevant, diluted, and generally far-fetched than ill-chosen words can make it. Yet somehow, the world of appearance in the novel has got to *seem* actuality. (Welty, *Three Papers on Fiction* 5)

Suzanne Marrs, a professor and Welty's friend, testifies to Welty's success in recreating place when she writes that readers believe in Phoenix Jackson, the central character in "A Worn Path," because they "recognize and believe in the world that she inhabits" ("Eudora Welty's Photography" 288). Even details such as Welty's choice of names are tied to real life and, occasionally, to actual news coverage: "When I first began writing I didn't realize the importance of names. I would just name characters anything. And then I realized how much it mattered, for cadence. . . . The other day I was reading in the *Jackson Daily News* the list of people arrested for drunk driving. There was this man whose name was Quovadis something. 'Quovadis, whither goest thou.' It's just wonderful" (Devlin and Prenshaw, eds., *Welty* 11).

Wherever her literary gifts originated, there is no doubt about Welty's prolific career. She won a Pulitzer Prize in 1973 for *The Optimist's Daughter*, and among her works are *The Robber Bridegroom, The Wide Net and Other Stories, Delta Wedding, The Golden Apples, The Ponder Heart*, and *Losing Battles*. Her short story collection *A Curtain of Green*, featuring an introduction by Katherine Anne Porter, contains some of her most beloved work, including "A Worn Path" and "Why I Live at the P.O." It is because of his devotion to "Why I Live at the P.O." that software developer Steven Dorner named his e-mail program Eudora. *One Time, One Place: Mississippi in the Depression* and *Eudora Welty Photographs* feature more than three hundred of her pictures, and *One Writer's Beginnings* is a memoir based on lectures she presented at Harvard University.

Welty, Cather, Ferber, Mitchell, and Porter are a few of the women who moved from newspaper writing to writing fiction. All deserve far more critical attention than they have received in order for readers to understand more about the pathways between journalism and fiction. What is truthful may be different from what is factual, and it is through a study of literary journalism that the gray area—the borderland that lies between fiction and nonfiction—may be best explored.

5

Representative Women
of the Alternative Press

As often as they work in libraries, special collections, and archives, those who conduct research on women in journalism also rummage through laundry baskets full of family photographs or comb through stacks of recipes and old bills for news clippings. Closets, attics, basements, and garages are often treasure troves. On one hand, that reality increases the excitement of discovering material. On the other hand, of course, it bears testimony to the fragility of important records often ignored by family members and to the transitory quality of photographs, diaries and journals, manuscripts, newspaper clippings, personal notes, and other resources.

Linda Steiner has commented that for nearly 250 years women "have recognized the value of establishing and operating their own communications media, literally making their own meaning and communicating it to one another across space and over time." To some extent, their use of alternative media has been prompted by an "inability—or reluctance" to use mainstream media, which have been "hostile to women's attempts to negotiate for themselves alternative visions, definitions, ways of being" ("The History and Structure" 121). Moreover, women are empowered by "producing and supporting their own women-controlled, women-oriented media," which are "oppositional, alternative, resistant in both product and process" (Ibid. 121, 123). In most cases, women's media are established by activists who are "not neutral observers distributing information commodities," and, as publications with specific target markets, women's print media are not profit-driven, although subscription rates are carefully overseen (Ibid. 124, 126).

Gaye Tuchman and Rodger Streitmatter join Steiner in emphasizing the role of women in the alternative press. Tuchman addresses the origins of the women's movement and the ambivalence many of its founders shared about dealing with established media organizations dominated by men. The "easy access to the news media requiring ongoing contacts between a reporter and a news source, such as those provided by beats" was intrinsically problematic for women activists. "Those who plan disruptive events do not have these contacts, because they are frequently suspicious of the media or may have other reasons, such as possible arrest, for *not* cultivating contact" (*Making News* 141). It is certainly true that "standard reportorial practice legitimates those with institutional power" (Ibid. 142). Furthermore, "issues and occurrences generated by any social movement are necessarily subjected to the frame of the conventional news narrative" when relegated to beat and general news reporters (Ibid. 154).

Streitmatter focuses on the way African American women factor into journalism history and how their experiences differ from those of their white counterparts:

> The evidence that there has been a tradition of sisterhood of cooperation and similarity of experience between white and black women is far outweighed by the evidence that there has been a tradition of tension. Some of the privileges that white women have enjoyed have been at the expense of black women; some of the opportunities that white women have fought for—such as being allowed to enter the workforce—are ones that black women would have been only too happy to have forfeited generations ago. . . Foremost among these concepts is that African-American women historically have identified themselves first as members of an oppressed race, feeling the pain of racial prejudice more acutely than the pain of sexual prejudice. (*Raising Her Voice* 9–10)

The four narratives that make up this chapter are in thematic rather than chronological order. The story of Hazel Brannon Smith (1914–94), a Mississippi journalist who has been discovered by competent and learned historians, appears first. A Pulitzer Prize–winner, Smith provides an example of the impact that a woman—although a segregationist during the civil rights movement—could have on legal equality between races. A person of courage and commitment to journalistic principle and human compassion, Smith transformed Mississippi politics and newspaper history in spite of her ideological limitations.

Phyllis Austin (1941–) is a contemporary activist and journalist who lives and writes in Maine. Known to many in journalism—especially those who write about human equality and environmentalism—Austin writes about people as much as she writes about landscapes. Like one of her favorite writers, Terry Tempest Williams, she profoundly understands the connection between those who love the land and those who champion ecological advances. In addition, she believes deeply in the power of the press to inform and persuade.

Caroline Nichols Churchill (1833–1926) alienated as many people as she influenced but founded newspapers during a time when most women considered such a feat impossible. Churchill's quick temper and quick wit made her memorable as a feminist editor. One of her newspapers, the *Queen Bee*, should be added to lists of important historical documents.

Betty Wilkins (1919–86) was denied membership in a prestigious Colorado women's press club because of her race but was unfazed by the experience. Although her name appeared in the *Denver Post* because of the discrimination she faced, her life merits inclusion in history books for reasons unrelated to that painful event. Throughout her long, happy, and productive life, Wilkins wrote local political and social news and advocated for African Americans in her community and throughout the nation.

Representing regions from the Deep South to the Northeast to the West, Hazel Brannon Smith, Phyllis Austin, Caroline Nichols Churchill, and Betty Wilkins are not-so-secret sharers whose work must be considered part of the canon of American journalism. From the 1800s to the present, these women symbolize women journalists whose stories are being uncovered daily and whose photographs, diaries and journals, manuscripts, newspaper clippings, and personal notes now are part of the historical record. This chapter is a tribute to these women and to those whose narratives remain to be told.

Civil Rights Journalism: Hazel Brannon Smith

It is tempting for those in many disciplines—including sociology, history, journalism, media studies, literature, American studies, and women's studies—to write of everyday citizens as if they were somehow more courageous, more spiritual, more committed, or less concerned with the opinions of others than the average person might be. Little appeals more to the American sensibility than a tale about overcoming insurmountable odds in the interest of a higher goal. The phrase *overcoming insurmountable odds* suggests the possibility that things that *cannot* be surmounted might, in fact, be surmounted by heroes. The more Detective Columbo–like the hero, the better the story and the more surprising the heroism.

Some descriptions of Hazel Brannon Smith lean toward hero worship. Although Dudley Clendinen's is based on fact, the truth is more complex:

> Eleven of the fifteen awards for editorial writing from 1946 to 1971 went to Southern editors, and the issue that fired 10 of them was race. Only one recipient, Hazel Brannon Smith, owner and editor of the *Lexington Advertiser,* was a woman, but none was any braver. She had fought the back-shooting segregationist sheriffs and other dark lights of the Delta for 10 years before she won the [Pulitzer Prize] in 1964. She endured personal ostracism, bombing and economic boycott until her husband's career and her own finances were ruined, until the unrepaired roof over her press fell in, until she ran out of money and finally lost her mind to old age. ("In the South" 18)

This study resists the temptation to build a monument to Mississippi editor and columnist Hazel Brannon Smith—at the same time that it acknowledges her acts of quiet and not-so-quiet courage. Smith remained in the Deep South as long as she could but was devastated by her husband's death and the loss of her Tara-like home, her friends, and her livelihood. Her sister aided her, penniless and suffering memory loss, in retirement. Smith was all too human. She did not overcome insurmountable odds; those she faced were insurmountable. Smith second-guessed herself, and although she embraced journalistic principles, she sometimes did so too little and too late. She worried about her neighbors' and friends' reactions and suffered and raged against the loss of financial security and community respect.

Smith did not consider herself to be a champion of civil rights—in fact, she did not believe in integration. She was an unlikely hero, and, ironically, although her life's work was spent telling the stories of others, her own life proved more dramatic, sensational, and controversial than many of the stories she told. Smith considered herself an average person who tried to exercise the tenets of good journalism—fairness, balance, and broad and accurate representation of her community. Respecting those tenets did not make her a hero, but it did make her a good journalist.

After advertisers and readers drove her from the newspaper industry, Smith won a Pulitzer Prize. She was also featured in a made-for-television movie and a documentary. By the end of her career she had been an officer in, or member of, numerous professional organizations and won awards from many of them. Among the groups were the Mississippi Press Women, International Conference of Weekly Newspaper Editors, Mississippi Press Association, National Newspaper Association, National Editorial Association, National Federation of Press Women (NFPW), Mississippi Council of Human Relations, and U.S. Civil Rights Commission.

Smith also won the Elijah Parish Lovejoy Award for Courage in Journalism in 1960, given by the journalism department of Southern Illinois University; was named "Mississippi Woman of the Year" in 1964; and was selected to Who's Who in America in 1968–69. She won the top editorial award from the NFPW in 1948, 1955, and 1961; was named a Woman of Conscience by the National Council of Women in 1964; served as secretary of the Holmes County, Mississippi, Democratic Executive Committee from 1940 to 1948; and was a delegate to the Democratic National Convention in 1940 and 1944. In addition, she won the Golden Quill Editorial Award from the International Conference of Weekly Newspaper Editors for an editorial on a black bombing victim who had tried to vote in Holmes County (the man, Hartman Turnbow, was arrested and falsely charged with arson). The editorial was selected from fifteen thousand submissions from across the world.

Accolades are only part of Smith's story. In fact, during her career as a reform journalist, she was treated as a pariah by local politicians and residents and had crosses burned on her lawn. Her office was firebombed as well. Smith did not leave her profession voluntarily. She was driven out. Even in hindsight, she underestimated the impact of what, for her, was simple human fairness and adherence to quality journalism.

At one point, Smith owned four small newspapers in Mississippi. Ira Harkey, a newspaper editor who was run out of the South, writes of her, "She is now a courageous and eloquent speaker for civil rights and in 1964 won the Pulitzer Prize for her long-time editorial opposition to misused official power" and refers to his colleague's being "unmercifully persecuted for objecting to the killing of a Negro by a local law officer" (*The Smell of Burning Crosses* 80). The persecution involved a July 8, 1954, front-page story, "Negro Man Shot in Leg Saturday in Tchula; Witness Reports He Was Told to 'Get Goin' by Holmes County Sheriff." In that report, Smith denounced a local sheriff, Richard F. Byrd, as unfit to occupy office. It was her belief that Byrd shot twenty-seven-year-old Henry Randall, an African American, in the leg without provocation, and on July 15 she wrote an editorial, "The Law Should Be for All," about the incident:

> The laws in America are for everyone—rich and poor, strong and weak, white and black and all the other races that dwell within our land. . .
> This kind of thing cannot go on any longer.
> It must be stopped.

> The vast majority of Holmes county people are not rednecks who look with
> favor on the abuse of people because their skins are black. . .
> [Sheriff Byrd] has violated every concept of justice, decency, and right in his
> treatment of some of the people in Holmes county. He has shown us without
> question that he is not fit to occupy that high office.
> He should, in fact, resign. (Kaul, "Hazel Brannon Smith" 295)

Byrd did not resign. Instead, he sued for libel. An all-male, all-white jury
fined Smith $10,000 on October 12, 1954, although the state supreme court
overturned the decision on November 7, 1955. In the time between the judgment and the appeal, Smith refused to budge, calling the sheriff a liar and
saying he had "no more remorse than an egg-sucking dog" (Ibid.).

Because of this and other of Smith's activist editorials, the White Citizens
Council pressured advertisers to boycott her publications, a ban that lasted
for ten years. As Matthew J. Bosisio writes,

> The pressure also continued, intensifying in bits and pieces. Smith's husband
> was fired as administrator of the county hospital, in spite of a petition signed
> by the entire medical staff demanding he be retained. Her house was vandal-
> ized. Someone firebombed the back of her newspaper office. Another bomb
> hit the *Northside Reporter,* a small weekly she owned in Jackson. After re-
> ceiving several threats of injury, she began sleeping with a gun close at hand.
> One night, she was greeted with a burning cross on her front lawn. ("Hazel
> Brannon Smith" 75)

Sam G. Riley maintains that Smith's enemies in Lexington, Mississippi,
founded the *Holmes County Herald* in 1958 in an attempt to drive her newspaper out of business (*Biographical Dictionary* 304). Chester Marshall, general manager of two of Smith's newspapers, *The Advertiser* and the *Durant
News,* became editor of the *Herald,* which began publication in 1959. Smith
was forced to mortgage some of her business and personal property, reduce
staff, and borrow money in order to continue publishing (Moritz, ed., "Hazel
Brannon Smith" 385).

By the time Smith began to suffer memory loss (perhaps due to the on-
slaught of Alzheimer's) in 1985, she had filed for bankruptcy and owed
$250,000, including $34,000 in newspaper printing bills. On one occasion,
"She got lost en route from Lexington to a mandatory bankruptcy-court hear-
ing in Jackson in November, and her bankruptcy case was dismissed for her
failure to appear. The bank foreclosed, taking her newspaper and repossessing
Hazelwood [Smith's home]; her furniture was auctioned. In February 1986

Smith's sister quietly took her back to an obscure and penniless retirement in Gadsden, Ala." (Kaul, "Hazel Brannon Smith" 300).

In spite of powerful opponents, Smith was not without friends and supporters. Several prestigious southern editors, including Nelson Poynter Jr. of the *St. Petersburg Times,* Mark Ethridge of the *Louisville Courier-Journal,* Ralph McGill of the *Atlanta Constitution,* and J. N. Heiskell of the *Arkansas Gazette,* were among those who banded together to try to protect her (Riley, *Biographical Dictionary* 304). In 1961, Pulitzer Prize–winner Hodding Carter II, publisher of the *Delta Democrat-Times* in Greenville, Mississippi, formed a committee (including Ethridge, McGill, and Heiskell) to help raise funds to offset Smith's losses in advertising. In addition, the *Columbia Journalism Review* established a fund to ensure the survival of her newspaper, the *Lexington Advertiser,* and black subscribers collected almost $3,000 to help her remain in business (Moritz, ed., "Hazel Brannon Smith" 385).

In spite of their help, Smith "borrowed heavily and mortgaged her home to keep publishing" (Riley, *Biographical Dictionary* 304) and in the 1970s had to sell two of her newspapers. In the fall of 1985, she filed for bankruptcy and closed her last two. "Eventually she found herself a pariah to whites and to blacks, an ally they no longer needed" (Ibid.).

Smith's best-known newspaper was an independent weekly in Holmes County, the *Lexington Advertiser,* which Smith purchased in 1943 and closed in 1985. Lexington, Mississippi, was a small, rural town in the 1940s; even in 1999, it had only 2,227 residents. Barbara Isaacs and Kevin Nance quote June Durff, assistant director of the Holmes County Chamber of Commerce, as saying that Lexington, Mississippi, is important largely because Smith once lived there: "She's kind of put us on the map" (Isaacs and Nance, "Other Lexingtons").

In all, Smith bought four Mississippi newspapers, beginning in 1936 with the *Durant News,* which became profitable within four years of her leadership. She owned the newspaper until 1985. Smith purchased the *Banner County Outlook* in 1955 and was forced to sell it in 1977 and the *Northside Reporter* in 1956, selling it in 1973. The *Northside Reporter,* a Jackson, Mississippi, weekly, was firebombed in 1964 while Smith was attending the Democratic National Convention (Downs and Downs, *Journalists of the United States* 318). Smith also helped to edit the monthly *Baptist Observer* for the largest African American Baptist association in Mississippi.

"Through Hazel Eyes," Smith's front-page column, began in 1936 and ran throughout most of her career, earning her national recognition. In 1964 she became the first woman to win a Pulitzer Prize for editorial writing. In her column, Smith "attacked social injustices and promoted unpopular causes" (Moritz, ed., "Hazel Brannon Smith" 384). Those causes included support for a local venereal disease treatment clinic and opposition to slot machine operators, bootleggers, gamblers, and corrupt local politicians. Arguing that newspapers in the South had "largely ignored our responsibility to our Negro citizens," Smith grieved about the emotional and financial toll of her beliefs on her and her family. "God has been with me," said the lifelong Baptist. "If he hadn't, I'd be insane or dead" (Ibid. 386).

In spite of her notable achievements, it is important not to deify this hard-working woman of conviction. She "gloried in being a newspaperwoman" (Kaul, "Hazel Brannon Smith" 291), but Smith, like many of her southern neighbors, believed in the separation of the races. Late in her career she supported the influx of civil rights workers into her state, commenting that "these young people wouldn't be here if we had not largely ignored our responsibilities to our Negro citizens" (Moritz, ed., "Hazel Brannon Smith" 385). It is questionable, however, how far Smith was willing to go in her quest for justice for all. In an early editorial, "The South's Racial Problem" (July 1943), she wrote:

> The white man and the black man have dwelt together in peace and harmony in the south for many, many years, because each has known his place and kept it. Each has had his own ideals, customs, and habits and they have not conflicted. . . as some of our meddling friends would have us believe. . .
>
> The vast majority of the colored race in the south know that the white man is his friend; when he is in trouble the first person he goes to is a white friend. And the white friend doesn't let him down. He values highly the friendship of his negro friends. . .
>
> But the south and America are a white man's country and both races know it. . .
>
> Southern white people are at last beginning to recognize the existence of trouble incited by people from the outside who have made a second carpet-bagging expedition into the south under the guise of the New Deal. . .
>
> We in our own way and in our own time as best we can will work out a better world for both ourselves and the negro in the south. But we will not be hamstrung nor dictated to by the group in this nation who would tell us how to run our elections and our state. (Kaul, "Hazel Brannon Smith" 292–93)

Smith eventually advocated equal rights for all American citizens but never became a "true integrationist" (Riley, *Biographical Dictionary* 304). Furthermore, she was strongly anticommunist and supported Sen. Joseph McCarthy. In a 1952 editorial Smith argued that the election of Dwight D. Eisenhower would cause a "thorough housecleaning that will rid our national government of all the pinks and reds and the pro-Soviet sympathizers that have been feeding at the expense of the American taxpayers for so long" (Kaul, "Hazel Brannon Smith" 294). She was clearly "an ultraconservative states' rights Dixiecrat" (Ibid.).

There is little doubt that Smith was conflicted about issues of race in the South. She urged segregation but supported equality before the law; she could not understand how the two beliefs could be contradictory. She opposed the integration of schools following *Brown v. Topeka Board of Education* in 1954, observing, "We know that it is to the best interest of both races that segregation be maintained in theory and in fact—that where it isn't maintained trouble results"(Ibid.). Smith also argued, however, that the South should have worked harder to maintain and fund schools for blacks. Smith also was capable of strong attacks on racist attitudes, even when she had trouble spotting similar feelings in herself. In the summer of 1964, for example, a week after the disappearance of three civil rights workers in Mississippi, she appeared on a panel for the American Newspaper Women's Club in Washington, D.C. "You don't have to have a sheet to belong to the Klan," she informed the audience. "It's as much a state of mind as anything else" (Moritz, ed., "Hazel Brannon Smith" 385).

One reason for her internal conflict may have been what some critics consider the inability to reconcile segregation with Christian beliefs about love, tolerance, and justice. Kaul also suggests that "her views moderated when her law-and-order brand of Christian morality confronted the racial bigotry and violence that erupted during the mid 1950s" ("Hazel Brannon Smith" 300–301). It is clear, however, that throughout most of her writing, Smith advocated separation of the races. In one of the most extreme examples, she attacked the "half-baked ideas" of the New Deal and the South's abandonment of "white supremacy principles" by urging the separation by race of blood at blood banks. "Good negro citizens. . . no more want white blood in their veins than does the white man want negro blood," she maintained. "The communistic influences that would mix the two do not have the interest of either at heart" (Ibid. 293).

The end of Smith's life redefines tragedy. "Her house was taken from her, leaving her with nothing but the remnant of a career started more than forty years earlier and now brought to an unceremonious end," and when she closed the newspaper in 1985, "nothing was written about her departure"

(Bosisio, "Hazel Brannon Smith" 80). Smith's husband, Walter, died in 1983, and in 1986 she moved to the Gadsden, Alabama, home of her sister, Bonnie Geer. After her sister died, she then moved to Cleveland, Tennessee, to live at the Royal Care Nursing Home, where her niece was director of nursing. In April 1994, ABC broadcast *A Passion for Justice: The Hazel Brannon Smith Story,* a documentary tribute to her life. "Smith watched the movie in silence from her nursing home that April day. Less than a month later, on 14 May, she was dead. She was eighty" (Ibid). Smith died at the nursing home and was buried in Forrest Cemetery in Gadsden.

Although she was recognized for her contribution to equal rights and was honored with a Pulitzer Prize for editorial writing in 1964, Smith occasionally fell victim to prevailing social norms and racist attitudes. She was human and sought to live up to the tenets of her profession in a difficult and dangerous time. She was also courageous and continued to believe in herself despite the familiar social, political, and religious supports shifting around her.

She never wanted to be a "crusading editor" (Kaul, "Hazel Brannon Smith" 293) and held racist beliefs, but the *New York Times*'s obituary praised Smith's crusading spirit and "stance against racism." The obituary appeared on May 16, 1994, and was datelined Cleveland, Tennessee:

> For 20 years, she prospered as a country editor, crusading against bootleg racketeering and becoming known for her broad-brimmed hats and her Cadillac convertible. . .
>
> As a result of her stands, Mrs. Smith's newspaper became the target of an economic boycott, and the segregationist White Citizens Council started an opposition paper. The boycott lasted 10 years, drained Mrs. Smith financially and eventually forced *The Advertiser* to close. But she continued to speak out against racism and bigotry. ("Hazel Brannon Smith" B8)

Women journalists who risk their personal safety and their careers for their principles are the focus of this chapter. Separated by time, by class, by race and ethnicity, and by geography, they often share more than they realize. It is perhaps not such a formidable step from the civil rights movement in Mississippi to the women's movement and a crusade for the environment in Maine.

Environmental Journalism: Phyllis Austin

Phyllis Austin is happiest guiding a kayak down a river or hiking along a mountain trail. When Austin, whose home is near Brunswick, Maine, does go indoors, it is to write about the outdoors. A feminist, environmental writer, and social activist since the 1970s, she is a tenacious advocate for the land and considers the entire state of Maine as her hometown.

Austin, a full-time reporter at the *Maine Times* beginning in 1974, has covered everything from land use regulation to public utilities, fisheries, the North Woods, the paper industry, private lands, the Allagash Wilderness Waterway, Baxter State Park, oil refineries, and the divestiture of land. Her work for the *Maine Times* continued until the newspaper folded in 2002. Since then, she has written for the *Maine Environmental News* on the Web, produced one book, and is working on a second. She is also coeditor of *On Wilderness: Voices from Maine* (2003), which has been featured on Boston's WCVB-TV program *Chronicle*. Almost forty writers, artists, and photographers combined their talents to produce the book about environmental issues in Maine.[1]

"The wilderness book came about because of anti-wilderness politics in Maine," Austin says. "In the nineties especially, there was a deliberate attempt in state government and industry to denigrate the word 'wilderness' and to eliminate it as much as possible. My chapter in the book tells this story. "Inspired by Terry Tempest Williams' book on Utah's Red Rock wilderness politics, I knew that it was time to speak out against 'disappearing' the word 'wilderness' and the designation of parts of the North Woods as wilderness," she remarked in a telephone conversation in 2004.

"Consider this book, then," she and coeditors Dean Bennett and Robert Kimber, urge, "our attempt—and an attempt of the authors and artists represented here—to reclaim wilderness both as a word and as a reality on the land. We think it is time to raise a collective voice in praise of wilderness and all it means to Maine people—its enchantment and mystique, its place in our history, and its contributions to our cultural heritage" (*On Wilderness* xi). In her essay "Dirty Word," which appears in the book, Austin explains the sense of urgency that led to the book: "We have long been too polite, too apologetic, and too fearful. There will be no chance of establishing large wilderness landscapes in Maine's future unless we fight for them—as if this were our last chance" (Ibid. 55).

Austin invited Bennett and Kimber to help her with the book and then asked writers, poets, photographers, and artists to contribute their work. The names and affiliations of those involved are significant. Collectively, they represent not only the wide range of professions of those concerned about the environment but also illustrate the extensive number of friends, acquaintances, and colleagues with whom Austin has worked and her influence on environmentalism, ecofeminism, and alternative newspapers.

Although still under the spell of more than five thousand lakes, a breath-taking coastline, and acres of dense woodland, Austin is not always optimistic about the future of her chosen home. Certainly, decades of investigative journalism have taught her to be wary. "Maine is a mythical place," she comments. "It is the land of Thoreau and Paul Bunyan, a land of dark, foreboding woods. It has also become a crucible for recreation in the Northeast, and the tourist industry will grow to meet an ever-growing demand. Even the paper companies are going into recreation," she told me in the summer of 1997.

Her hard-hitting, alternative newspaper stories have a readership dedicated to preserving the state as if it were their own backyard, and Austin makes no apologies for representing environmental zealots or writing deeply personal, opinionated prose. "My audience is a segment of people who work for state government and for advocacy groups, who are interested in things as close to the earth as possible, who are interested in protecting a way of life," she added. "Maine is my community, my hometown."

In addition to being senior writer for the *Maine Times,* Austin has written for publications that include the *Boston Globe, Backpacker, AMC Outdoors, Washington Post, Northern Woodlands, Wild Earth, Los Angeles Times, SELF, New England Business Review, Down East,* and *Yankee.* Her unflagging commitment to environmental concerns carries over into her freelance assignments. In a 1997 piece for *Outdoors,* the Appalachian Mountain Club's magazine, for example, she writes about the "breakup of Maine's large tracts of timberland into smaller parcels destined to be scalped of timber, laced with roads, and carved into subdivisions" ("Diamonds Aren't Forever" 16).

Austin's writing ability does not stop with powerful active verbs, however; even descriptive excerpts from her work belie the intensity of her convictions. In 1991, for example, she wrote, "A rare golden eagle sails on wings seven feet across and lands in a spruce on the east side of Old Blue Mountain's broad summit. While airborne above the 3,600–foot mountain, she had spotted her tree and picked out the jutting branch, her eyes many times sharper than ours. From her lofty vantage point, she feels the sun's warmth and surveys a huge forested territory that cradles some of western Maine's most exquisite scenery—the Rangeley Lakes to the north, the Mahoosucs to the South and the Presidential Range in neighboring New Hampshire to the west" ("Battle for the Northern Forest" 1).

Similarly, in a 1988 story on tourists' overuse of Acadia National Park Austin describes the "surf-pounded cliffs, thick forests, glacier-carved valleys and lakes, and bald eagles gliding over gentle air currents." To solicit reader interest in preserving Acadia, she comments that the "people crush is four times the population of the state and 1,000 times the year-round population of Bar Harbor, the island's largest town" ("Acadia's Cry for Help" 1, 8).

A resident of Maine since 1969, Austin has spent almost three decades learning about the state and its people. "Too often journalists cover the moment," she maintains. "They read a document and talk to five people, but they don't really know anything about an issue," she told me in the summer of 1997. The immersion has paid off, both in the responses of sources who know of her deep investment in the topic and the responses of loyal readers. Moreover, her commitment to the *Maine Times* was obvious in statements she made about the publication: "The *Maine Times* is here, and we have a presence in this state. . . . Over time, we figure into legislative decisions."

Austin also has spent her career promoting the advancement of women. "The *Maine Times* wouldn't have survived without the energy of women," she maintained. One of several women who contributed to what she calls the "feminist consciousness" of the publication, Austin is proud of colleagues Peggy Fisher, Lucy Martin, and others, all of whom worked for women's rights in the early 1970s.

By the mid-1970s, the *Maine Times*'s staff had covered stories about local female artists and political activists, the absence of women on the Maine Supreme Court, women in labor unions and vocational schools, and women employed in social work and teaching. In one account, she attacked the Cumberland Club, at that time an all-male organization in Portland: "There are two doors to the Cumberland Club. The white-columned front entrance through golden oak doors is reserved for members, men only. Wives or female guests of the members must enter through the black-painted side entry. By way of both entrances passes the cream of Portland's social and business set. They don't mind which door they use, just so they get in" ("A Visit to the Exclusive Cumberland Club" 8).

Some journalism textbooks, such as *A Place in the News: From the Women's Pages to the Front Page* by Kay Mills (1990), feature Austin as a feminist rather than an environmental writer, a logical categorization, Austin said, because the *Maine Times* "was writing about women's issues when no one else was."

Austin's life-long commitment to the power of print media began early. After graduating from Meredith College in Raleigh, North Carolina, she worked for a small newspaper in Selma, North Carolina, and then was hired by the *Raleigh News and Observer* to write for its women's section and cover city and business affairs. After employment with the Associated Press from 1966 to 1973 in South Carolina and Maine, she joined the *Maine Times* on October 4, 1974, six years to the day after the publication was founded in Topsham, Maine.

In addition to championing the environment and women, Austin crusades for equal rights for all people. A native of Four Oaks, North Carolina, Austin told me in the summer of 1997 that she was "the first woman in South Carolina covering race riots during the 1960s. There I was, wearing my dresses and heels. It was a momentous time. I drove home at night through fog rising from the river, past men wearing helmets and carrying guns."

While working for the AP, Austin moved from Columbia, South Carolina, to Augusta, Maine, where she covered politics for four years. During this time, her interest in environmental issues began, and she covered topics such as the development of nuclear power plants. "Obviously, my success in focusing on environmental issues coincided in South Carolina and Maine with the rise of the national environmental movement," she commented.

After spending these years "finding a voice," when she took the job with the *Maine Times* she learned not only to have an opinion but also how to defend it to readers. She also learned to admit to mistakes: "It was an important transition for me in every way. I had practiced being objective at the AP. At the *Maine Times* everyone had an opinion—I knew I had to get one."

As the *Maine Times* provided help in finding a voice and a professional home, Austin helped make the publication into a transforming voice in state politics. The history of the newspaper parallels changes in Austin's life and illustrates the editorial and geographical transitions an alternative newspaper often makes in order to survive. "Phyllis works harder on stories than any other journalist I've known," says Douglas Rooks, editor of the *Maine Times* from 1995 to 2000 and now a freelance writer, editor, and consultant. "Unlike many writers, she really does use the empirical method, interviewing dozens and even scores of people before she closes in on the facts—what can really be known about a given subject. The words 'tireless' and 'dogged' can certainly be used to describe her pursuit of a story. But what's most striking to me is her humility, her understanding that our knowledge is incomplete but that a journalist must do her utmost to fill in as many blanks as possible" (e-mail to author, Aug. 8, 2005).

By the time the *Maine Times* ceased publication in 2002, circulation had fallen from a high of eighteen thousand in 1988 to fewer than four thousand subscribers and some newsstand sales, according to the *Portland Press Herald* and *Editor and Publisher*. Women gave the publication an edge in dealing with women's issues, but its owners and publishers were men. Peter Cox and John N. Cole, founders and editors in 1968, set up offices in Topsham.

Cox bought out Cole's share of the newspaper in the 1970s, and then Dodge Morgan, a businessman and world-class sailor, bought the newspaper from Cox in 1985 and moved the operation to Portland in 1994. There it shared an office with his other newspaper, the *Casco Bay Weekly.* In 1997 a group of businesspeople purchased the paper and moved it from Portland to Hallowell, a small community outside Augusta.

Rooks, who edited the newspaper for many years, moved with it from Portland to Hallowell. At the time, Austin said she believed the alternative weekly would become an even more potent voice for the environmental movement as it moved toward its thirtieth anniversary. Rooks recalls that during his time as editor the staff was committed to coverage of environmentalism "broadly defined": "We asked questions such as, 'How do we live?' 'How do we develop the community?' 'How do we provide public services?' We don't hate people and worship trees" (Ibid.).

Austin appreciated the symbolic significance of the publication's move from upscale Portland to Hallowell, with its inviting restaurants and antique shops. Moreover, because Hallowell is close to the state capital, it provides access to the legislature and various government offices. The owners of the *Maine Times,* however, struggled unsuccessfully to rebuild the newspaper's advertising, distribution, and readership and eventually sold it. Chris Hutchins, heir to an oil company fortune in Maine, then bought the newspaper in 1999 and moved it to Bangor. Soon after, he closed the newspaper and established a monthly magazine, also called the *Maine Times,* but it, too, failed.

"The lesson of the *Maine Times* is the lesson of every nuts-and-bolts business. You have to create yourself—find your own success—and then keep in touch with the clientele and grow together," Austin commented. "You don't leave your loyal advertisers: Stay with the breadmakers and the weavers. They were small in the 1960s, and they're small in the 1990s."

Austin's love for the *Maine Times* continues, and although she celebrates its contributions to the state, she doubts the newspaper will be reborn. "The *Maine Times* is not likely to rise from the ashes," she says. "In hindsight, where the *Maine Times* went wrong was in not having a plan of succession to carry on the fine work the paper did from 1968 into the early nineties. *High Country News,* which is very much like the *Maine Times,* was excellent at insuring its future through careful planning." It is impossible to estimate how much legislation resulted from investigative articles published in the *Maine Times,* but Austin is convinced the newspaper had a profound impact: "The *Maine Times* cut frontier paths into many issues over the years. We covered it. We uncovered it. We did something about it."

Mills and other media critics acknowledge the contributions that Austin and others like her have made to American journalism. In the early 1970s, for example, the women at the *Maine Times* published an issue devoted almost totally to women's issues. "We put out a sequel in the mid-1970s, and we would not have put the energy into that if we weren't women," Austin maintains. She believes that women write the kinds of stories that put the *Maine Times* on the journalistic map because they "see a story immediately, they know it affects their lives, their relationships. It's really where the heart is. When we covered those things, we were vitally interested in them, and they touched our lives, and we knew they touched others' lives. We knew their importance. They're not at arm's length, as it so often is with men who do these stories" (Mills, *A Place in the News* 248).

Journalists, politicians, and residents of Maine are among those who celebrate Austin's role in protecting the state's resources. Karin Tilberg has served as the deputy commissioner of Maine's Department of Conservation, which oversees 650,000 acres of parks, historic sites, and public lands and manages four waterways. Of Austin she says,

> I have found Phyllis to have a rare array of talents that include devotion to detail and fact-finding, a deep passion for her work and the subject matter of her articles, and a fine-tuned intuition for what stories will be of lasting importance. What is perhaps most amazing is that over time, the intensity of these qualities has not diminished. Her stories, taken together, chronicle the key events in Maine over decades specifically in the arena of environmental protection and conservation. So much of importance would have gone unchronicled and largely unnoticed by the public had it not been for Phyllis Austin. (e-mail to author, Aug. 9, 2005)

In addition to professional responsibilities in retirement, Austin plans to continue hiking and "tending to the spirit." Because her longtime partner Anne Dellenbaugh was diagnosed with cancer in 1996 (and her father and sister died of cancer), she also writes personal essays about health ("forays into the world of the body"). "Cancer is not just something happening to us," she noted in the the summer of 1997. "It's happening to everyone. We have only so much life. I'm learning to be realistic and thoughtful about some of my decisions."

The personal essays are also a result of nearly dying in a cross-country skiing accident in 1984. Since that event, when she was impaled through the abdomen vertically by a tree branch, Austin has endured eleven surgeries. The near-death experience and other personal experiences have changed and challenged her. "It isn't easy . . . to let go and be open to constant change," she writes. "But coming to terms with the birth and death in each moment creates a harmony within. It is the path I've chosen to a fuller, wiser heart" ("Impaled" 128).

Austin continues writing regularly for the *Maine Environmental News,* a bimonthly independent online publication begun in March 1998 and from the Maine Environmental Policy Institute in Hallowell. The nonprofit institute researches environmental challenges and reports to policymakers and the public. The online publication includes news, news features, features, press releases, and action alerts from organizations and governmental agencies dealing with topics as varied as forestry, agriculture, and marine life. She has written about coyotes, vehicular access to Baxter State Park, the state's hut-and-trail system, conservation, forestry, tourism and Monhegan Island, logging, and other issues.

She is also at work on a book about Buzz Caverly and Baxter State Park, home to forty-eight mountains, including Mount Katahdin. The park, which is financially independent of the state or federal government, was donated to the people of Maine by Percival Proctor Baxter, a former governor. The park is the fourth-largest state park in the United States. Caverly began working in the park in 1960 as a ranger, became a supervisor in 1968, and then took over the preserve in 1982. "Buzz, with just a high school education, started his summer ranger's job at twenty-one years old and grew up with the park. His is a Horatio Alger story," Austin commented during interviews in 2004 and 2005, "and his life and career are truly unique. I've woven his personal rise—including many tribulations—into the life of the park behind the scenes and the issues that galvanized the public to regard Baxter as a sacred place."

When she is not writing, Austin and Dellenbaugh enjoy the home they built on Mere Point Bay in Brunswick, a half mile from the house where Austin lived for twenty years; they also hike in Hawaii, Utah, Alaska, and Scotland. Dellenbaugh runs an outdoor business that sponsors trips to wilderness areas, and she also counsels others dealing with serious illness.

Because of numerous writing deadlines, Austin rarely has the time to reminisce. When she does, she speaks from the heart about the contributions she made to the environment and what she still hopes to accomplish:

> In looking back over my career, I have been most fortunate to have worked during the rise of environmentalism and for a paper that initiated investigative newspaper coverage in Maine in so many areas, such as public utilities, agriculture, and transportation. We were driven by an energy and passion for

being able to effect institutional and governmental change in the late sixties, the seventies, and into the eighties. The *Maine Times* staff was creative, bright, indefatigable, and honest. We really did feel the public service expectations of our job, which naturally paid much less than regular newspaper jobs.

My work generated hope in me—hope for life around me and for the world—that we were in a progressive move toward equality, justice, and all those good things. While *Maine Times* was thriving, I had the satisfaction of knowing that I was an agent of change by the stories I chose to write, especially on the environment. But it was an influence that I knew had a short life.

As I contemplate the newspaper business today, I can't fathom how difficult it is to be a starting journalist—the corporate ownership, the scandals of false reporting, the restrictions on the truth. My one regret is that *Maine Times* did not survive the failures of its owners/guardians. I like to believe that my work influenced decisions, especially in the environmental arena, for a time. With *Maine Times* "retiring" before I have, I don't get to complete my journey. I am hoping that the Baxter book, and perhaps others to follow, will complete my body of work.

Austin received an Alicia Patterson Foundation Journalism Fellowship in 1986, in Washington, D.C., during which she researched and wrote about Maine's paper industry; the John S. Knight Foundation Journalism Fellowship in 1989 and 1990 at Stanford University, during which she took courses in business, civil rights law, architecture, and the environment; the Japan Press Association Fellowship in 1990, during which she spent two weeks studying Japan's environmental issues; and another Knight Fellowship in 1991 at University of Maryland, during which she took a course on national environmental issues.

Her numerous awards include the Natural Resources Council of Maine Conservation Award for "outstanding work to protect Maine's environment" in 1989; a distinguished service award from the University of Southern Maine in 2000; and, all in 2001, the Maine Press Association Award for investigative reporting, the Sierra Club Environmental Reporting award, and the Mary Hartman Award from the University of Maine for environmental reporting.

Her highest tributes, however, come from those with whom she has worked. Will Sugg, head of the Maine Environmental Policy Institute, maintains that "Phyllis' work has been essential in framing and informing the debate for policymakers and citizens on wilderness and conservation issues in Maine for nearly thirty years. It is hard to imagine where North Woods issues in Maine would be without her work. She is as much a part of the landscape here as a lynx or a remote mountain lake" (e-mail to author, Aug. 30, 2005).

Austin has amassed a formidable portfolio, a notable list of awards and honors, and the accolades of colleagues. Her focus, however, is on her life's work: persuading others through her writing that they are responsible for protecting the world. One recent project, for example, concerns including immigrants from Africa and Asia in environmental initiatives necessary to preserving Maine's beauty:

> They come with their own history and sense of landscape, and Maine's is truly foreign to them. I can imagine the day when the executive director of the Maine Audobon Society will be a woman who came to Maine as a child from Somalia or Ethiopia.
>
> How will these children, as well as their parents, learn about Mt. Katahdin, Moosehead Lake, the Appalachian Trail, moose and loons to the point that they cherish them as much as I do and want to protect them forever? These ethnic communities are part of the new face of Maine, and it's crucial that we include them in the family of environmentalists. (August 2004)

From Phyllis Austin, a contemporary writer, philosopher, and activist, we move from the twenty-first century to the nineteenth and early twentieth centuries and from Maine to Colorado. With all their differences, what binds Austin to Caroline Nichols Churchill is her belief in the power of newspapers to drive social issues and her commitment to feminism.

A Feminist Crusader: Caroline Nichols Churchill

Caroline Nichols Churchill had the passion of a revival minister, the commitment of a crusader, and the hope and steadfastness of a saint. She was not universally popular. Only occasionally could she make a living as a journalist, and she died without having gained the widespread recognition she craved. Her writing is redundant; her tone, strident; and her style, unimaginative. But Churchill believed in equality for women even when she stood alone. Unflinching and unapologetic, she communicated her beliefs by founding two Colorado newspapers and writing several books.

Never wavering in her demand that women transform themselves, their homes, their relationships, their professions, and their society, Churchill wrote in the *Queen Bee* on January 9, 1884: "Show the world that simply because we are women we are not compelled to be mother to some man's children. . . . When women vote they will make all the laws regulating marriage. . . . A woman will be no more tied at home than a man will." She then added, "'Oh! haste the glad day, but do not idly sit waiting for it. If it comes at all we must work for it with strong hands and joyful hearts.'"

And it was with strong hands, a joyful heart, and a will of steel that Churchill wrote, edited, published, marketed, and distributed her newspapers, the *Colorado Antelope* (1879–82) and the *Queen Bee* (1882–1926). It would be difficult to find a woman more committed to the tenets of alternative media. No evidence suggests that Churchill pursued a job in traditional journalism, but the limited information about her personal life and professional career indicates a woman who would have been impatient with prevailing news practices, would not have welcomed the direction of male editors, and wanted to pour her energies into her own publications and make her own rules.

Churchill was colorful, committed, and very public in her support for the equality of women and the role of journalism in transforming public opinion. While interviewing sources and distributing her newspapers she traveled across Colorado and the rest of the West, trying to increase her circulation base and soliciting advertising. Determined to use journalism to champion women's rights, Churchill also was a teacher and a pioneer. Had she lived during another time, she would no doubt have considered herself a feminist as well. In addition to her newspapers, more than fifty thousand copies of her two books, *Little Sheaves* and *Over the Purple Hills,* have been sold.

Churchill's autobiography, *Active Footsteps,* describes a life and time now lost—one in which activism and journalism were nearly synonymous and a reporter's point of view was assumed. Gaye Tuchman deals with the origins of the women's movement and the ambivalence many of its founders shared about dealing with established media organizations dominated by men. The "easy access to the news media requiring ongoing contacts between a reporter and a news source, such as those provided by beats," she writes, was intrinsically problematic for women activists. "Those who plan disruptive events do not have these contacts, because they are frequently suspicious of the media or may have other reasons, such as possible arrest, for *not* cultivating contact" (*Making News* 141).

Tuchman is correct when she argues that "standard reportorial practice legitimates those with institutional power" (Ibid. 142) and excludes journalistic activists such as Churchill. Furthermore, when women are relegated to careers as beat and general news reporters, "issues and occurrences generated by any social movement are necessarily subjected to the frame of the conventional news narrative" (Ibid. 154) and may lose the impact they might otherwise have.

A quotation from *Active Footsteps*—"it is a queer world, any way; many of us never get used to it" (119)—provides an apt summary of the motivation for Churchill's life and work and supports the purpose of establishing an alternative medium. She makes clear that she identifies with those who have been made to feel peripheral. As an outcast, she would betray herself in choosing to relay a radical message via traditional media. In her "queer world," Churchill was a force to reckon with as she challenged accepted notions and modeled energy, radical thinking, and courage, unsettling many of those targeted by her newspapers. In the August 9, 1882, issue of the *Queen Bee*, for example, Churchill raged against men who use their wives for the services they provide: "Sweet woman, come into my kitchen and serve me, and let me do as I please, no matter what, if it is to trot thee out of the back door after thy beauty has faded entirely in my service and I will get another" (4).

She also realized that the power structure would not reward women imprisoned in their homes while men had the option of working in the public sphere and exchanging their wives for younger models. "Is Marriage a Failure?" she asked in a *Queen Bee* column published on June 26, 1889. "If we keep track of the divorce courts," she explained, "we see that many more women than men desire freedom from the matrimonial bonds. Why? Because women are coming to look upon the wedding ceremony as a legal bond and ask that they be freed from the tyranny of the men who treated them like slaves."

The layout and design of the *Queen Bee* were as notable as its content. The lefthand column of page one consisted of sayings ("above all things man should keep sober") and mottoes that were brief and varied. In one issue, for example, one could read about politicians; a woman who remarried on her deathbed; teachers' pay; New Mexico history; a Fort Collins fix-it shop; the election of women in Pueblo, Colorado; the significance of a woman's age; and child labor law. Poetry and song lyrics were interspersed among the stories on page one.

Churchill's pride and determination can be illustrated by the hyperbolic manner in which she described the *Queen Bee* at the top-righthand side of its masthead: "*The Queen Bee* has the largest circulation of any weekly paper published between Kansas City and San Francisco." Relying on circulation and advertising, Churchill asked that businessmen support her newspaper because it provided them with inexpensive exposure and appealed to women readers. In the July 5, 1882, issue, she wrote, "THE Queen Bee, being the only paper in the state advocating Woman's Political Equality and Individuality, makes it the best and cheapest advertising medium. Business men will consult their own interests by advertising in it."

Churchill was hyperbolic about herself as well. When women gained the vote in Colorado in 1893, the headline on the *Queen Bee*'s front page was "Western Women Wild With Joy Over Colorado's Election." By 1893, Churchill began to claim political equality for women in Colorado and took a great deal of credit for their strides. "While it is difficult to measure how big a part the *Queen Bee* actually played in this victory," historian and biographer Joan Swallow Reiter writes, "Modesty never stopped the publisher from saluting herself. In her autobiography she stated, 'It is not at all likely that another woman on the continent could under the same conditions accomplish as much'" (Editors of Time-Life Books, *The Women* 220).

Taking on controversial topics, Churchill lived and published without apology. The subheading for her newspaper was, after all, "Devoted to the Interests of Humanity, Woman's Political Equality and Individuality." One example of her theory that men are to blame for the plight of the world appeared in the April 11, 1883, issue, where Churchill blamed the "Indian Question" on men and commented that "war and bloodshed are the results, and women have always been the worst sufferers." Soon after, in 1884, she wrote columns that carried the headlines "Give Women the Ballot!" and "We Shall Vote."

Churchill's commitment to journalism and public well-being prompted a life-long interest in politics. Above all, she argued for women's freedom in the political sphere and demanded nothing less in the home. In *The Women*, a revised edition of *Woman of the Century*, a collection of 1,500 biographies, Reiter notes, "Eclectic in her choice of weapons, newspaper publisher Caroline Churchill used everything from mawkish poetry to serious political reporting in an effort to rally Colorado women behind equal rights" (220).

One important woman whom Churchill featured in the *Queen Bee* was Harriett N. Prewitt. Profiled in the October 10, 1883, issue, Prewitt was described as "A Woman of Talent" and "the first real newspaper woman in this country." She was said to have "held out as she could against the extreme measures of secession, but when she did haul down her Union flag she became one of the boldest, bravest defenders of the Southern cause." Born in Stillwater, New York, Prewitt was educated at Willard Seminary at Troy. Of particular interest to Churchill was the fact that Prewitt left her three children and the *Yazoo City* (Mississippi) *Whig* in order to take a position at the *Yazoo City Banner*. Such stories make the *Queen Bee* an essential historical document as well as a chronicle of daily events.

Churchill was born on December 23, 1833, in Canada. Married for approximately a decade to a Canadian, she gave birth to their daughter in 1852. She remained with her husband until he died in 1862. During this time, she taught during the summers and sewed during the winters. When her husband died, her sister took their daughter "indefinitely" (Churchill, *Active Footsteps* 21). In 1869 Churchill became ill with consumption and soon after moved to California, where she lived from 1870 to 1876, the year she went to Chicago to begin writing *Over the Purple Hills;* she then spent two years in Texas and also lived in Missouri and Kansas until 1879. At that point she visited Denver and decided to stay, presumably because of her health (Ibid.).

In 1879, Churchill founded and became editor of the *Colorado Antelope,* which she edited for three years, first as a monthly and later as a weekly, before she began to publish the weekly *Queen Bee* in 1882. The *Colorado Antelope* was published on credit and sold for 10 cents a copy; the *Queen Bee* relied upon subscriptions and donations. Mary Winter, a *Denver Post* lifestyles editor, wrote in 1992 that Churchill chose the name *Colorado Antelope* "because a little deer is so difficult to overtake" ("Lifestyles" 33). The newspaper boasted a circulation of a thousand and was published from October 1879 to June 1882. All thousand copies of the first pressrun were sold by noon, and "the little paper soon had a very fair subscription list, and some advertising. . . . In publishing the monthly paper there were men entirely incredulous as to a paper succeeding published by a woman. There were those who would buy and read the paper and steadily oppose its publication" (Churchill, *Active Footsteps* 83, 85). Subscribers paid $1.50 a year for the *Colorado Antelope,* which occasionally lapsed in publication.

The first issue featured three columns. There was a poem in the upperlefthand corner, a humorous feature about Leadville, Colorado, and stories about Churchill's travels in Texas. On page two, column one, Churchill published an editorial that stated, "It is our opinion that every State in the Union should have a live feminine paper published at the Capital and that such paper should be liberally sustained. As the acquisition of women to the educational department has raised the standard of education and general cultivation, so the acquisition of women to the journalistic department will advance the standard of journalism. It is not good for man to be alone in journalism any more than in any other enterprise." Moreover, "woman was given to man as a civilizer." In column three she added, "There will always be women content as slaves because they have neither the will nor the ability to think or act for themselves. . . . What is life worth if we are to be so cramped as not to half develop our faculties. Let us develop."

With the *Colorado Antelope* Churchill began to disseminate a message of equality between women and men. The undated volume one, number two from the first year of publication stated in "Editorial Notes" on column two: "A man says, waiting for the train is the most irksome thing a *man* can do. A woman says, waiting for the train is the most irksome thing a *person* can do." Churchill believed gender differences to be especially obvious in the cultural lexicon. In "Advice to Young Men" in column three, for example, she challenged males to do housework well: "Do not imagine yourself a born dictator because you happen to belong to the ruling class and have inherited a pair of pantaloons. . . . Learn to cook, wait on table, make beds artistically, and wash."

In 1881, struggling for funding, Churchill provided two reasons for readers to support the *Colorado Antelope*. First, "It places whiskey and tobacco outside the pale of a high civilization, as it should," and, second, "Women have been wonderfully patient with the peculiarities of the masculine press, have helped to sustain it when it was her worst enemy." There would be an "aching void in the hearts of the people of Denver" if the newspaper folded (volume three, number four, page seven, columns two and three).

Churchill failed in her quest to keep the newspaper afloat, however, and on July 5, 1882, the *Colorado Antelope* was superseded by the *Queen Bee*. In 1909 she moved to Colorado Springs and continued to publish the latter publication, somewhat sporadically, until her death in 1926.

Throughout Churchill's life, travel played an important role in her development as a person and a writer. She wrote of Boulder, Silverton, Ouray, Pueblo, and Georgetown, among other Colorado cities, in her autobiography. She mentions trains, snow, maple sugar, and the silver panic of 1893, and then she discontinued publication: "There was nothing to do, and nothing to do with. The silver mines, the principal industry of the State, were shut down" (*Active Footsteps* 172). Churchill supported the Populist Party in Colorado and credited herself with helping bring about suffrage in both Idaho and Utah ("Mrs. Churchill's papers were extensively read in all those localities" [Ibid. 213].)

Two of her books rely heavily upon her pilgrimages throughout the West. Published in 1874, *Little Sheaves: Gathered While Gleaning After Reapers* is composed of letters about travel. *Over the Purple Hills: Sketches of Travel in California* (1884) deals with her experiences in Yosemite, the Napa Valley, San Francisco, Stockton, Lake Tahoe, Vallejo, Monterey, and San Jose.

Active Footsteps, a blend of personal narrative and description of travel, is one of Churchill's most interesting texts. She described herself as "five-foot-four inches tall, thirty-two inches at the bust and twenty-nine inches at the waist, with very brown hair and not very abundant; study eventually caused it to fall. . . . Not really great in anything but perseverance, firmness and self-respect" (23). *Active Footsteps,* Christiane Fischer observes, "contains many pronouncements on life in general and on the condition of women in particular, which are interspersed here and there, and are always striking by their sharp and pithy character. . . . She found it hard to make a place for herself in a man's world" (*Let Them Speak for Themselves* 167). In one line from the book Churchill called men a "master class" and said they "seldom lose a chance to insult a woman who has the ability for something besides service to his lordship" (Ibid.). Calling the work "vaguely chronological," Fischer comments, "Mrs. Churchill jumps from one subject to the next without any transition; her descriptions are not especially compelling, her stories and anecdotes are not frequently arresting, but her ideas concerning the condition of women are so provocative that they make the book well worth reading" (Ibid.).

Occasionally, reporters at other newspapers covered Churchill, among them the *Colorado Springs Gazette* and *Sierra Journal,* published in Rosita, Colorado. The August 11, 1907, issue of the *Gazette* revealed that Churchill, then seventy-four, had purchased a home in Colorado Springs. She was described on page eight as being "alert and vigorous as ever":

> In Mrs. Churchill, the equal suffrage cause has always had a dauntless champion, and beyond doubt she was an important factor in bringing it about for Colorado. She came rightfully by her aggressive and courageous characteristics, for her grandfather on her father's side, William Nichols, was a naval officer under King George III, and participated in the Revolutionary war. On her mother's side, Mrs. Churchill is of Holland and German descent, and her ancestors who settled in America were noted for their fine farms and their homespun linens.

The *Sierra Journal* provided much more detail when its editors published "Mrs. Catherine Spiteful Churchill" on May 11, 1882, accusing her of having a fierce temper and making it clear that she could be difficult. The *Sierra Journal's* lead story was in the top-lefthand corner of the newspaper's first page. A typical combination of news and opinion, it described the arrogance of the *Colorado Antelope* "editress":

> Mrs. Catherine Churchill, the editress of the *Colorado Antelope,* visited Rosita a few weeks ago, as she has done beforehand, and, in accordance with her usual custom made the rounds of the town, visiting all the gin mills and beer halls and the various business houses of the town, and in the course of

her perigrinations went into the dry goods establishment of C. F. Blossom & Co., where she met Miss Addie Jordan, the daughter of the junior member of the firm, and solicited her to subscribe for the *Antelope*. Miss Jordan told her that she did not wish the paper and would therefore not subscribe for it, whereupon Catherine with the odor of the gin mills which she had visited for the sake of obtaining through the means of her wonderful "cheek" a few subscriptions to her paper or selling a few copies of it, informed Miss Jordan that if it was not for such women as herself (Mrs. Churchill) that she (Miss Jordan) would now be working over somebody's washtub, and that to such women as herself was due all the elevation that women of the present day have attained to and became so offensive in her manner that Miss Jordan very properly, no doubt, asked her to leave the house and Catherine sailed forth very wroth and informed many of our people that Miss Jordan would catch it in the next issue of the *Antelope*. The May number of the *Antelope* has been received in this office and we note the fact that Mrs. Churchill is really the vixen that her actions here denoted her to be. We have not the inclination to inflict on our readers the mess of garbage and silly excrescences of Mrs. Churchill's pen. It contains neither sense nor taste and is only the frothy-vaporing of a petulant woman—a "disposition to" be revenged for a merited rebuke, administered by a sensible young lady, and in this Mrs. Churchill has showed herself to be possessed of, in an eminent degree, a quality of petty vindictiveness. Her uncalled for attack on Miss Jordon [*sic*] was premeditated and was not, as she would have her readers believe, written with a view of elevating her sex.

Publishing her obituary, *The Trail: A Magazine for Colorado (Organ of the Society of Sons of Colorado and Societies of Daughters of Colorado and the Territorial Daughters)* was among the last newspapers to refer to Churchill. Will C. Bishop of Denver was its editor and publisher. Headlined "The Passing of the Pioneer," the obituary read:

93 years old, Colorado's pioneer woman suffrage leader, and for fifty-eight years publisher of the *Colorado Antelope* and later the *Queen Bee,* official publications in Colorado for the movement, died in Colorado Springs at the home of her sister, Mrs. A. D. Kingsley, on June 10.

Mrs. Churchill was born in Whitby, Canada. She came to Denver in the early days, and in 1867, when 37 years of age [*sic*], conceived the idea of publishing the *Colorado Antelope,* advocating woman suffrage. Although bedfast for the last year, she continued publication of the *Queen Bee,* which replaced the *Antelope,* until a few months ago.

There is no doubt that equal rights for women and issues in marriage were the topics that dominated Churchill's fledgling newspapers and gave her significant notoriety in the West. Excerpts from the *Queen Bee* include statements that attest to the revolutionary quality of the feminist newspaper. The July 5, 1892, issue informed readers that "there are women so shrewd as to manage to make a husband support them. There are others smart enough to take care of themselves and husbands too." Given that the newspaper was published a century before women's equality would be assumed to exist in the United States, Churchill was prescient in saying, "It is considered a dreadful thing for a woman to marry a man for his money. It should be full as mean a thing for a man to monopolize a woman's time so that she cannot make money for herself." Even more admonitions were provided in the December 13, 1882, issue:

> Some time ago the Silver Plume *Coloradoan* published a long harangue about woman's inferiority to man, and among other nonsense said that even in fashionable life she was falling off so much in producing children as to alarm the gravest thinkers.
>
> Now if the editor of that journal would instruct men as to their duties in bringing up the children. . . he would be doing the race a more consistent service. As to woman's inferiority physically, no person of sense pretends to claim that woman could make as great a prize fighter as man, and no person of common sense would give this as a reason for enslaving women.

Similar in tone and content was "What Men Need Wives For" in the July 12, 1882, *Queen Bee.* Men, in Churchill's opinion, seek "courage, sympathy, and love," but some "seek for nothing further than success in housework." Of such men, she said, "Justly enough, half of these get nothing more."

With the *Queen Bee,* Churchill became even more tireless in advocating for women's rights than she had been in the *Colorado Antelope.* An activist whose interests were broader than woman suffrage, "She frequently battled against social injustice and spoke out for Denver's Chinese, who in the 1880s were often blamed for taking mining jobs from whites" (Winter, "Lifestyles" 33). Connecting her advocacy for the Chinese with her desire to see women as equal to men, she said, "The Chinaman's greatest crime seems to be his superior industry, sobriety and living within his income. The same objection is frequently mooted in the case of women" (Ibid.; Churchill, *Active Footsteps* 87). Some sources even reported that during the Hop Alley Riot in 1881, Churchill nursed a wounded Chinese man at her newspaper office and that another man died on its floor. In the July 12, 1882, *Queen Bee,* she published "Chinese Pete" and admonished, "It is well for us not to despise the counsels of different nations, or their customs or costumes, even though they come to us by individual example and from the lowly."

In addition to race and ethnicity, Churchill was concerned about issues of class. In "The Lower Classes" on July 26, 1882, she referred to poor people as "nature's nobility" and wrote: "If there were a class of human beings on earth who may be properly denominated low, it is that class who spend without earning, who consume without producing, who dissipate on the earnings of their fathers or mothers or relatives without being anything in and on themselves." The August 9, 1882, issue included a feature entitled "The Widow's Sewing Machine: A Story of Love, Pride and Poverty," which indicated her respect for the widow's sacrifices.

At the center of Churchill's message was the idea that women are equal to men. In the preface to *Active Footsteps,* written with great bravado and in the third person, she observes that "slavery of any character is a most pitiable condition: that of woman keeps the entire race at a low standard" (n.p.). Of herself, she says, "Mrs. Churchill was married in the early fifties. People did not know what else to do with girls, as there were few avenues of employment for them. A husband was selected, and, however inappropriate, the girl was expected to conform to the condition" (19).

Churchill's advocacy for adult women suggests a quite logical concern about how girls were raised in America near the turn of the century. She often advised them in her columns. The December 1879 *Colorado Antelope,* for example, provided "Advice to Young Girls": "Remember that the heart of man is deceitful above all things and desperately wicked" and "Do not be afraid of work, but at the same time do not make a drudge of yourself for anyone. Society does not sufficiently appreciate what woman does in the way of work to pay her for ruining her personal beauty" (page two, column three). The August 1880 issue contained "Only a Girl," Churchill's poem celebrating girls:

> . . . And I will pray to Heaven, on bended knees
> That every child henceforth may be a boy;
> That every father's heart may leap with joy;
> But 'ere in scorn you breathe 'only a girl!,'
> Look lest you cast aside the greater pearl.

A column by Ada M. Bittenbender, president of the Nebraska Woman Suffrage Association, appeared in the July 19, 1882, *Queen Bee,* along with a "Charity to Children" column. The following issue (July 26, 1882) contained "Charming Girls," in which Churchill recommends that girls pursue their talents, gain an education, and read voraciously: "If you go through life a flying butterfly, how will you be spoken of by and by? I own that it is nice to eat, drink and be merry, and be courted and flattered by all your friends, but how much better to cultivate character, sense and true womanliness?" (1).

To some extent Churchill was as much a construction of her own imagination as she was a living, breathing woman who held progressive ideas. Certainly, she lived during an era when most readers were unconvinced about her warnings and prophecies. Compounding the problem of making every argument a battleground was her elevated self-esteem:

> The pioneer settlers of Colorado well know that for industrial effort, or rather endeavor, this woman could never be surpassed. For physical strength she might have been outdone, but never in plucky effort to overcome almost insurmountable obstacles and difficulties. . . . The fact that men hold in supreme selfishness all the great avenues of influence, the pulpit and the press, with the learned professions, rankled in her mind until to get even with the arch enemy of the race became the prime object of existence. (*Active Footsteps* 79–80)

When Churchill is remembered, it will be as much for her personality as for her newspapers and books. Her commitment and sense of humor were powerful tools, whether in daily life or prose. A few historians have referred to Churchill's contributions and praised her. Fischer suggests that the "strong personality" exhibited in Churchill's writing "constitutes their main interest" and adds, "She was a most unusual woman, who cared nothing for housekeeping and seemed uninfluenced by the sentimental effusions about the 'home' which are so characteristic of 19th-century popular writings in America. Her ideas concerning women's place in society were extremely advanced for the times; she was constantly fighting against traditional ideas and rebelled at the existing conditions" (*Let Them Speak for Themselves* 166).

Churchill's sense of humor was often evident, although it was frequently at the expense of men. On page three, column three of the December 1879 *Colorado Antelope,* she reported, "Mr. Palmer of New York city, a portrait painter, is in the city, painting the pictures of Colorado's Governors and ex-Governors. They are all handsome men—in oil." And in the January 1880 issue she referred to herself as the "oldest and handsomest editor in the U.S."

The newspapers attest to their publisher's passion and assertiveness during a time when deference to others was a measure of a woman's gentility and place in society. Churchill's beliefs and adversarial approach, however, guaranteed serious disputes and regular attacks. "Espousing her own brand of blunderbuss feminism, the crotchety Mrs. Churchill used her paper to rail against men ('the arch enemy of the race'), to push vocational education for girls and to advocate pensions for mothers with dependent children" (Editors of Time-Life Books, *The Women* 220). Although Churchill overstated herself for effect—she wrote, for example, that "women should remember that all the evils of society are caused by the bad management of men, and women are greatly to blame for folding their hands and permitting this state of things" (Winter, "Ahead of Their Time" 1)—she was far ahead of her time.

Despite the limited biographical material available, any critical article about Caroline Nichols Churchill reveals that she was a symbol of the lives and contributions of many women who built careers and fostered social change while working for newspapers. Her life suggests the range of age, racial and ethnic identity, and political and social opinions held by the women who championed specific causes in the American press. Churchill will be remembered as a crusader who founded, wrote for, edited, marketed, and distributed two alternative newspapers. She also demonstrated that the media provide an effective tool for political, social, and cultural change.

African American Newspapers and Betty Wilkins

On July 30, 2005, a family gathered for swimming and a picnic near the sparkling waters of the Aurora, Colorado, Reservoir. With temperatures in the high nineties, the children chased one another into the waves while their parents, aunts, uncles, and grandparents reminisced. One of the threads that connected them was the life of the late Betty Wilkins of Denver, an African American journalist who in the 1960s became a lightning rod for prejudice. It is Wilkins's love and faith that her family remember, and it is her contributions to journalism and her community that make her story essential in a study that deals with media secret sharers who are too often overlooked.

The story of Betty Wilkins, a committed journalist who worked on weekly and daily newspapers and in radio, is important in its own right and a reminder of the often untold narratives about women of color in media. These narratives—acknowledged to be largely absent from the journalistic canon—are emerging slowly as media historians work their way through manuscripts and microfilm in library archives and special collections. Furthermore, the story of Betty Wilkins is humbling because it reminds people that many whose lives emerge from research have been discovered accidentally. How many more stories have been lost entirely or temporarily overlooked in scrapbooks, letters, and storage boxes forgotten in attics or basements?

Jane Rhodes accounts for some of the reasons that African American journalists have been overlooked and quotes scholars such as James Carey who suggest the oversight is an "embarrassment" to media history ("Mary Ann Shadd Cary" 211). Rhodes suggests that "losing African American women in the scholarship" is "particularly ironic given the explosion of interest in African American women's history and literature" (Ibid.). Although her focus is primarily on the nineteenth century, it is Rhodes's hope that—beyond paying attention to newspaper articles by African American women who advocated for a cause—scholars will begin showing more interest in the "people who produced them" (Ibid. 212).

Two newspaper clippings in the Western archives of the Denver Public Library are among the reminders of Wilkins's legacy. When two members of the Colorado Press Women resigned when that organization refused to admit an African American newspaperwoman as a member in 1960s, Wilkins found herself the target of discriminiation in the midst of what had been a prolific career in journalism.

Wilkins was a Denver resident and had worked for six years as associate editor and society editor for *The Call*, a "Negro weekly" published in Kansas City and distributed throughout the West. Colleagues described her as being "very well qualified" for membership, and one women who resigned commented that Wilkins's qualifications "outrank those of most of us." She was, she told reporters, surprised by the rejection, as were many of the members in the CPW:

> Two members of the Colorado Press Women have resigned over the organization's refusal to admit a Negro newspaperwoman as a member, *The Denver Post* learned Tuesday.
>
> Mrs. Sue Mosier, women's editor of radio station KFKA in Greeley and president of the 100–member organization, said she expects more resignations over the rejection of Mrs. Betty Wilkins, 3681 E. 31st Ave., whom Mrs. Mosier described as "very well qualified" for membership.
>
> Mrs. Wilkins has been associate editor and society editor in Denver for the past six years for *The Call*, a Negro weekly published in Kansas City and distributed throughout the West.
>
> Her membership in the organization, made up of newspaperwomen, free lance writers and other [sic] in allied fields, was proposed last June. Her application was tabled until a meeting last Saturday at the Denver Press Club.
>
> Five "no" votes were cast against Mrs. Wilkins, believed to be the first Negro to seek membership, in a written ballot among the more than 20 members present, *The Post* learned.
>
> The organization's by-laws provide that three "no" votes rule out membership.
>
> One of those who resigned over the incident was a former national board member and last year's state president, Mrs. Helen Fletcher Collins, 627 S. Corona St. The other woman's name has not been disclosed.

Mrs. Collins, assistant editor of the *American Horologist and Jeweler,* handed her written resignation to Mrs. Mosier and walked out of the meeting after the vote was announced.

Mrs. Wilkins' qualifications "outrank those of most of us," she charged.

She told *The Post* she left the national board over the same issue and "didn't want to be affiliated with an organization which has racial prejudice."

Mrs. Wilkins said she had not been officially notified of the club's action and refused comment.

Mrs. Mosier said she planned to tell Mrs. Wilkins in person Wednesday.

She expressed embarrassment over the incident and said she believes that if Mrs. Wilkins' membership were proposed again in six months she would be made a member.

She said the case has sparked a move to change the club's bylaws so that a majority vote in favor of admission—rather than three votes against an applicant—will determine membership.

She said the group's membership includes members of some minority groups and that the club's annual scholarship recently was awarded to a Japanese girl. ("Press Women Resign" 3)

The story that appeared on the third page of the *Denver Post* the following day was headlined "Ban on Membership Shocking to Negro":

A Negro newspaperwoman who was refused membership in the Colorado Press Women said Wednesday she was "shocked" by the organization's action.

"It just doesn't seem possible this would happen in Colorado," said Mrs. Betty Wilkins, 3681 E. 31st Ave.

Mrs. Wilkins is Denver society editor for *The Call,* Negro weekly published in Kansas City, Mo., and distributed throughout the West.

TWO MEMBERS QUIT

She is the first Negro to seek membership in the organization, made up of newspaperwomen, free lance writers and others in allied fields.

Five "no" votes were cast against Mrs. Wilkins in a secret ballot Saturday at a Denver meeting attended by about 20 of the group's 100 members.

The organization's bylaws provide that three "no" votes rule out membership.

Two members immediately resigned over the incident, charging that Mrs. Wilkins was rejected because of her race.

"I entered the journalistic field with the belief that this was one of the more liberal professions—and now to be faced with this," Mrs. Wilkins said. "I would have expected such treatment in Mississippi, but Colorado supposedly has a reputation of being a liberal mecca."

CHANGE SOUGHT

As a result of the incident several members of the organization have suggested changing the bylaws so that a majority vote in favor of admission, rather than three votes against a prospective member, would determine membership.

If this were done, Mrs. Wilkins said, she would permit her name to be proposed for membership again.

Understanding this humiliating episode in Denver media history is important in contextualizing the life and contributions of African American women, including Betty Wilkins. As Streitmatter notes throughout *Raising Her Voice,* the stories of deserving African American women journalists are told against the backdrop of prejudice and hatred in the larger society. The surprise and sadness that await researchers of African American life often mirror the surprise and sadness that Betty Wilkins confronted when she was rejected for membership in a women's journalism organization.

The bylaws of the Colorado Press Women in 1960 dictated that if a candidate received more than three no votes, she would be rejected. Of the twenty women present on the day of the election, five voted against Wilkins in a secret ballot. Because of this case, the bylaws were changed the following year, allowing election by simple majority. There are no public records that disclose whether Wilkins ever reapplied or was admitted (there are no membership lists that date to the 1960s), but her daughter, Margaret Wilkins-Fields, believes Wilkins was eventually granted membership.

Streitmatter could be describing Wilkins when he writes, "From the early 1800s to today, the American woman of African descent has raised her voice in both the black and the white press. The research summarized in this book adds a new chapter to an evolving depiction of the African-American woman as a defiant, strong-minded, and independent individual who refused to be a silent victim" (*Raising Her Voice* 2–3). A Christian who believed in forgiveness, compassion, and equality, Wilkins persevered after the public rejection of her application. She worked for media organizations that included radio and newspapers; raised six children; remained active in her local congregation, Zion Baptist Church; and founded numerous social and service groups.

Wilkins could not believe that professional women in Colorado could reject her for membership in their organization. The pain she felt is similar to that Streitmatter describes of other African American women journalists, as is the courage that drove her to contribute to her community. As Streitmatter observes:

> The picture I paint is not always a pretty one. Each portrait is a case study of the triumph of the human spirit, but each is sketched against the backdrop of a society rife with prejudice, injustice, and hatred. It is precisely because of these factors that American historians have, until recent decades, largely ignored women of African descent. The chroniclers of this country's evolution—most of whom have been white men—generally have discounted black women as long-suffering victims who not only endured their oppression and degradation but passively submitted to it. Because of the prejudice against these women, they have been perceived as powerless and dismissed as unimportant. Only recently have researchers begun to document that, in reality, many African-American women steadfastly refused to accept their subjugation and, indeed, helped to shape this nation's history. During the last decade, scholars have documented that black women resisted the emotional, physical, and sexual oppression of slavery and that they provided important leadership in the anti-slavery, women's suffrage, and modern civil rights movements. (Ibid. 2)

Research into the life of Betty Wilkins was easier than other partial biographies for several reasons. First, *The Call* has been preserved in archives and is available on microfilm through interlibrary loan from several universities, including Colorado State University in Fort Collins. Second, I was able to locate several of Wilkins's children, and one in particular expressed great interest in preserving her mother's contributions to journalism. Streitmatter is correct, however, in noting that "searching for information about members of a minority group that has been denied its history can be difficult, frustrating, time-consuming—and fruitless." As he suggests, "Relatively few African-American newspapers have been preserved, and research libraries contain the personal papers of only a handful of black women" (Ibid. 6).

It is useful to embrace Streitmatter's conclusions, particularly his contention that "the history of the black press, grounded in a tradition of advocacy, is closely intertwined with the history of black America" (Ibid. 3). Wilkins was not just an African American journalist reporting the events of the day; she was an advocate for her community and wanted to make the world more welcoming to her children's generation. "She wanted to have something to do with Negro rights and making things better so that her children and everyone else's children didn't have to struggle," says Wilkins-Fields. "She would say that everything would be the same for everybody by and by" (e-mail to author, July 26, 2004).

Streitmatter argues that African American women journalists are success-ful because black men "historically have been relatively accepting of black women as coworkers" and black women "historically have been accustomed to being economically independent and self-sufficient" (*Raising Her Voice* 10). Black men, Wilkins-Fields comments, advocated for her mother and were "inspirational in her work. Afro-American men were supportive in every way, for it wasn't long before they noticed that to be on Betty's side was to be on the right side" (e-mail to author, July 26, 2004).

Wilkins was a friend of local politicians and ministers, including former Denver Mayor Wellington Webb, and she allied herself with local social and political causes. She solicited the help of nationally known African American leaders as well, including Jesse Jackson, Al Sharpton, and Ralph Abernathy, and was acquainted with celebrities and entertainers such as Mahalia Jackson.

Like many other media historians, Streitmatter notes the importance that religion and education have had on the lives of African American women. That was certainly true in the case of Wilkins, who had been a member of Zion Baptist Church in Denver for thirty-eight years at the time of her death in 1986 and long served as publicity chair for the church. "The lives of many of these women, like those of many American women of African descent, have been firmly anchored in the church, and they were drawn to journalism by a sense of religious mission" (*Raising Her Voice* 146), Streitmatter writes. Not surprisingly, when she was in Denver to enjoy the family reunion at the Aurora Reservoir, Wilkins would spend Saturday with her family and Sunday with her family in worship. "Having been a preacher's daughter, raised in the church, and taught to be active and not just a roll member, Mama stepped out on her faith daily," said Wilkins-Fields. "She would use her training as her backdrop when speaking to others and giving advice. She was always willing to do whatever it took to get the church through" (e-mail to author, July 26, 2004).

There is no doubt that Wilkins believed in the power of the pen or type-writer to right social injustice. Indeed, as Streitmatter suggests, African Amer-ican women are drawn to journalism because that profession has a "potential for helping to bring about racial reform. Since the first black newspaper was founded in 1827, the African-American press has served to sustain the spirit of its readers as they have endured the heavy burden of racial oppres-sion. African-American journalists have chronicled instances of physical and psychological abuse, interpreted policies that have veiled discrimination in housing and employment, and represented the conscience of the black com-munity" (*Raising Her Voice* 141).

Like Wilkins, many black women drawn to journalism defied the rigid genres in traditional news reporting. Because of her belief in the life-changing potential of journalistic writing and her desire to speak personally to readers, Wilkins rejected straight news stories and opted to write columns or influence the public through radio. "Contributing to the forces that attracted these strong-willed, independent-minded women to journalism," Streitmatter adds, "was a tradition much more pronounced in the black press than in the white: interpretive reporting. None of the women described in this book allowed herself to be confined to the limited scope of 'objective reporter.' Instead, each brought her own perspective to her work. Some wrote editorials, others wrote columns, and still others wrote what could be called intepretive news stories" (Ibid. 144–45).

Wilkins was born on March 31, 1919, in Braddock, Pennsylvania, and died October 2, 1986, one of the two children of the Rev. Thomas Reed and Bertha Lee Carpenter. As the October 8, 1986, program printed for her funeral at Zion Baptist Church states, "The early training in a Christian home, coupled with an abiding faith in God, provided her the stamina and spirit to succeed." Wellington Webb and other Denver dignitaries are listed as Wilkins's pallbearers. She was buried in Fort Logan National Cemetery in Denver.

In addition to journalism and community activism, Wilkins also raised six children. Gloria Josephine Williams Jackson died in 2002; Raymond L. Evans of Aurora, a funeral director and building and grounds supervisor for Zion Baptist Church, retired after thirty-two years with a brewing company and is also deceased; Robert Wendell Wilkins Jr. of Denver works for a moving company; Donald Eugene Wilkins also of Denver, a retired police officer and former chief petty officer with the U.S. Navy, works for a waste management company; Patricia Lynn Wilkins; and Margaret Wilkins-Fields of Cleburne, Texas, is a technician and secretary in a cardiac intensive care unit and a graduate of the Dallas Institute of Mortuary Service.

As generations of Wilkins's family interacted at the reunion and reminisced about her, it became clear how important family is to all of them. An excerpt from the funeral program reads, "It was often said that 'one might be smarter to unleash hell and all its fury rather than bother one of Betty's kids.'" Wilkins was married three times, to Raymond L. Evans Sr. in 1934, with whom she had two children before their divorce; to Robert Wilkins in 1946, with whom she had four children; and to Harvey Bender, whom she married in 1979 and who is listed as a survivor. At the time of her death, she had twenty-one grandchildren and seventeen great-grandchildren.

Wilkins had little formal education, although she was a demonstrably strong writer. She attended the Emily Griffith Opportunity School and Wilberforce University and graduated from the Denver Opportunity School of Journalism in 1957. Her media career was rich and varied. She hosted a two-hour gospel show on KFML Radio in Denver; was the Denver editor for *The Call* for eighteen years; was a society columnist for KDKO Radio; and was also a society editor for the *Denver Weekly News* for fifteen years, reporting church, civic, and community events. In the funeral notice, *Weekly News* publisher Freeman (Cosmo) Harris recalled, "When Betty joined me, I got more than a columnist. I was given a mother, a friend, and a hard worker."

Wilkins's children often—perhaps inadvertently—played a role in her media success. When she was a guest on the radio gospel show, she had to persuade one of her sons, usually Donald, to drive her to Twenty-third Street and Broadway on Sundays at 4 A.M.—and then wait for her to finish the broadcast. "This started her Sunday mornings in good fashion," Wilkins-Fields comments (e-mail to author, July 26, 2004). The children also delivered newspapers that included her stories to black churches in Denver. Wilkins's son, Raymond Evans, recalls that he and his siblings walked or biked to the churches and left stacks of newspapers on front steps (interview with author, Aug. 19, 2003).

Wilkins was also extensively involved in her community. She was president of the Sophisticates Social and Civic Club, which raised money for scholarships for girls from single-parent homes, provided aid for seniors, and made food and clothing available to the needy; vice president of the Astro Jets, a social and fundraising organization devoted to education; a member of the Jane Jefferson Democratic Club, Denver mayor's Council on Human Relations, Bronze Daughters of America, Pond Lilly Club, LaBella Art and Literary Club, and Delta Mothers and Patrons Club; founder of the State Association of Colored Women's Clubs; and a past president of the Denver Federation of Colored Women's Clubs. She also belonged to the Negro Council of Women (sometimes referred to as the Council of Negro Women).

In addition, Wilkins had membership in the Denver Press Club, Zion Circle Seven, and Denver Beauty Guild; served as a black delegate for the Democratic Party in 1968 and 1972 and a committeewoman in East Denver for twenty years; chaired volunteers for the United Negro College Fund; and was a member of the charter committee for the Syl Morgan-Smith annual awards program and a life member and public relations chair of the National Association for the Advancement of Colored People.

Her service as a delegate for the Democratic Party is especially significant. Few African Americans were as invested in state and national politics as

Wilkins was. "Use the phrase 'black delegate' in the book," Wilkins-Fields urges. "This was a hard-earned title during that time. This was a time when blacks were just being accepted and allowed to participate in politics openly" (e-mail to author, July 25, 2004).

Wilkins's awards were as plentiful as her memberships. She won the Syl Morgan Smith Community Award Trophy (1976), a public relations award from the Astro Jets (1977), the Miss Bronze Daughters Award (1958), the Robert L. Vaden Award (1972), the Harriet Tubman Distinguished Service Award (1973), a woman of the year award (1972), a community award from the Metropolitan Club (1979), and a hall of fame award from May D&F, a department store where she worked for many years (1980).

Finally, Wilkins founded the Ten Best Dressed Black Women of Colorado organization to "lift the Black woman's self-esteem," according to the funeral program. Publications describing the group lauded the women as those "who are dressed correctly at all times for all occasions." Her funeral program cites her as saying, "Beauty is beauty, and Black women are indeed beautiful." For twenty-eight years she selected the best-dressed black women for *The Call* and *Denver Weekly News* and, ultimately, staged an elaborate production for the competition. "Never again," reads the funeral program, "would beautiful Black women be intimidated by callous [*sic*] print and electronic media which failed to acknowledge their presence and accomplishments."

During several interviews in the summer of 2004, Evans described his mother, their relationship, and her contributions to the communities she served. Most important, he talked about the kind of person Wilkins was:

> She was first at everything. She was the proudest woman in the world. We had the right bringing up. She raised us so that we would not be an embarrassment to anyone, and she taught us to stand on our own. A loving Christian woman, she guided every one of us. She was supportive of her kids and of her church. She showed us what it takes to make it. She wanted us to get an education and not expect anything from anyone. I couldn't ask for a better mother than the one I had. She taught us not to wait for anyone to give you anything.

Wilkins-Fields and her siblings may not fully understand their mother's significance to journalism history. "Thank you," Wilkins-Fields says, however, "for finding my mother to be so interesting and wanting to make journalism students of the future aware of her" (e-mail to author, July 24, 2004). Betty Wilkins will not be remembered as only a journalist. She was also a committed activist who transformed her community and worked for equality for all disenfranchised people. "She never liked the title or label of 'activist,' but indeed she was one," observes Wilkins-Fields. "She would just do things that she saw or thought needed doing . . . Mom did things with such grace" (e-mail to author, July 26, 2004).

This description of Betty Wilkins symbolizes the lives of other African American women who built careers and fostered social change while they worked for newspapers during the civil rights movement. The newspapers and radio stations for which Wilkins worked were "alternative" to those who study traditional, corporate-owned, metropolitan dailies and contemporary radio stations but not for her and the rest of African American community. Her place in media history is secured because of her activism and contributions to journalism. It is likely, however, that had Betty Willkins been able to attend the July gathering of her extended and extensive family, she would consider them as her greatest legacy.

The snapshots of women of the alternative press in this chapter are symbols for the many women who built careers and fostered social change while working for newspapers. The short biographies are in no way inclusive, although they are representative and suggest the range of age, racial and ethnic identity, and political and social opinions held by women who championed a particular cause. In the case of Betty Wilkins, the publications for which she worked were not "alternative" in any sense of that word, although her role as an activist is reason enough to include her in this chapter. Phyllis Austin and Caroline Nichols Churchill, however, are crusaders who allied themselves with particular newspapers that are considered alternative and who believed that the press is an effective tool for political, social, and cultural change. Hazel Brannon Smith relayed an alternative message in traditional newspapers that were significant community voices.

6

The Lesbian Press

History was made February 13, 2004, at San Francisco City Hall when Del Martin, eighty-three, and Phyllis Lyon, seventy-nine, took their wedding vows and became the first same-sex couple to be officially married in the United States. A group of twenty, many in tears, watched as the two women who have been together for five decades wed. The wedding was made possible by Mayor Gavin Newsom, who said San Francisco should take the lead in providing marriage rights to gays and lesbians.

Many newspaper accounts mentioned that Martin and Lyon had been gay rights activists throughout their lives, although few related the contribution the two women made to a lesbian magazine, *The Ladder,* which profited from the women's journalistic experience. Martin had been a reporter for the *San Francisco Chronicle* while in high school and had taken journalism courses at San Francisco State College; Lyon had been editor of the *Daily Californian,* the University of California at Berkeley's newspaper. Graduating with a journalism degree in 1946, Lyon then covered the police and city hall beats for the *Chico* (California) *Enterprise.* Later, she edited two trade journals.

This chapter discusses five lesbian publications: *Vice Versa, The Ladder, Focus: A Journal for Lesbians, Sinister Wisdom,* and *Lesbian Connection.* What it cannot possibly do is profile all the courageous, determined, committed women who founded lesbian publications without society's support and with few (if any) advertisers. Their stories are more interesting than the histories of publications, unless one remembers that the publications resulted from collectives of editors and readers in the emerging lesbian community.

The lesbian publications featured in this chapter are the legacies of women who defied those who said they did not have enough experience, enough money, or a broad enough readership to succeed. In many cases the publications failed, but for a time they were beacons for women who struggled with their sexual identities and were determined to build a broader, more politically responsive community.

It is important to note that not all lesbian magazines suffered financial difficulties. The editor of *Lesbian Connection,* Margy Lesher, said, "I started *Lesbian Connection* back in '74, and I would have to say that while money is always a challenge, we've basically been fairly successful financially" (e-mail to author, Sept. 5, 2001). The editors were requesting a $27 donation for an individual subscription by 2004; the publication remains free to readers who choose not to pay or cannot do so. Most lesbian publications, however, struggled financially, and financial constraints often led to in-fighting among editors and occasionally to the demise of the publications.

Although under threat in an inhospitable economic climate, lesbian publications often succeeded, in part because they belong to a broader tradition of alternative newspapers, magazines, newsletters, and journals. David Armstrong writes that the "history of feminist media and the media of lesbian feminists and gay men inspired by the women's movement closely paralleled that of other alternative media: There developed a creative core of radical outlets, limited in resources but significant in influence" (*A Trumpet to Arms* 226). His summary is accurate, both in its reference to the limited financial resources most editors faced and the significant impact of the publications on the gay-lesbian-bisexual-transgender (GLBT) community.

Critics such as Armstrong and Jennie Ruby have commented extensively on the manner in which alternative media fill an information gap and attract readers who have been marginalized or made invisible by the mainstream press. Ruby, for example, discusses *off our backs,* a radical-feminist monthly news journal in Washington, D.C., that was founded in 1970. She considers such publications important specifically because they "provide an alternative to the mainstream suppression of women's news, women's actions, and women's lives" ("Off Our Backs" 52).

Rodger Streitmatter also comments on the ways in which lesbian publications often resembled those initiated by other marginalized groups, both in the motives of the founding editors and the content and marketing of the publications. He also focuses on another distinctive contribution of publications for lesbians and gays as they sought to provide an accessible platform for as many readers as possible:

> *Vice Versa* also was similar to the early African-American press, as well as the women's suffrage and women's liberation presses, in its attempt to provide an open forum for diverse voices from within the community. Just as African-American and feminist journals allowed their respective audiences the voices the mainstream press denied them, this historic lesbian magazine welcomed readers to express themselves—even to the point of sometimes sacrificing writing quality. [The editor and publisher of *Vice Versa*] never succeeded in attracting as many contributors as she would have liked, but her publication established, nonetheless, the open forum as a central element in the lesbian and gay press. (*Unspeakable* 16)

Until the 1990s, the gay and lesbian press has been neglected by media scholars (even those specializing in the history of alternative media), although it shares numerous ideologies and goals with African American, Native American and feminist publications.[1] The oversight is particularly ironic in light of the sheer number of gay and lesbian publications and readers. By the late 1980s, total circulation for gay publications in America had topped one million; in the 1990s, approximately 850 publications boasted more than two million subscribers (Ibid. 279, 339).

Although it is true that publications targeted to gay males historically were glossier, had more consistent advertising income, and claimed higher circulations than lesbian periodicals, the number of lesbian newsletters, newspapers, and magazines also grew significantly between 1947 and 1994. According to *Our Own Voices: A Directory of Lesbian and Gay Periodicals,* however, the total circulation of the lesbian press in 1975 was only fifty thousand, less than the readership of *The Advocate* alone. Gay male publications at the time claimed fifteen thousand subscribers (Ibid. 158). As Streitmatter comments, "By the mid-1970s, the gay male press was becoming a financially lucrative institution; while the lesbian press remained a labor of love—and impoverishment" (Ibid. 185).

It is important not to measure the impact of the lesbian press in terms of circulation figures and profit margins, though. Nor should it be diminished with a simplistic comparison to the gay male press. Joan Nestle, cofounder of Lesbian Herstory Archives in New York, has argued persuasively that the impact of the lesbian press "cannot be measured in mere numbers." An omen of the approaching revolution, early lesbian publications altered forever the lives of women who resided in what Nestle calls "isolated communities from coast to coast" (Ibid.).

This chapter chronicles the origin, growth, and disappearance of four significant lesbian publications—*Vice Versa, The Ladder, Focus: A Journal for*

Lesbians, Sinister Wisdom—over a nearly fifty-year period. It also includes a brief description of *Lesbian Connection,* a publication that in 2004 celebrated its thirtieth anniversary. These magazines illustrate varied genres in lesbian publishing history and represent three distinctly different geographical areas. As symbols of the efforts of lesbian journalists and creative writers, the publications represent mimeographed newsletters, news and issues magazines, literary journals, and activist publications that began to gain a loyal readership. They also symbolize emerging lesbian communities on the West Coast, in the East, and in the Deep South and span the inauspicious beginnings of the lesbian press and its rapid growth.

The chapter also examines their reason for being and traces their achievements, placing them in a broader cultural context. It separates their influence from that of dominant lesbian news magazines such as *Lesbian Tide;* more erotic publications such as *Bad Attitude, Lesbian Contradiction* or *On Our Backs;* and newspapers such as *Lavender Woman.* It is important to note that the editors of these publications were usually white and concerned with representing their own interests, and the publications often floundered because of dissension among the editors as much as because of the lack of advertising support or a reliable circulation base.

Although a few gay publications profoundly influenced public policy (especially during the 1960s), lesbian newsletters and magazines, although often tied to politically active organizations, existed primarily to help individuals come to terms with a homophobic world and provide social connections and essential support systems. Less financially secure than their counterparts in the gay male magazine industry, lesbian publications were labors of love and rarely survived.

Vice Versa, The Ladder, Focus: A Journal for Lesbians, and *Sinister Wisdom* were designed to provide a forum for lesbians who, before they set out to change the world, sought to believe in themselves and in each other. It is true that magazines such as *The Ladder* listed news events and promoted rallies and other gatherings that both united the lesbian community and spawned activism, but their primary goals were support for a new and fragile lesbian community and encouragement for isolated, closeted lesbians scattered across the nation.

Providing education, encouraging positive self-identity, spurring political action, and building community motivated editors of early gay magazines, such as *ONE* and *Mattachine Review,* just as they did editors of other alternative media.[2] There are, however, significant differences between the gay-lesbian press and the alternative media: their emphasis on design, use of visual images, high level of internal editorial discord, merging of advertising and editorial content, desire to inform and amuse, and use of language unique to their community and "largely unintelligible to heterosexual society" (Ibid. 112–14).

In some ways the lesbian press offers an even more striking contrast to alternative publications. Lesbian editors and writers, for example, could not agree about whether it was more advantageous for individual lesbians to assimilate into the existing culture or rebel against it. Such ideological differences understandably led to disastrous infighting and fragmented editorial purpose. Although they provided an open forum for diverse voices, as did the alternative press, early lesbian publications began as social conduits rather than catalysts for broad social activism. Furthermore, many advertisers shunned the publications because they represented small circulations among women struggling for economic equality and contained what some advertisers considered immoral content. Newsstand sales for lesbian publications were unthinkable in the 1940s and 1950s.

Just as damaging to the survival of lesbian publications was the fact that even during the social revolution of the 1960s—ostensibly a period when the work of lesbian editors and writers would appear less radical—the lesbian press found only sparse acceptance in mainstream women's publications. Lesbians continued to be seen as a politically and economically weak subgroup of the feminist movement.

Lesbians found little acceptance by publications, whether those they assumed would be sympathetic to their cause or those that were mainstream. Heterosexual feminists, however, found homes in New Left media during the 1960s and in their own periodicals in the late 1960s and early 1970s. By the late 1970s, feminist issues began making their way into popular women's magazines as well. Five feminist publications in 1968 grew to 228 newsletters, newspapers, and magazines by 1971. By 1973, there were 560 feminist publications, including *Ms.*, and they often imitated the "confrontational tone of leftist underground newspapers" (Beasley and Gibbons, *Taking Their Place* 7). Still, feminists did not necessarily embrace lesbian concerns.

Mainstream newspapers also ignored lesbian issues in their women's pages during the 1950s and 1960s and also in their thinly disguised "lifestyle" pages during the 1970s. "Lesbian issues, alternatives to conventional marriage, and feminism as it affected women of color fit poorly, if at all, within the confines of lifestyle/women's pages" (Ibid. 23).

In spite of these obstacles, however, the lesbian press has survived. It continues to build community, document social struggle, and give a voice to lesbians from coast to coast.

Vice Versa

Two publications, *Vice Versa* and *The Ladder,* are called the "first" magazines for lesbians. Both were born during a ten-year period during which lesbians had been given what literary critic Lillian Faderman calls a "new outlaw status" (*Surpassing* 20). Love between women, Faderman comments, was considered a "disease" during the 1940s and 1950s, and women "who were professedly lesbian generally internalized those views. This was reflected in their own literature, which was full of self-doubts and self-loathing until the 1960s" (Ibid.).

Heterosexuality was so normative after World War II, in fact, that a lesbian's positive experiences with another woman would rarely displace her internalized societal expectations. Even after lesbians had managed businesses and supported the war effort, they could hardly conceive of homes without men. Because earning a living was a logical priority for middle-class lesbians, any hint of being gay jeopardized those livelihoods. As Trisha Franzen writes, "Most of these women had only seen or heard of a future at home with husband and children. Though they felt they wanted to be independent, have adventures, and love women, neither their home communities nor the larger culture provided words or positive images of women doing what they themselves wanted to do" (*Spinsters and Lesbians* 104).

Given the prevailing cloud of cultural disapproval, therefore, the appearance of *Vice Versa* was nothing short of miraculous. Certainly, its creator had no intention of launching a controversial social movement. She was lonely and hoped the publication would help her make contact with other lesbians and prevent having to rely on the bar scene. During the 1940s and 1950s, lesbian bars were often raided and their patrons were harassed and even raped by police; those women dressed in men's clothing were sometimes arrested.

Vice Versa, typed and mimeographed by "Lisa Ben" (an anagram of "lesbian"), was printed monthly in Los Angeles from June 1947 to February 1948. Neither Lisa Ben's name nor address appeared in the publication. The title came from the fact that homosexuality was considered a "vice" and from the fact that the lesbian lifestyle was the opposite ("versa") of the established norm (Streitmatter, "*Vice Versa*" 5). In her first issue, Lisa Ben explained the purpose behind her effort:

> Have you ever stopped to enumerate the many different publications to be found on the average news stands? . . .

> Yet, there is one kind of publication which would, I am sure, have a great deal of appeal to a definite group. Such a publication has never appeared on the stands. News stands carrying the crudest kind of magazines or pictorial pamphlets appealing to the vulgar would find themselves severely censured were they to display this other type of publication. Why? Because *Society* decreed it thus.
>
> Hence, the appearance of VICE VERSA, a magazine dedicated, in all seriousness, to those of us who will never quite be able to adapt ourselves to the iron-bound rules of Convention. ("In Explanation" 1)

The publication, which Wayne R. Dynes called "an early clandestine effort" (*Encyclopedia* 104), died after only nine issues when its editor, sole reporter, and publisher was given a new job and had less time to work on the newsletter. Moreover, she had accomplished what she had hoped: "I was discovering what the lesbian lifestyle was all about, and I wanted to live it rather than write about it. So that was the end of *Vice Versa*" (Streitmatter, "*Vice Versa*" 8).

As a gesture of commitment to Lisa Ben's closeted community, *Vice Versa* deserves its place as one of this country's two early lesbian publications. As the editors of *The Alyson Almanac: A Treasury of Information for the Gay and Lesbian Community* described Lisa Ben's work, "She typed each issue manually, making as many carbons as possible, during her lunch break at RKO Studios. Copies were then distributed . . . *Vice Versa* was remarkably open for its time: The subtitle read 'America's gayest magazine'" (21). Ben, who lives in Burbank and uses her pseudonym, recalls:

> I had an awful lot of fun putting it together. I would use carbon paper, because in those days we didn't have such things as a Xerox or even a ditto machine. And I would put in the original and then seven copies, and that's all the typewriter would take legibly.
>
> And I would type it out during working hours. I never had enough work—I was a fast typist. And my boss would say, "Well, I don't care what you do if your work is done. But I don't want you to sit there and knit or read a magazine. I want you to look busy." (Brandt, "Lisa Ben" 8)

When she finished printing the first few copies, Ben gave them to friends and asked them to pass the copies along. "I never sold it," she says. "I just gave it to my friends, because I felt that it was a labor from the heart, and I shouldn't get any money for it" (Ibid. 9).

The Ladder

Lisa Ben's "labor from the heart" preceded *The Ladder,* a longer-lasting, more influential publication, by only a few years. Soon after *Vice Versa* disappeared, the women of San Francisco's Daughters of Bilitis chapter created *The Ladder,* which was published continuously for sixteen years.[3] Founded in October 1955, the group produced its first issue in October 1956. The title of the new publication "was chosen because it was seen as a means lesbians could use to climb out of the 'well of loneliness' that Radclyffe Hall's popular novel had depicted as their plight" (Streitmatter, *Unspeakable* 22).

By this time, homosexuals had become what Faderman calls a "particular target of persecution" (*Odd Girls* 140). The focus in America during the 1950s was on family values and loyalty to the status quo. Gays in the government and the military were outed and labeled communists or worse.

Leaders of Daughters of Bilitis, established as a social club, were Del Martin and Phyllis Lyon. They decided that their group, in addition to providing a sense of community, should dedicate itself to changing public attitudes about lesbians. Lyon served as the first editor of *The Ladder,* and in 1960 the governing board of the Daughters of Bilitis appointed Martin as coeditor.

Given the hostile political climate, it was, perhaps, understandable that in its early years *The Ladder* was mailed in a plain envelope to members of the Daughters of Bilitis. Well aware that they were treated with suspicion and sometimes open scorn by society, the group struggled desperately to encourage assimilation and emphasize that lesbians are normal, productive citizens. One of the stated purposes of the Daughters of Bilitis, which was composed predominantly of white, educated, middle-class women, was to promote "the integration of the homosexual into society by . . . advocating a mode of behaviour and dress acceptable to society." That integrationist statement appeared as part of four goals of the organization in all early issues of *The Ladder.*

Little by little, the leaders of the organization began to recognize that a lesbian's acceptance by society often came at the expense of her self-identity. As part of its activism, for example, the Daughters of Bilitis picketed the State Department in 1965 to call for gay rights at the Pentagon, White House, and other federal institutions. The group also picketed the federal building in San Francisco on July 3, 1968, demanding an end to governmental employment discrimination against gays and lesbians. The events subsequently were covered in *The Ladder.*

The Ladder's shift to a more militant position came too late, however, for many young lesbians unconcerned about public approval and determined to place blame where they believed it belonged: on a closed-minded society. Many abandoned the magazine. As Faderman explains, young lesbians "associated *The Ladder* with the politics of adjustment" (*Surpassing* 380). "There had been no existing groups that represented the ideals of these young activist lesbians," Faderman comments. "Despite their relatively militant rhetoric of the late 1960s, DOB and *The Ladder* could not recover from their conservative image, and they were seen as too poky for the new activists. . . . *The Ladder* stopped publication in 1972, not only because of internal difficulties but also because they had failed to appeal to younger women, who were more interested in the numerous militant gay and lesbian-feminist magazines that were now available" (*Odd Girls* 197). Faderman even cites one *Ladder* reader who in January 1988 called the publication an "old conservative rag" (*Surpassing* 384). Yet it is hard to discount the importance of *The Ladder* in the history of lesbian publications. The October 1961 issue celebrated the sixth anniversary of the organization that had begun in 1955 with eight women. By then, the Daughters of Bilitis had chapters in San Francisco, Los Angeles, New York and New Jersey.

In 1963, the organization called for a change, saying *The Ladder* should stop being merely a newsletter for members of the Daughters of Bilitis. Barbara Gittings, who had founded the New York chapter, became editor from 1963 to 1966. Under Gittings the publication allied itself with more militant gay civil rights groups and began to challenge prevalent views among psychiatrists, the clergy, and other professionals that homosexuality is an illness or sin that needs to be cured or eradicated. "We came," Gittings says, "to the position that the 'problem' of homosexuality isn't a problem at all. The problem is society" (Streitmatter, *Unspeakable* 51). As Kristin Gay Esterberg comments:

> The period from 1956 to 1965 showed enormous changes in *The Ladder* and the women who wrote for it. From its earliest years, when proclamations that lesbians were mentally ill or unnatural went virtually unchallenged, *The Ladder* grew into a forum for lesbians who wished to replace those conceptions with more positive images. From its earliest years, *The Ladder* shows the power of the psychiatric and medical professions to control the terms of the debate around homosexuality and their ability to cause enormous harm to many lesbian women. ("From Illness to Action" 78)

Early covers of *The Ladder* were line drawings with typed copy. As a result of Gittings's influence, however, the publication began to have more representative covers, including a photograph of two women holding hands (October

1964). Gittings also changed the name of the publication to *The Ladder: A Lesbian Review* in 1964.

After disagreement over editorial emphasis and other issues, Phyllis Lyon and Del Martin once again took the reins of *The Ladder* in September 1966. Citing a September 10, 1993, interview with Gittings, Streitmatter notes that one reason for the shift in editorial leadership was that Gittings disagreed with the leadership of Daughters of Bilitis about the "for adults only" disclaimer that always appeared on *The Ladder*'s cover and removed the wording without the group's consent. "[The organization] chastised Gittings for making such a radical change without their approval, and then hand stamped 'for adults only' on every copy before distributing them. After three-and-a-half years of such disputes, the old guard removed Gittings from the editor's position in 1966 and reverted to a more conformist editorial philosophy" ("Lesbian and Gay Press" 158).

In the fall of 1968, Barbara Grier ("Gene Damon") became editor of the publication that now featured articles, short stories, reviews, editorials, and columns. In 1970 she, too, broke with Daughters of Bilitis in an effort to create a more independent journal with activism at its center. By 1971 topics included butch-femme issues, lesbian activists in the women's movement, Angela Davis, and ethnic issues. The publication featured work by Georgia O'Keeffe and other well-known artists, musicians, and writers.

Predictably, financial difficulty plagued the publication. In the October–November 1968 issue, Damon made her first request for financial and editorial support ("Bluntly, we must have money" 33). "Don't wait until there is no LADDER to help" appeared on the inside back cover of the August–September 1969 issue. The plea was restated on the inside front cover in December–January 1970–71: "THE LADDER, though written, edited, and circulated by volunteer labor cannot survive without money. . . we need to keep alive the only real Lesbian magazine in the world."

In the April–May 1971 issue, Damon requested editorial help and financial support: "It's true, WE CAN'T stop publishing in terms of need—but we will have to if we run out of money. We are the only magazine in the country that deals honestly with the needs of the Lesbian, and the only women's liberation publication that deals honestly with all women" (4). Citing controversial content that made advertising difficult to solicit, she added, "We have no expense of any kind except the actual cost of the printing and binding and mailing of the magazine. Everything else is a labor or an expense given out of love. . . . We are also at the point where we can be forced to stop existing at all" (Ibid.).

As with numerous other lesbian publications, however, the pleas were to no avail. The final issue of *The Ladder*, August-September 1972, included an angry message from Damon: "After 16 complete continuous years of publication, there are to be no more issues. . . . To those of you who have supported us . . . we simply wish the best in the future. For those of you who have casually read us through the years, indeed sometimes intending to subscribe, but not ever quite getting around to it, we wish you whatever you deserve and leave it to your own consciences to decide just what that might be" (3).

The demise of *The Ladder* provides support for Streitmatter's assertion that marketing gay and lesbian publications was particularly challenging:

> Marketing the magazines was a problem as professional magazine distributors refused to touch a gay publication. . . . Despite their daunting commitments of time and energy that totaled more than forty hours a week, none of these journalists was paid. Finances were a recurring problem. The publications depended on the membership dues of their respective homosexual-rights organizations for financial support, because heterosexual-owned businesses refused to advertise in them. ("Lesbian and Gay Press" 144)

The Daughters of Bilitis printed only two hundred copies of the first issue of *The Ladder*, the mailing list consisting of other lesbians whom members knew personally. In spite of its inauspicious origin, *The Ladder* survived its early years and for a time became a unifying element in the fledgling lesbian community. Its success is traceable in large part to the fact that its original editors, Lyon and Martin, were trained journalists.[4]

The Ladder and its short-term predecessor *Vice Versa* inspired and united a group of women who desperately needed a social and political center. Both publications were important "first" lesbian magazines for quite different reasons. *Vice Versa* was the signature of one woman's search for connection with others like her, whereas *The Ladder* was a source of information for its growing lesbian audience. It represented not just one woman but a group united by conviction and committed to individual development and collective social change.

The Ladder did not set out to be a trailblazer as much as it did to be a service publication for lesbians, but its contributions have caused debate among media scholars. Some, such as Dynes, believe that it was primarily concerned with the emotional health of individual readers: "The pages of *The Ladder* reflected the priority that DOB attached to personal problems of the individual lesbian, especially the one living in isolation far from the subculture of the large cities. The magazine reported political news, but was never meant to be a political journal, and so the publishers shunned advocacy, devoting space instead to poetry, fiction, history and biography" (*Encyclopedia* 137). Others argue that articles in *The Ladder* dealt with controversial issues—such as lesbian parents, lesbians in heterosexual marriages, and lesbians dealing with job and salary concerns—that are profoundly political. Claire Potter comments that "Lesbian journals have always been political as well as cultural acts. Their editors created community with every word put on paper; each mailed edition was an attack on isolation and the social judgement of deviancy" (*The Lesbian Periodicals Index* vi).

Although designed to serve the needs of various groups, the editors of publications begun by the Daughters of Bilitis never lost sight of individual gay women who struggle daily with institutionalized prejudice. "My Daughter Is a Lesbian" in the July 1958 issue symbolizes that goal. Proud of her daughter, whom she describes as intelligent, strong and determined, Doris Lyles writes, "There are no two more normal persons alive than my daughter and her charming associate" (4).

By the time *The Ladder* ceased publication in 1972 it had been transformed from a chapter newsletter to a forty-five-page publication with a national and international circulation of approximately 3,800. The publication ran reviews, news, a calendar, short stories, and letters.

Since then, Grier and Donna J. McBride have produced *The Index to* The Ladder, making the publication more accessible to those interested in history, culture, literature and gay and lesbian theory. The full set of *The Ladder* was reissued with a complete index in 1975. In 1976 Grier also published *Lesbiana: Book Reviews from* The Ladder, *1966–1972*, and with Lee Stuart she produced the first edition of *The Lesbian in Literature: A Bibliography* in 1967, which was reprinted in 1981.

When *The Ladder* disappeared, editors of the *Amazon Quarterly*, founded in Oakland in 1972, stepped in to fill the void and asked all former *Ladder* subscribers for help. By the time it, too, ceased publication in 1975, numerous other lesbian publications had taken hold, including literary journals such as *Focus: A Journal for Lesbians*.

Focus

Focus: A Journal for Lesbians was preceded by a monthly, eight-page newsletter, *Maiden Voyage*. Appearing in 1969, the mimeographed *Maiden Voyage* was distributed until February 1970. At that point, two Daughters of Bilitis members in Boston created *Focus: A Journal for Gay Women*, which they produced on their own offset press. By March, *Maiden Voyage* had become *Focus: A Journal for Gay Women.*

Focus: A Journal for Lesbians was a pioneer publication in the quest for gay and lesbian rights that occurred in the United States during the 1960s and early 1970s. Following on the heels of more established and more prestigious publications such as *The Ladder, Focus: A Journal for Lesbians* began as the mouthpiece for the Boston chapter of Daughters of Bilitis but gained a reputation as an innovative collection of poetry, short stories, and essays by and about lesbians.

In celebration of the first five years of *Focus: A Journal for Gay Women,* the staff in December 1974 compiled a detailed history of the Boston chapter of Daughters of Bilitis, and it was with great pride that the editors and readers of *Focus* recognized their parent organization. By noting the success of the group, members were also paying tribute to their own courage in the face of public ridicule and hostility. While pushing for social acceptance, lesbian readers had begun to unite and be more confident about their self-worth.

When the Massachusetts Daughters of Bilitis group was founded in 1969, there was no gay movement in the Boston area. To gain readers, lesbian activists in the area mailed fliers to the area subscribers of *The Ladder* and advertised in a local underground newspaper, *Boston after Dark,* and on a talk show on what was then WMEX radio. At the time, according to the December 1974 issue of *Focus,* "Virtually everyone involved in the gay movement used pseudonyms," and members were "afraid of getting into trouble if they rented a post office box for the group" (2).

In December 1973, subscribers could buy the magazine for $3.50 a year—$4.50 if they elected to receive the publication in a brown wrapper. Most early covers featured innocuous line drawings. In October 1973, for example, the cover illustration alluded to the popular *Peanuts* cartoon strip by Charles Schulz and featured Lucy and a friend saying, "Who needs Charlie Brown?" Other covers featured benign photographs, such as the gay pride flag in July 1973.

Soon after, though, the activist focus of the literary journal became hard to miss. Coverage of timely news and schedules of local gay events were taken over by the *Gay Community News* in 1973, freeing *Focus: A Journal for Gay Women* to devote itself to encouraging civil rights for gays. In February of that year, the editors reproduced the cover of the December-January 1969–70 issue of *The Ladder* in order to stress the history and solidarity of the lesbian community. That issue also included a quotation from Radclyffe Hall's controversial novel *The Well of Loneliness,* which attested to the growing numbers of visible lesbians and a culture that "dare not disown" them.[5]

Gradually, editors and readers became vocal advocates of gay rights. The March 1971 issue quoted one woman as saying, "We had gotten used to the smell of moth balls, the darkness of that lonely closet somehow seemed more comfortable than putting our jobs and families on the line" (10). By the mid-1970s, women were putting their jobs and families, as well as their reputations, firmly on the line. Having celebrated their anniversary with a party on December 8, the editors began to create covers that reflected the group's growing pride and public visibility. In 1977 a line drawing of women kissing appeared, and by 1979 a nude woman was featured.

With the December 1977 issue, the name of the publication, and its emphasis, changed. *Focus: A Journal for Lesbians* was born, and the magazine became even more literary and political in emphasis.

In February 1980, *Focus: A Journal for Lesbians* and the Daughters of Bilitis cut financial ties, and editors devoted themselves to particular controversial topics for each issue. The March–April 1981 issue, for example, was a "Special Sexuality Issue."

Finances, however, remained a constant pressure, and in the September–October 1983 issue, editors advised, "*Focus,* America's oldest literary journal for lesbians—and, therefore, the world's oldest literary journal for lesbians—needs subscribers." There was also a P.S.: "Monetary donations in any amount are always appreciated, too" (6). The plea mirrors those in other centrally important lesbian publications such as *The Ladder* and *Sinister Wisdom,* where requests for financial support from the editors were common. It is not surprising that *Focus: A Journal for Lesbians* disappeared. It is far more surprising—with its limited resources and the limited editorial experience of its editors—that it persevered for more than a decade and waged a successful war against rising publication prices, competition, falling circulation and social disdain.

Decreased circulation, unpredictable advertising revenue, and increasing publication costs, however, took their toll. In 1983 the message on the inside front cover read: "To Our Readers: Somewhat to our surprise, we have finally come to grips with our financial situation and, perhaps even more important, with our own fatique [sic]. After twelve years in continuous publication, FOCUS is ceasing with this issue . . . thank you AND GOOD-BYE." It was the end of one of the most supportive lesbian publications in the early gay rights movement. Although it remained a low-gloss publication throughout its history, *Focus: A Journal for Lesbians* had evolved into far more than an organizational newsletter. It lasted for twelve years, and its editors produced 112 issues between March 1971 to November–December 1983.

Focus: A Journal for Lesbians weathered identity crises, financial turmoil, and a changing cultural landscape during more than a decade of publication. As Potter observes, "While some themes remain constant, each decade of Lesbian publications reflected the influences of a changing time, a history of a people within a history of a country" (*The Lesbian Periodicals Index* vi).

By the mid-1970s, *Focus: A Journal for Lesbians* and *The Ladder* had made lesbian publications far more common. The lesbian community had become more connected and more politically aware. What would be the next challenge? What about a lesbian magazine designed, written and published in the Deep South? The possibility, as one of the founding editors later said, was like "raising pineapples on the North Pole."

Sinister Wisdom

Sinister Wisdom began in February 1976, when Harriet Desmoines and Catherine Nicholson received a telephone call inviting them to a lesbian writer's workshop in Knoxville, Tennessee. As Desmoines wrote in the spring 1977 issue, "Catherine and I brazenly announced that we were starting a magazine. The women appeared to believe us, and we taped ideas for the first issue" (99).

In addition to being concerned that neither knew much about publishing, they also questioned the wisdom of starting a publication in Charlotte, North Carolina. In an editor's note in the spring of 1977, Desmoines commented, "Earlier this year it dawned on us that we were publishing a journal of Lesbian writing in the hometown of 'Praise the Lord' television network and that this was somewhat akin to raising pineapples on the North Pole. Our solution? Move to New York, move to Boston, move to L.A., move to San Francisco! Finally, we decided to just stay where we were. For one thing, it freaks out people in the Bay area. For another, most Lesbians live, love, work and politic outside the metropolitan centers" (100). Thus, for July 1976, volume one, number one, the editors decided on *Sinister Wisdom* as the publication's title, taking the name from *The Female Man* by Joanna Russ, and the first lesbian publication in the land of magnolias and mint juleps was born. Little did they know that by 1987 *Sinister Wisdom* would call itself a "political journal for radical lesbian feminists" (*The Alyson Almanac* 241).

Desmoines and Nicholson informed readers in the first issue, "We're lesbians living in the South. We're white; sometimes unemployed, sometimes working part-time. We're a generation apart . . . *Sinister Wisdom* is also our political action. We believe that writing of a certain consciousness has greater impact when it's collected, when several voices give weight, harmony, and countermelody to the individual message" (3–4). Introducing the next issue, they dedicated the publication to "lesbians, who have been without faces, without voices, without a validating herstory" (72). The masthead promised essays, fiction, poetry, drama, reviews, and graphics and stated as its mission the development of the lesbian imagination in politics and art.

Touting itself as *Sinister Wisdom: A Journal of Words and Pictures for the Lesbian Imagination in All Women,* the publication began to enlist artists and writers such as Audre Lorde, Rita Mae Brown, and Adrienne Rich; Mab Segrest provided assistance with editing. The fall 1976 issue was dedicated to Barbara Grier, who, after twenty years at *The Ladder* became editor of the Naiad Press, the largest feminist-lesbian press in the United States.

Sinister Wisdom survived its first year. In the spring 1977 issue Desmoines wrote that the publication had begun "at point zero: isolation and ignorance. We decided to make a magazine because we wanted more Lesbian writing, we wanted more friends, and we wanted to express the power we felt building up inside ourselves, that was both us and not-us. (We didn't want much, just everything)" (99). Defying lack of experience and geography, the group had not only survived but also prevailed.

By the summer of 1978, *Sinister Wisdom* was printing the work of reputable writers such as Judy Grahn, Jane Rule, Carol Seajay, Andrea Dworkin, and Gloria Anzaldua, but there were warnings of financial problems. In the summer 1978 issue, the editors included a plea for subscriptions and urged, "Without [you], *Sinister Wisdom* dies of a broken pocket book" (2).

In the spring of 1980, *Sinister Wisdom* announced new editors, Michelle Cliff and Adrienne Rich, and a new place of publication, Amherst, Massachusetts. Cliff wrote the "Notes for a Magazine" for volume 17 in the 1981 issue and promised a revolutionary commitment to social revolution (2–4). "In their first issue, in 1976," Rich added, "Harriet and Catherine described the founding of *Sinister Wisdom* as a political action. We reaffirm that purpose here" (4). With that began the revolutionary contribution of *Sinister Wisdom.* In a new emphasis on the disenfranchised within the lesbian community itself, the editors began to focus on specific topics. For example, a combined issue (number 22–23) was entitled "A Gathering of Spirit" and featured Native Americans. Melanie Kaye/Kantrowitz continued that tradition through the number 29–30 issues with a "Jewish Women's Anthology," a 336-page effort.

In volume 24, published in the fall of 1983, Cliff and Rich, who had devoted two years to the publication, resigned. Rich, who had rheumatoid arthritis for thirty-three years, said she was in too much pain to continue her editorial responsibilities: "I have been slowed down by physical pain and its impact on the spirit" (3). Kaye/Kantrowitz and Michaele Uccella took over as editors of a publication that would ultimately boast a circulation of four thousand.

The new editors Kaye/Kantrowitz and Uccella wrote in volume 25 of winter 1984, "We will try, during our time with *Sinister Wisdom,* to make her—like a good dyke—both tough and sensitive" (3). By late 1985, Kaye/Kantrowitz was the sole editor and publisher. When she left the publication in the winter of 1987 with volume 31, she described trying to bring "great emphasis on class issues and on the experience of working class women" (3).

Sinister Wisdom then was headed by Elana Dykewomon, who published in the thirty-third issue what she called "Notes for a Magazine: A Dyke Geography." Taking over in the fall of 1987, Dykewomon wrote, "*Sinister Wisdom* is a place. A country. To which lesbians add their own villages, their own geography, issue by issue" (volume 33, 3). Dykewomon produced topical collections dealing with friendship, the disabled, Italian American women, class, lesbians of color, and lesbian relationships. Berkeley, California, became the place of publication.

In the summer 1991, issues 43–44 celebrated the history of the publication from 1976 to 1991 with a "Fifteenth Anniversary Retrospective." The issue was, Dykewomon wrote, "a marker of our movement: small and bright, bobbing in a difficult channel, sometimes obscured by waves and weather, showing direction" (5). By that point the publication had been through seven editors, six changes of address, and what the editor called "all those Republican years" (8). Its 368-page issue was testimony to the survival of the community it represented. In a letter for the issue, Harriet (Desmoines) Ellenberger, reminisced:

> We began it in Charlotte, North Carolina (a more unlikely place you could not pick) in utter (and I do mean utter) isolation. . . . It was an act of love. . . . For me, *Sinister Wisdom* was never really about lesbian community. It was never really about art or politics either (since, for starters, the distinction between the two is not clear to me). It was about transformation, nothing less. It was about releasing the power of passionate love between women through language and image, words and pictures, with the intent of saving the earth and her creatures, including ourselves, from destruction. (8–9)

With issue 46 (spring 1992), *Sinister Wisdom* became a tax-exempt corporation and seemed financially solvent. By issue 51 (winter 1993–94), however, the warnings began again: "This place, *Sinister Wisdom,* is in danger of closing down" (5). Like *Focus: A Journal for Lesbians* and *The Ladder, Sinister*

Wisdom could not withstand falling subscription rates and rising publication costs. It, too, disappeared, but not without making substantial contributions to the history of gay publications in America.

Lesbian Connection

Lesbian Connection began when one or more women of lesbian collective Ambitious Amazons realized they needed to communicate with a broader audience. "It occurred to us that no matter how many artists created lesbian albums, books, or posters, or how many activists organized lesbian groups, centers, or conferences, it all would be basically pointless if other lesbians had no way of knowing these things existed," said Margy Lesher, editor of *Lesbian Connection*. "In an attempt to fill this need for a worldwide lesbian communications network, we decided to start *Lesbian Connection*, a free worldwide magazines for lesbians" (correspondence with author, Dec. 9, 2003).

The group decided that the magazine should be written by readers, not editors who saw themselves as "caretakers of this forum" and not as writers (Ibid.) In October 1974 in East Lansing, Michigan, the women mimeographed and mailed four hundred copies of the first issue. That number grew to 1,200 copies by the third issue and then to 12,500 copies by 1982. Today, the editors print more than twenty-five thousand copies of each issue. *Lesbian Connection* has a circulation of twenty thousand and an annual budget of $400,000. Most of the funds that support *Lesbian Connection* today come from donations, with less than 20 percent coming from advertising.

In 1975 the women calculated that each pressrun of *Lesbian Connection* cost approximately $110 to produce; as of 2003, the estimate was more than $70,000. Although the publication boasts that it is "Free to Lesbians Worldwide," the "suggested donation" is $4.50 a copy. Following the request on the cover is the phrase "more if you can, less if you can't."

The only original founder still involved with *Lesbian Connection*, Lesher and her partner were touring the country in 1973 and were frustrated by the lack of information about lesbian communities in the cities they visited. The next year, trying to publicize a lesbian conference, Lesher realized how hard it was to advertise a local event in national lesbian publications. "We saw a need for getting the word out, across the continent, about what lesbians were doing," she commented in 1999. "Though none of us considered ourselves writers, we came up with the idea of starting a publication" (e-mail to author, Dec. 8, 1999).

The editors decided that *Lesbian Connection* would be a forum for readers.

"We envisioned it as a place to be able to announce what was going on for lesbians, which would encourage more things to happen for lesbians," said Lesher. "We wanted to try to encourage the growth of the lesbian movement" (unpublished history 1999).

Aware of the financial difficulties of other lesbian publications, Lesher is proud that her publication is financially solvent and has survived for more than three decades. It is, however, clear that *Lesbian Connection* has also suffered down times. "Even though *LC* has enjoyed a long existence," Mary Detwiler observes, "it hasn't always been easy. In the early summer of 1975, the Ambitious Amazons wrote in their letter to *LC* readers that the money reserves were almost depleted, which meant there wasn't enough to continue publishing the magazine. The Ambitious Amazons estimated they needed $865 to get the next issue out. Readers responded with donations equaling $1,150.25" (Ibid.).

Lesbian Connection "committed itself—as no publication before or since— to reaching the broadest possible spectrum of American lesbians" (Streitmatter, *Unspeakable* 247). With an "open submission policy" (Ibid. 268), its editors encouraged readers to address controversial personal and political topics, including lesbian adoption and service in the military. According to Detwiler, readers continue to debate issues such as incest, abuse, sadomasochism, money and relationships, alcoholism, custody, and personal appearance (unpublished history 1999).

Unlike other publications of the genre, *Lesbian Connection* provided a "Contact Dykes" section that made available the names and telephone numbers of women across the country willing to provide information about lodging, restaurants, and activities to other women traveling to their area. In 1975, fifteen women were listed in the directory; by 1987, there were five hundred; and in 1997, more than a thousand women from more than twenty countries were included. As of 2003, the publication boasts 1,500 listings and contacts from every state and from twenty-four countries.

Detwiler observes that *Lesbian Connection* had much in common with other lesbian publications of the 1970s, but offering the publication free to all lesbians and asking donations from those who could afford to pay was not a common strategy in the gay and lesbian press. "We figured people would support it once they saw it," comments Lesher. "Our point was to help the lesbian movement grow. Accessibility was important. Being free was important. We didn't want a lack of money to stop anyone" (Ibid.).

Copies of *Lesbian Connection* are mailed to subscribers and are placed in women's bookstores and women's centers throughout the country. The multicolored sheets of paper (printed on both sides) are folded in half and stapled. In addition to the popular "Contact Dykes" portion, over the years section headings have included "Articles and News," "Letters," "Responses," "Bits and Pieces," "Ads and Announcements," "Groups, Organizations and Services," and "Regional Festivals and Other Gatherings." It now takes nine women working full time to produce the publication, which includes announcements, news clippings, opinions, articles, and letters. *Lesbian Connection* provides information about lesbian cultural events, conferences, music festivals, publications or newsletters, and record, film, television, and video reviews.

The Importance of Lesbian Publications

As *Lesbian Connection* continues publication, we must acknowledge the obvious market for publications by and about lesbians. No one realized that a mimeographed publication called *Vice Versa* would be the forerunner to more than 2,600 lesbian publications. Some—such as *Lesbian Tide* and *The Furies*—were often more incendiary than *Sinister Wisdom* and certainly more controversial than *Vice Versa*, *The Ladder*, and *Focus: A Journal for Lesbians*. Others, such as *Gay Community News* with its sixty thousand subscribers, were better known. And some lesbian literary magazines, such as *Conditions*, were as influential as *Focus: A Journal for Lesbians*. Certainly, numerous lesbian publications had short lifespans, including *The Furies, Amazon Quarterly, Lavender Woman*, and *Lesbian Tide*.

The significance of *Vice Versa, The Ladder, Focus: A Journal for Lesbians*, and *Sinister Wisdom*, however, cannot be overstated. They represent four genres—a mimeographed newsletter, a news and issues magazine, a literary journal, and an activist publication, respectively. They also represent lesbian communities on the West Coast, in the East, and in the Deep South (with publication bases scattered throughout the nation).

Most important, however, they document the lesbian press as something that began primarily to connect isolated, closeted women to one another and provide them with a voice. Few editors dreamed that their efforts would encourage participation in what would become a potent social movement. Certainly, Lisa Ben, whom Streitmatter calls "mother of the lesbian press," never expected that *Vice Versa*, a "tiny magazine she created to combat her own loneliness, would play a singular role in a social movement that would help define the second half of the twentieth century" (*Unspeakable* 13, 16).

Lesbian publications have never been profitable, nor have they rivaled mainstream publications or competed with the more successful, glossy gay male periodicals. As Lyon said of *The Ladder*, however, it "broke the silence. Finally. Before it came along, there was absolutely nothing about lesbians in the major press" (Ibid. 39).

Vice Versa, The Ladder, Focus: A Journal for Lesbians, Sinister Wisdom, and *Lesbian Connection* are among the alternative publications that helped lesbians build communities, and they gave readers ways to combat feelings of marginalization (*The Ladder* even inspired what lesbians called "Ladder parties," gatherings where they read, reacted, and felt accepted). The publications gave voice to a nearly silent minority and disseminated news about events that spawned profound social change. For such reasons it is impossible to gauge the importance of lesbian newsletters, magazines, journals, and newspapers in terms of circulation figures, income, or even the longevity. Instead, it is the five decades of the lesbian press and its impact on readers that most accurately measures its worth.

Conclusion

Metaphorically, women continue to seek rooms of their own in which to think, plan, dream, create, define themselves, think about others, and feel safe.

Literally, however, women already are authentically present to themselves and others, and they already inhabit the physical spaces they have created for themselves in the academy, corporate world, home, and elsewhere.

Scholars will continue to discover, write, and reposition narratives of women in journalism, and the news industry will continue to undergo significant (some would say cataclysmic) change.

As I indicated in the introduction, my Ph.D. degree in English was awarded at the same time that *The Norton Anthology of Literature by Women* first was published in 1985. The anthology provoked both excitement about all that remained for me to learn and terror that I knew so little about a field of study to which I had dedicated myself.

It has been helpful throughout my career to hear other women acknowledge how slow they were to "catch on," to "get it," to discover the essential contributions made by women in the arts and humanities, in the social sciences, in the hard sciences, in their communities, and in the broader society. As Virginia Woolf examined the official public record of what women had accomplished in 1942, she wrote facetiously, "For it is a perennial puzzle why no woman wrote a word of that extraordinary literature when every other man, it seemed, was capable of song or sonnet" (*A Room of One's Own* 1376). This book is the result of a collective recognition that women editors, publishers, reporters, columnists, and photographers are no better represented in the scholarship than women in fiction and other creative and critical fields have been.

Chapter 1 is devoted to the representative women in journalism who excelled and whose stories are part of the scholarly and public discourse. For every woman whose story media historians unearth, however, thousands more await discovery. As Woolf suggests in *A Room of One's Own,* perhaps William Shakespeare had a sister, and perhaps she, too, could write a sonnet or create characters such as Hamlet.

Future research will no longer simply tabulate how many women entered journalism during a particular period but will address what they contributed. Did they slip into prescribed roles to accommodate male owners, publishers, and editors in mainstream media? Or did they quietly and not so quietly transform the face of newsgathering and writing? Specifically, what stories and photographs and editorial responsibilities were they assigned—and why? Published excerpts and photographs, accompanied by meticulous textual and visual analysis, are overdue.

Chapter 2 is devoted to the women of society news and women's pages. If women's pages reappear (or disappear entirely), scholars should continue to explore the differences between hard news and soft news with all that those terms imply. They should continue to ask whether news about sports, car accidents, war, and the economy belongs to men and whether health, the welfare of children, entertainment, and food and furnishings remain the province of women. The definition of what constitutes news of interest to men and to women has remained remarkably constant since the first women's pages. What will happen next in American newspapers and online journalism—and why?

Chapter 3 analyzes writing of women in literary journalism. As long as Joan Didion, Sara Davidson, Susan Orlean, and others continue to captivate readers, extended nonfiction studies will most assuredly become less gendered. For now, though, it bears watching which works of fiction and nonfiction elementary school children are exposed to, which are on the bestseller list of the *New York Times,* and which are recommended to forums such as *Newsweek's* "My Five Most Important Books" (and who those contributors are). How often are they books by women—and which women? How books are selected for Oprah Winfrey's book club, for the Book-of-the-Month Club, and as featured works by book store chains is also of interest.

Chapter 4 chronicles the lives of women journalists who chose fiction. Although gender will continue to claim a central place in this research, a study of the borderland between journalism and fiction remains compelling.

What is truthful may be different from what is factual, and the gray areas between genres will be useful in the continued study of lesser-known women poets, short-story writers, essayists, and novelists who learned their craft in American newsrooms. The line between fiction and nonfiction continues to be less distinguishable, so what does that mean for the future of literary study?

Ideas for research into the alternative press—chapters 5 and 6—fairly leap from the page. Linda Steiner, a journalism historian, maintains that women invested themselves in alternative media with enthusiasm, "literally making their own meaning and communicating it to one another across space and over time." She also suggests that women's use of alternative media has been motivated by "inability—or reluctance" to use mainstream media because those media have been "hostile" to women's ways of defining themselves and the world around them ("The History and Structure" 121).

What alternative media have sprung up during the writing and production of this volume? How many print or broadcast products represent a particular racial or ethnic group? How many newsletters, magazines, newspapers, and online texts for lesbians and bisexual women will appear as more and more feel safe to come out, express themselves, and build communities? Furthermore, how many women who agitate for peace, for the safety of animals, for the protection of the environment, and for other causes are now sitting at computers or walking along quiet lanes in contemplation of what they might write in order to inform or motivate others?

"Drawing her life from the lives of the unknown who were her forerunners," Woolf writes, "she will be born" (*A Room of One's Own* 1383). Ultimately, *Women in American Journalism: A New History* is dedicated to the known and unknown women who traveled outside their comfort zones to gather news, who wrote and redefined news, and who in the process created art. It is dedicated to the forerunners and, especially, to those who have yet to be born.

Notes

Chapter 4: Women Journalists Who Chose Fiction

1. The dedication to R. Thomas Berner's *Writing Literary Features* reads: "This volume is dedicated to the late Joseph Jay Rubin, Professor Emeritus of American Literature, whose course on Masters of American Literature included journalists, which encouraged me." The fact that the two fields are so consistently separated in American literature survey courses merits examination, although that is not Berner's goal. The term he prefers in his book designed for journalism students is *literary newswriting* (1). Ronald Weber entitled his book *The Literature of Fact* but subtitled it *Literary Nonfiction in American Writing,* and he describes the field as "nonfiction with a literary purpose" (1). In *A Sourcebook of American Literary Journalism: Representative Writers in an Emerging Genre* Thomas B. Connery separates new journalism and literary journalism and defines the genre as "nonfiction printed prose whose verifiable content is shaped and transformed into a story or sketch by use of narrative and rhetorical techniques generally associated with fiction" (xiv). John Hellmann's *Fables of Fact: The New Journalism as New Fiction* provides a provocative discussion of a journalist's responsibility to provide a personal instead of a corporate explanation for events and restates the impossibility of objectivity as the public and the media once understood it. His prose is clear and direct: "Almost by definition, new journalism is a revolt by the individual against homogenized forms of experience, against monolithic versions of truth" (8). Unfortunately, Hellmann deals extensively with only Norman Mailer, Hunter S. Thompson, Tom Wolfe, and Michael Herr and, like others, omits important women in the field.

2. One of the most surprising examples of sexist language is Shelley Fisher Fishkin's *From Fact to Fiction,* in which she writes, "Where the formulaic newspaper story allowed the reader to distance himself from the people about whom he read,

the poem or novel encourages emotional intimacy with them" (9). Throughout the introduction of John Hellmann's *Fables of Fact* he assumes a reporter or editor to be male, as in: "The same is true for any reporter, no matter how unobtrusive he may be" (6). Such examples may be explained as an author's use of a male pronoun to include both sexes, but numerous feminist critics have documented the difficulty female readers have in associating with male nouns and pronouns. In the case of books dealing with literary journalism—books that often either omit or underrepresent women—the damage is compounded by the use of exclusionary language.

3. Connery's *A Sourcebook of American Literary Journalism* is a thorough collection documenting the work of thirty-five literary journalists, four of whom are women, Dorothy Day, Lillian Ross, Joan Didion, and Jane Kramer. Fishkin's *From Fact to Fiction* chronicles the news and fiction writing of Walt Whitman, Mark Twain, Theodore Dreiser, Ernest Hemingway, and John Dos Passos. Norman Sims's two books, *The Literary Journalists* and *Literary Journalism in the Twentieth Century,* feature two sets of writers who belong under the broad banner of "Literary Journalists." In the former, he showcases thirteen contemporary literary journalists (three of whom are women) and lists five characteristics of literary journalism. In the latter, he features essays by scholars interested in Ernest Hemingway, John Steinbeck, and John McPhee. Also included are essays dealing with the inherent political quality of writing and definitions of literary journalism. Others such as Howard Good (*Acquainted with the Night*) have examined the portrayal of journalists in American fiction.

4. Willa Cather wrote an obituary about fellow journalist Eugene Field (1850–95) that includes Cather's view of her early experience in journalism. "Eugene Field," she writes, "was only a journalist. The American newspaper was his task and his curse, as it has been of so many brilliant men. Journalism is the vandalism of literature. It has brought to it endless harm and no real good. It has made an art a trade. The great American newspaper takes in intellect, promise, talent; it gives out only colloquial gossip. No man can write long for any journal in this country without for the most part losing that precious thing called style. Newspapers have no style and want none" (Slote, ed., *The Kingdom of Art* 332).

5. Kathryn Adams Sexton chronicles Katherine Anne Porter's years as a reporter for the *Rocky Mountain News* in Denver in her 1961 unpublished thesis completed at the University of Colorado, "Katherine Anne Porter's Years in Denver." In it, she organizes eighty-one bylined articles by Porter and interviews many who knew Porter during 1918 and 1919 in Denver. The articles are divided into reviews of dramatic productions, reviews of operas and concerts, profile interviews, and light special-assignment stories. Either Porter was not capable of writing hard news or her editors seriously underestimated her ability. Of course, the case may also be made that the writing of reviews and features—often considered by editors the domain of women reporters for women readers—may need to be taken more seriously as being of interest for readers of both sexes.

6. The fictional episodes included in *Pale Horse, Pale Rider* are often autobiographical. One is particularly important in understanding where Porter found herself as she struggled to carve out a career in a male-dominated newsroom. In it, Mary Townsend, the society editor, and Miranda (Porter's acknowledged personal voice) fail to please their male editors when they are assigned to cover an elopement. As their punishment, they are assigned to cover news considered important only to women. Although they may have failed to cover the human interest story well, young reporters of any gender are susceptible to the young women's errors, and the fashion or theater beat should not be "punishment" for poor judgment.

7. Interviewed about the time she spent working for the WPA, Welty responded, "I worked directly under another publicity agent who knew a lot more than I did. He was a professional newsman, named Louis Johnson. He's dead now. He was senior publicity agent. I was junior publicity agent—which also indicated I was a *girl*. We sometimes traveled together, and he did the news work and I did feature stories, interviews, and took some pictures" (*Photographs* xxv).

Chapter 5: Representative Women of the Alternative Press

1. Contributors include Neil Rolde, author of *The Interrupted Forest*, a history of the Maine Woods, and member of the Maine House of Representatives; Gary Lawless, co-owner of Gulf of Maine Bookstore in Brunswick and editor and publisher of Blackberry Books; John McKeith, a New England landscape photographer; Robert Kimber, author of numerous books and magazine articles for publications such as *Audobon and Field and Stream;* Jon Luoma, an artist and illustrator; Frank Graham Jr., an author and field editor of *Audobon* since 1969; D. D. Tyler, former illustrator for the *Maine Times* and an artist; Mitch Lansky, author, founder of the Maine Low-Impact Forestry Project, and contributor to the *Atlantic Forestry Review;* Chris Ayres, a Maine newspaper, magazine, and commercial photographer and chief photographer at the *Maine Times;* Karin Tilberg, deputy commissioner of the Department of Conservation; Kent Wommack, executive director of the Nature Conservancy's twelve-thousand-member Maine chapter; Charles Fitzgerald, wood products manufacturer, store owner, and organic farmer; Robert Shetterly, former illustrator for the *Maine Times* and president of the Union of Maine Visual Artists; Bernd Heinrich, author; Tom Higgins, professor of art at the University of Maine at Farmington; Greg Shute, Wilderness Programs Director for the Chewonki Foundation in Wiscasset; Bill Curtsinger, a photographer and photojournalist with more than thirty articles in *National Geographic;* Robert M. Chute, a poet; Alexandra and Garrett Conover, canoe, snowshoe, and toboggan guides; Bunny McBride, anthropologist and author; Bill Silliker Jr., photographer for *National Wildlife, Outdoor Photographer, Outdoor Life,* and other magazines; Bob Cummings, environmental affairs reporter for the *Portland Press Herald* and *Maine Sunday Telegram* for many years; Marguerite Robichaux, a painter; John Lund, publisher of the *Maine Sportsman* and former Maine

attorney general; Jerry Stelmok, canoe builder; Malcolm Hunter Jr., professor of conservation biology in the Department of Wildlife Ecology at the University of Maine; Kate Barnes, Maine's first poet laureate; Margaret Campbell, a graphic designer and illustrator; Susan Hand Shetterly, author of essays, children's books, short fiction, and articles; John N. Cole, who died on January 8, 2003, founding editor of the *Maine Times* and editor of newspapers in Kennebunk and Bath-Brunswick; Jym St. Pierre, Maine director of RESTORE: The North Woods, a conservation organization; Lloyd Irland, president of a forest economics and marketing consulting firm in Winthrop; Dean B. Bennett, professor of science and environmental education at the University of Maine in Farmington and an author; and Franklin Burroughs, a former English professor and an author.

Chapter 6: The Lesbian Press

1. In "Creating a Venue for the 'Love That Dare Not Speak Its Name,'" Streitmatter lists "standard histories" of the American media that omit reference to the gay and lesbian press (444). They include Emery and Emery, *The Press and America* (7th ed.) and Folkerts and Teeter, *Voices of a Nation* (2d ed.). Streitmatter also lists several histories of alternative journalism, including Glessing, *The Underground Press in America*; Kessler, *The Dissident Press*; and Leamer, *The Paper Revolutionaries*. The gay and lesbian press also is omitted from *Media in America* (2d ed), ed. Sloan, Stovall, and Startt. The eighth edition of *The Press and America*, however, includes two references to the gay and lesbian press. The importance of Streitmatter's *Unspeakable* cannot be overstated, and such a study is certainly overdue.

2. The Mattachine Society, established in 1950 in Los Angeles and the first organization for gays, took its name from "matachin" or "matachine" (to mask oneself). ONE, Inc., established in Los Angeles in 1952, sought to unify the national gay community. In January 1955, the San Francisco chapter of the Mattachine Society began a journal, *Mattachine Review*, that lasted until 1966. ONE, Inc., published *ONE Magazine*, considered by many the first successful gay magazine in America. It had its debut in 1953 and achieved a circulation of five thousand before ceasing regular publication in 1968. The *ONE Institute Quarterly of Homophile Studies*, which replaced it, ceased publication in 1973.

3. The Daughters of Bilitis took their name from *Bilitis*, the Hellenic form of *Ba'alat*, the female counterpart of Baal in Semitic mythology, and from Pierre Louys's *Les Chansons de Bilitis* (1894). After Louys's death, *Les Chansons de Bilitis inedites* and *Las Chansons secretes de Bilitis* appeared in 1929 and 1931, respectively. Unlike the first novel, the others contained explicit lesbian eroticism. The heroine of the novels lives in Mytilene on the Island of Lesbos and writes elegies to her beloved Mnasidika, having learned to write poetry at the feet of Sappho. The national Daughters of Bilitis organization began in the 1950s as a reaction to a growing and organized cry for gay

civil rights. Its related organizations for gay men included the Mattachine Society and ONE, Inc.

The Daughters of Bilitis, Mattachine Society, ONE, Inc., and other groups such as Homophile Action League used their publications to encourage membership, debate issues, and announce both demonstrations and social events. The three organizations worked together to fight discrimination and end the stereotypes of gays and lesbians.

4. Having earned a journalism degree from the University of California at Berkeley in 1946 and working for the *Chico* (Calif.) *Enterprise,* Lyon served as the first editor. In 1960 the governing board of the Daughters of Bilitis appointed Martin as editor. Martin studied journalism at San Francisco State College and had been a reporter for the *San Francisco Chronicle.*

5. *Focus,* February 1973, cover. The full quotation is, "We are / coming / And our name / is legion / You dare not / disown us."

Works Cited

Allen, Patrick, ed. *Margaret Mitchell: Reporter.* Athens, Ga.: Hill Street Press, 2000.

Alyson Publications. *The Alyson Almanac: A Treasury of Information for the Gay and Lesbian Community.* 2d ed. Boston: Alyson Publications, 1990.

Armstrong, David. *A Trumpet to Arms: Alternative Media in America.* Los Angeles: J. P. Tarcher, 1981.

Austin, Phyllis. "Acadia's Cry for Help: There's No Money and No Plan To Save the Park from Overuse." *Maine Times,* Sept. 2, 1988, 1+.

———. "Battle for the Northern Forest." *Maine Times,* Aug. 23, 1991, 1+.

———. "Diamonds Aren't Forever: Developers Mine the Maine Woods." *Outdoors: The Magazine of the Appalachian Mountain Club* 63 (June 1997): 16–17.

———. "Impaled." *Yankee* (Jan. 1990): 76–79, 126–28.

———. "A Visit to the Exclusive Cumberland Club (By the Side Door)." *Maine Times,* March 12, 1976, 8+.

———. Interviews with author (e-mail and personal). Summer 1997, 2004–5.

———, Dean Bennett, and Robert Kimber, eds. *On Wilderness: Voices from Maine.* Gardiner: Tilbury House, 2003.

Avery, Donald. "The Colonial Press." In *The Media in America: A History,* 4th ed. Edited by William David Sloan and James D. Startt, 35–48. Northport, Ala.: Vision Press, 1999.

"Ban on Membership Shocking to Negro." *Denver Post,* Sept. 14, 1960, 3A.

Bartimus, Tad. "Bullets and Bathrooms." *Media Studies Journal* 15 (Summer 2001): 8–15.

Beasley, Maurine H. "The Emergence of Modern Media." In *The Media in America: A History,* 4th ed. Edited by William David Sloan and James D. Startt, 281–300. Northport, Ala: Vision Press, 1999.

———. "Recent Directions for the Study of Women's History in American Journalism." *Journalism Studies* 2 (2001): 207–20.

———, and Sheila J. Gibbons. *Taking Their Place: A Documentary History of Women in Journalism*. Washington: American University Press, 1993.

Ben, Lisa. "In Explanation." *Vice Versa*, June 1947, 1.

Berendt, John. *Midnight in the Garden of Good and Evil*. New York: Random House, 1994.

Berner, R. Thomas. *The Literature of Journalism: Text and Content*. State College, Pa.: Strata Publishing, 1999.

Bohlke, L. Brent, ed. *Willa Cather in Person: Interviews, Speeches and Letters*. Lincoln: Nebraska University Press, 1986.

Bosisio, Matthew J. "Hazel Brannon Smith: Pursuing Truth at Her Peril." *American Journalism* 18 (Fall 2001): 69–83.

Bradley, Patricia. *Women and the Press: The Struggle for Equality*. Evanston: Northwestern University Press, 2005.

Brandt, Kate. "Lisa Ben: A Lesbian Pioneer." *Visibilities* (Jan.–Feb. 1990): 8–10.

Bridge, M. Junior. "What's News?" In *Women and Media: Content, Careers, and Criticism*. Edited by Cynthia M. Lont, 15–23. Belmont, Calif.: Wadsworth, 1995.

Capers, Charlotte. Interview with Eudora Welty. Mississippi Department of Archives and History, Jackson, Oct. 26, 1971.

Churchill, Caroline Nichols. *Active Footsteps*. Colorado Springs: Mrs. C. N. Churchill Printer, 1909.

———. *Little Sheaves Gathered While Gleaning After Reapers: Letters of Travel Commencing in 1870 and Ending in 1873*. San Francisco: Mrs. Caroline M. Churchill, Publisher, 1874.

———. *Over the Purple Hills; or, Sketches of Travel in California, Embracing All the Important Points Usually Visited by Tourists*. Denver: Mrs. Caroline M. Churchill, Publisher, 1884.

Clendinen, Dudley. "In the South—When It Mattered to Be an Editor." *Media Studies Journal* 9 (Winter 1995): 11–21.

Connery, Thomas B., ed. *A Sourcebook of American Literary Journalism: Representative Writers in an Emerging Genre*. New York: Greenwood Press, 1992.

Conrad, Joseph. "The Secret Sharer." In *Great Short Works of Joseph Conrad*, 365–404. New York: Harper and Row, 1966.

Curtin, William, ed. *The World and the Parish: Willa Cather's Articles and Reviews: Volumes One and Two (1893–1902)*. Lincoln: Nebraska University Press, 1970.

Davidson, Sara. *Cowboy: A Novel*. New York: Harper Collins, 1999.

———. "The Gray Zone." *Book* (July–Aug. 1999): 49–50.

———. *LEAP! What Will We Do with the Rest of Our Lives*. New York: Random House, 2007.

———. *Loose Change: Three Women of the Sixties*. Berkeley: University of California Press, 1977.

———. "Notes from the Land of the Cobra." In *Real Property*, 199–220. New York: Pocket Books, 1980.

———. "Real Property." In *Real Property*, 1–36. New York: Pocket Books, 1980.

"Death Claims Tough, Witty Post Reporter: Brimberg Spent 33 Years Covering News in Denver." *Denver Post*, Feb. 1, 1996, 1B, 5B.

Dellenbaugh, Anne. E-mail interview with author, Aug. 7, 2005.

Detwiler, Mary. Unpublished history of *Lesbian Connection*. Dec. 1999.

Devlin, Albert J., and Peggy Whitman Prenshaw, eds. *Welty: A Life in Literature*. Jackson: University Press of Mississippi, 1987.

Didion, Joan. *The Last Thing He Wanted*. New York: Vintage Books, 1996.

———. *Political Fictions*. New York: Alfred A. Knopf, 2001.

———. "Some Dreamers of the Golden Dream." In *Slouching Towards Bethlehem*, 3–28. New York: Quality Paperback Book Club, 1992.

———. *The Year of Magical Thinking*. New York: Alfred A. Knopf, 2005.

Dishon, Colleen. Telephone interviews with author, 1994, 2000–2004.

Domhoff, G. William. "The Women's Page as a Window on the Ruling Class." In *Hearth and Home: Images of Women in Mass Media*. Edited by Gaye Tuchman, Arlene Kaplan Daniels, and James Benet, 161–75. New York: Oxford University Press, 1978.

Douglas, George H. *The Golden Age of the Newspaper*. Westport: Greenwood Press, 1999.

Downs, Robert B., and Jane B. Downs. *Journalists of the United States*. Jefferson, N.C.: McFarland, 1991.

DuPlessis, Rachel Blau. *Writing beyond Ending: Narrative Strategies of Twentieth-century Women Writers*. Bloomington: Indiana University Press, 1985.

Dynes, Wayne R. *Encyclopedia of Homosexuality*. New York: Garland Publishing, 1990.

Editors of Time-Life Books. *The Women*. Text by Joan Swallow Reiter. Alexandria: Time-Life Books, 1978.

Emery, Michael, and Edwin Emery. *The Press and America: An Interpretive History of Mass Media*, 8th ed. Boston: Allyn and Bacon, 1996.

Epstein, Cynthia Fuchs. "The Women's Movement and the Women's Pages: Separate, Unequal, and Unspectacular." In *Hearth and Home: Images of Women in the Mass Media*. Edited by Gaye Tuchman, Arlene Kaplan Daniels, and James Benet, 216–21. New York: Oxford University Press, 1978.

Epstein, Laurily Keir, ed. *Women and the News*. New York: Hastings House Publishers, 1978.

Esterberg, Kristin Gay. "From Illness to Action: Conceptions of Homosexuality in *The Ladder*, 1956–1965." *Journal of Sex Research* 27 (Feb. 1990): 65–80.

Evans, Raymond. Interviews with author. Summer 2004.

Faderman, Lillian. *Odd Girls and Twilight Lovers: A History of Lesbian Life in Twentieth-Century America*. New York: Columbia University Press, 1991.

———. *Surpassing the Love of Men*. New York: Quality Paperback Book Club, 1994.

Fischer, Christiane. *Let Them Speak for Themselves: Women in the American West (1849–1900)*. Hamden: Archon Books, 1990.

Fishkin, Shelley Fisher. *From Fact to Fiction*. New York: Oxford University Press, 1985.

Folkerts, Jean, and Dwight L. Teeter Jr. *Voices of a Nation: A History of Mass Media in the United States,* 3d ed. Boston: Allyn and Bacon, 1998.

Franzen, Trisha. *Spinsters and Lesbians: Independent Womanhood in the United States*. New York: New York University Press, 1996.

Gilbert, Sandra M., and Susan Gubar. *The Norton Anthology of Literature by Women*. New York: W. W. Norton, 1985.

Givner, Joan. *Katherine Anne Porter: A Life*. New York: Simon and Schuster, 1982.

———. "Katherine Anne Porter, Journalist." In *Katherine Anne Porter*. Edited by Harold Bloom, 69–80. New York: Chelsea House, 1986

Glessing, Robert J. *The Underground Press in America*. Bloomington: Indiana University Press, 1970.

Good, Howard. *Acquainted with the Night*. Metuchen: Scarecrow Press, 1986.

Goodman, Ellen. "Exit Ron Reagan: Stage Right." In *Making Sense,* 393–94. New York: Atlantic Monthly Press, 1989.

Greenwald, Marilyn S. *A Woman of the Times: Journalism, Feminism, and the Career of Charlotte Curtis*. Athens: Ohio University Press, 1999.

Grier, Barbara. *Lesbiana: Book Reviews from* The Ladder, *1966–1972*. Reno: Naiad Press, 1976.

———, and Donna J. McBride. *The Index to* The Ladder. 16 vols. Reno: N.p., 1974.

———. *The Lesbian in Literature: A Bibliography*. Tallahassee: Naiad Press, 1981.

Hale, William Harlan. *Horace Greeley: Voice of the People*. New York: Collie Books, 1961.

Harkey, Ira B. *The Smell of Burning Crosses: An Autobiography of a Mississippi Newspaperman*. Jacksonville, Ill.: Harris-Wolfe, 1967.

Hartsock, John C. *A History of American Literary Journalism: The Emergence of a Modern Narrative Form*. Amherst: University of Massachusetts Press, 2000.

Hawley, Melinda D. "Is the 'Women's Section' an Anachronism? Affinity for and Ambivalence about the *Chicago Tribune*'s WomanNews." Presented at the Association for Education in Journalism and Mass Communication, Chicago, Aug. 1997.

"Hazel Brannon Smith." *New York Times,* May 16, 1994, B8.

Hellman, John. *Fables of Fact: The New Journalism as New Fiction*. Urbana: University of Illinois Press, 1981.

Hendrick, George. *Katherine Anne Porter*. New York: Twayne Publishers, 1965.

Henry, Susan. "Ann Franklin: Rhode Island's Woman Printer." In *Newsletters to Newspapers: Eighteenth Century Journalism*. Edited by Donovan H. Bond and W. Reynolds McLeod, 129–43. Morgantown: West Virginia University Press, 1977.

———. "Changing Media History Through Women's History." In *Women in Mass*

Communication: Challenging Gender Values. Edited by Pamela J. Creedon, 341–62. Beverly Hills: Sage, 1989.

Huntzicker, William E. "The Frontier Press." In *The Media in America: A History,* 4th ed. Edited by William David Sloan and James D. Startt, 173–96. Northport, Ala.: Vision Press, 1999.

Isaacs, Barbara, and Kevin Nance. "Other Lexingtons Offer Attractions for Travelers." *Lexington* (Kentucky) *Herald Leader,* Oct. 1, 1997.

Kaul, A. J. "Hazel Brannon Smith." In *Dictionary of Literary Biography: American Newspaper Publishers (1950–1990).* Edited by Perry J. Ashley, Vol. 127: 291–301. Detroit: Gale Research, 1993.

Keith, Don Lee. "Eudora Welty: 'I Worry Over My Stories.'" In *Conversations with Eudora Welty.* Edited by Peggy Whitman Prenshaw, 141–53. Jackson: University Press of Mississippi, 1984.

Kessler, Lauren. *The Dissident Press: Alternative Journalism in American History.* Beverly Hills: Sage, 1984.

Kitch, Carolyn. "The Work That Came Before the Art: Willa Cather as Journalist, 1893–1912." *American Journalism* 14 (Summer–Fall 1997): 425–40.

Krause, Marla. Telephone interviews with author, 1994.

Kunitz, Stanley J., ed. *Authors Today and Yesterday.* New York: H. W. Wilson, 1934.

Kurtz, Howard. *Media Circus: The Trouble with America's Newspapers.* New York: Times Books, 1993.

Laucella, Pamela C. "*McClure's:* The Significance of 1906–1912 on Willa Cather and Her Artistic Growth." Presented at the Association for Education in Journalism and Mass Communication, Washington, D.C., Aug. 5–8, 2001.

Leamer, Laurence. *The Paper Revolutionaries: The Rise of the Underground Press.* New York: Simon and Schuster, 1972.

Lesher, Margy. E-mail messages to author, Dec. 8, 1999, Sept. 5, 2001, June 16, 2004.

Lont, Cynthia M. *Women and Media: Content, Careers, and Criticism.* Belmont, Calif.: Wadsworth, 1995.

Lopez, Enrique Hank. *Conversations with Katherine Anne Porter: Refugee from Indian Creek.* Boston: Little, Brown, 1981.

Lueck, Therese L. "'Her Say' in the Media Mainstream: A Cultural Feminist Manifesto." *Journalism and Mass Communication Monographs* 6 (Summer 2004): 61–96.

Lule, Jack. "Myth and Terror on the Editorial Page: *The New York Times* Responds to September 11, 2001." *Journalism and Mass Communication Quarterly* 79 (Summer 2002): 275–93.

Lyles, Doris. "My Daughter Is a Lesbian." *The Ladder* 2 (July 1958): 4–5.

Lyon, Peter. *Success Story: The Life and Times of S. S. McClure.* Deland, Fla.: Everett/Edwards, 1963.

Macdonald, Myra. *Representing Women: Myths of Femininity in the Popular Media.* New York: Edward Arnold, 1995.

MacNeil, Robert. *Eudora Welty: Seeing Black and White.* Jackson: University Press of Mississippi, 1990.

"Marjorie Paxson." In *New Guardians of the Press: Selected Profiles of America's Women Newspaper Editors.* Edited by Judith G. Clabes, 121–29. Indianapolis: R. J. Berg, 1983.

Marrs, Suzanne. "Eudora Welty's Photography: Images into Fiction." In *Critical Essays on Eudora Welty.* Edited by W. Craig Turner and Lee Emling Harding, 280–96. Boston: G. K. Hall, 1989.

Marzolf, Marion. *Up from the Footnote: A History of Women Journalists.* New York: Hastings House Publishers, 1977.

Meese, Elizabeth A. "Constructing Time and Place: Eudora Welty in the Thirties." In *Eudora Welty: Critical Essays.* Edited by Peggy Whitman Prenshaw, 401–10. Jackson: University Press of Mississippi, 1979.

Meltzer, Milton. *Dorothea Lange: A Photographer's Life.* New York: Farrar, Straus, Giroux, 1978.

Mills, Kay. *A Place in the News: From the Women's Pages to the Front Page.* New York: Columbia University Press, 1990.

Molotch, Harvey L. "The News of Women and the Work of Men." In *Hearth and Home: Images of Women in Mass Media.* Edited by Gaye Tuchman, Arlene Kaplan Daniels, and James Benet, 176–85. New York: Oxford University Press, 1978.

Moritz, Charles, ed. "Hazel Brannon Smith." In *Current Biography Yearbook,* 384–86. New York: H. W. Wilson, 1974.

"Mrs. Catherine Spiteful Churchill." *Sierra Journal,* 11 May 1882, 1.

Orlean, Susan. "The American Man, Age Ten." In *The Bullfighter Checks Her Makeup: My Encounters with Extraordinary People,* 3–14. New York: Random House, 2002.

———. Introduction. In *The Bullfighter Checks Her Makeup: My Encounters with Extraordinary People,* ix–xv. New York: Random House, 2002.

———. *The Orchid Thief: A True Story of Beauty and Obsession.* New York: Ballantine Books, 2000.

———. Reader's Guide. In *The Orchid Thief: A True Story of Beauty and Obsession,* n.p. New York: Ballantine Books, 2000.

———. "Rough Diamonds: Fidel's Little Leagues." *The New Yorker,* Aug. 5, 2002, 34–37.

———. "Straight and Narrow." *Vogue* 192 (April 2002): 281–83.

"The Passing of the Pioneer." *The Trail: A Magazine for Colorado (Official Organ of the Society of Sons of Colorado and Societies of Daughters of Colorado and the Territorial Daughters)* 18 (Feb. 1926): 22.

Pauly, John J. "The Politics of the New Journalism." In *Literary Journalism in the Twentieth Century,* 110–29. Edited by Norman Sims. New York: Oxford University Press, 1990.

Pingree, Suzanne, and Robert P. Hawkins. "News Definitions and Their Effects on

Women." In *Women and the News.* Edited by Laurily K. Epstein, 116–33. New York: Hastings House Publishers, 1978.

Porter, Katherine Anne. *The Collected Stories of Katherine Anne Porter.* San Diego: Harcourt Brace Jovanovich, 1944.

———. *The Never-Ending Wrong.* Boston: Little, Brown, 1977.

———. *Pale Horse, Pale Rider.* New York: New American Library, 1967.

Potter, Clare. *The Lesbian Periodicals Index.* Tallahassee: Naiad Press, 1986.

"Press Women Resign after Negro Is Rejected." *Denver Post,* Sept. 13, 1960, 3.

Quindlen, Anna. *Living Out Loud.* New York: Random House, 1988.

Rhodes, Jane. "Activism Through Journalism: The Story of Ida B. Wells-Barnett." In *Women and Media: Content, Careers, and Criticism.* Edited by Cynthia M. Lont, 29–40. Belmont, Calif.: Wadsworth, 1995.

———. "Mary Ann Shadd Cary and the Legacy of African-American Women Journalists." In *Women Making Meaning: New Feminist Directions in Communication.* Edited by Lana F. Rakow, 210–24. New York: Routledge, 1992.

Ricchiardi, Sherry, and Virginia Young. *Women on Deadline: A Collection of America's Best.* Ames: Iowa State University Press, 1991.

Riley, Sam G. *Biographical Dictionary of American Newspaper Columnists.* Westport: Greenwood Press, 1995.

Robertson, Nan. *The Girls in the Balcony: Women, Men, and the* New York Times. New York: Random House, 1992.

Rooks, Douglas. E-mail message to author, Aug. 8, 2005.

Ross, Ishbel. *Ladies of the Press: The Story of Women in Journalism by an Insider.* New York: Harper and Brothers, 1936.

Ruby, Jennie. "Off Our Backs." In *Women and Media: Content, Careers, and Criticism.* Edited by Cynthia M. Lont, 42–53. Belmont: Wadsworth, 1995.

Russell, Dennis. "Baudrillardesque Impulses in the Impressionistic Journalism of Joan Didion." *Southwestern Mass Communication Journal* 16 (2000): 19–28.

Schilpp, Madelon Golden, and Sharon M. Murphy. *Great Women of the Press.* Carbondale: Southern Illinois University Press, 1983.

Schmidt, Peter. *The Heart of the Story: Eudora Welty's Short Fiction.* Jackson: University Press of Mississippi, 1991.

Schulman, Norma M. "Wrinkling the Fabric of the Press: Newspaper Opinion Columns in a Different Voice." In *Women and Media: Content, Careers, and Criticism.* Edited by Cynthia M. Lont, 55–67. Belmont, Calif.: Wadsworth, 1995.

Sexton, Kathryn Adams. "Katherine Anne Porter's Years in Denver." Master's thesis. University of Colorado, 1961.

Simpson, Peggy A. "The Washington Press Club Foundation's Oral History Project: Getting Women Journalists to Speak of Themselves, for Themselves, for Herstory's Sake." In *Women Transforming Communications: Global Intersections.* Edited by Donna Allen, Ramona R. Rush, and Susan J. Kaufman, 290–302. Thousand Oaks: Sage, 1996.

Sims, Norman. "The Art of Literary Journalism." In *Literary Journalism: A New Collection of the Best American Nonfiction*, 3–19. Edited by Norman Sims and Mark Kramer. New York: Ballantine Books, 1995.

———, ed. *Literary Journalism in the Twentieth Century.* New York: Oxford University Press, 1990.

———, ed. "The Literary Journalists." In *The Literary Journalists*, 3–25. Edited by Norman Sims. New York: Ballantine Books, 1984.

Sloan, William David, and James D. Startt. *The Media in America: A History,* 4th ed. Northport, Ala.: Vision Press, 1999.

Slote, Bernice, ed. *The Kingdom of Art.* Lincoln: University of Nebraska Press, 1966.

Smythe, Ted Curtis. "The Press and Industrial America." In *The Media in America: A History,* 4th ed. Edited by William David Sloan and James D. Startt, 197–220. Northport, Ala.: Vision Press, 1999.

Steiner, Linda. "The History and Structure of Women's Alternative Media." In *Women Making Meaning: New Feminist Directions in Communication.* Edited by Lana F. Rakow, 121–43. New York: Routledge, 1992.

———. "Stories of Quitting: Why Did Some Women Journalists Leave the Newsroom?" *American Journalism* 15 (Summer 1998): 89–116.

Streitmatter, Rodger. "Creating a Venue for the 'Love That Dare Not Speak Its Name': Origins of the Gay and Lesbian Press." *Journalism and Mass Communication Quarterly* 72 (Summer 1995): 436–47.

———. "Lesbian and Gay Press: Raising a Militant Voice in the 1960s." *American Journalism* 12 (Spring 1995): 142–61.

———. *Raising Her Voice: African-American Women Journalists Who Changed History.* Lexington: University Press of Kentucky, 1994.

———. "Transforming the Women's Pages: Strategies That Worked." *Journalism History* 24 (Summer 1998): 72–81.

———. *Unspeakable: The Rise of the Gay and Lesbian Press in America.* Boston: Faber and Faber, 1995.

———. "*Vice Versa:* America's First Lesbian Magazine." Presented at the Association for Education in Journalism and Mass Communication Conference, Washington, D.C., 9 Aug. 1995.

Sugg, Will. E-mail message to author, Aug. 30, 2005.

Tilberg, Karin. E-mail message to author, Aug. 9, 2005.

Tuchman, Gaye. *Making News: A Study in the Construction of Reality.* New York: Free Press, 1978.

———. "The Newspaper as a Social Movement's Resource." In *Hearth and Home: Images of Women in Mass Media.* Edited by Gaye Tuchman, Arlene Kaplan Daniels, and James Benet, 186–215. New York: Oxford University Press, 1978.

———, Arlene Kaplan Daniels, and James Benet. *Hearth and Home: Images of Women in Mass Media.* New York: Oxford University Press, 1978.

Tucker, Mary Louise. "Photography and Photographers." In *Encyclopedia of Southern Culture*. Edited by Charles Reagan Wilson and William Ferris, 94–100. Chapel Hill: University of North Carolina Press, 1989.

Webb, Joseph. "Historical Perspective on the New Journalism." *Journalism History* 1 (Summer 1974): 38–42, 60.

Weber, Ronald. *The Literature of Fact: Literary Nonfiction in American Writing.* Athens: Ohio University Press, 1980.

Welty, Eudora. *The Collected Stories of Eudora Welty.* New York: Harcourt Brace Jovanovich, 1980.

———. "One Time, One Place." In *The Eye of the Story: Selected Essays and Reviews,* 349–55. New York: Random House, 1978.

———. *One Writer's Beginnings.* Cambridge: Harvard University Press, 1984.

———. *Photographs.* Jackson: University Press of Mississippi, 1990.

———. *Three Papers on Fiction.* Northampton, Mass.: Metcalf, 1962.

"Welty Photos Show Another Side of Depression." *Denver Post,* 17 Dec. 1989, 1E.

West, Cassandra. E-mail interviews with author, Sept. 19, 2005, May 30, 2007.

Westling, Louise. *Eudora Welty.* Totowa, N.J.: Barnes and Noble Books, 1989.

Wilkins-Fields, Margaret. E-mail messages to author, 2005–6.

Williams, William Carlos. "Asphodel, That Greeny Flower." In *Asphodel, That Greeny Flower and Other Love Poems,* 19–42. New York: New Directions, 1994.

Winter, Mary. "Ahead of Their Time." In "Lifestyles." *Rocky Mountain News,* March 10, 1992, 1+.

Woodress, James. *Willa Cather: Her Life and Art.* New York: Pegasus, 1970.

Woolf, Virginia. *A Room of One's Own.* In *The Norton Anthology of Literature by Women.* Edited by Sandra M. Gilbert and Susan Gubar, 1376–83. New York: W. W. Norton, 1985.

Yeats, W. B. "The Second Coming." In *The Norton Anthology of Modern Poetry,* 2d ed. Edited by Richard Ellman and Robert O'Clair, 158. New York: W. W. Norton, 1988.

Index

JAN WHITT is an associate professor in the School of Journalism and Mass Communication at the University of Colorado, Boulder. She is the author of *Allegory and the Modern Southern Novel.*

The University of Illinois Press
is a founding member of the
Association of American University Presses.

———————————————————————————

Composed in 10.5/13 Adobe Minion Pro
with FF Meta display
by Jim Proefrock
at the University of Illinois Press
Manufactured by Sheridan Books, Inc.

University of Illinois Press
1325 South Oak Street
Champaign, IL 61820-6903
www.press.uillinois.edu